Aversion and Erasure

Aversion and Erasure

The Fate of the Victim after the Holocaust

Carolyn J. Dean

Cornell University Press

Ithaca and London

First published 2010 by Cornell University Press
First printing, Cornell Paperbacks, 2016

Library of Congress Cataloging-in-Publication Data

Dean, Carolyn J. (Carolyn Janice), 1960–
    Aversion and erasure : the fate of the victim after the Holocaust /
Carolyn J. Dean.
        p. cm.
    Includes bibliographical references and index.
    ISBN 978-0-8014-4944-4 (cloth : alk. paper)
    ISBN 978-1-5017-0563-2 (pbk. : alk. paper)
    1. Holocaust, Jewish (1939–1945)—Moral and ethical aspects.
    2. Holocaust, Jewish (1939–1945)—Influence.   3. Victims.
    4. Collective memory.   I. Title.
    D804.7.M67D43   2010
    940.53′1814—dc22   2010023525

Cornell University Press strives to use environmentally responsible
suppliers and materials to the fullest extent possible in the publishing of
its books. Such materials include vegetable-based, low-VOC inks and
acid-free papers that are recycled, totally chlorine-free, or partly composed
of nonwood fibers. For further information, visit our website at www.
cornellpress.cornell.edu.

Contents

Acknowledgments   vii

Introduction: Victims, Suffering, Identity   1

1. The Surfeit of Jewish Memory   31

2. French Discourses on Exorbitant Jewish Memory   58

3. Minimalism and Victim Testimony   101

4. Erasures   143

Epilogue   178

Index   185

Acknowledgments

I would like to thank those colleagues and friends who have invited me to present portions of this book at various venues, including Noël Bonneuil, Florent Brayard, Susan Brison, Brian Fay, Peter Fritzsche, Dominick LaCapra, Harriet Murav, Michael Rothberg, Alan Schrift, and Richard Wolin.

In addition, others have read this work and have improved it. I am deeply grateful to two anonymous readers at Cornell University Press, who provided generous and helpful reviews, and to Dominick LaCapra, from whose example I have learned a great deal. He read this manuscript with his usual care and pushed me to think differently about several important questions. Martin Jay also read some of this in a draft, and I am ever grateful for his steadfast support over so many years. Michael Rothberg kindly took the time to review the last chapter as it was unfolding and provided helpful references, and Warren Breckman and Peter Gordon read a version of Chapter One and provided incisive criticism. Alyson Cole proved a generous interlocutor as the book was in its last stages.

I would also like to thank Jane Pedersen and Laurie Bernstein for their solidarity. Rajiv Vohra allowed me sufficient summer time off from my administrative position to work on my research. Without that time I would have been unable to complete this book.

John Ackerman, the director of Cornell University Press, courageously took this manuscript in hand, was constantly reassuring, and went far beyond the call of duty in every way. I cannot thank John and the staff at the Press enough, including Susan Barnett, Candace Akins, and Kay Scheuer.

I would like to acknowledge the indomitable spirit of my mother, Harriet Katzman Dean, whose example continues to inspire.

I am most grateful of all to Francesca Trivellato.

Unless otherwise indicated, all translations are my own.

Chapter one originally published as "Against Grandiloquence: 'Victim's Culture' and Jewish Memory," *The Modernist Imagination: Intellectual History and Critical Theory,* ed. Warren Breckman, Peter E. Gordon, A. Dirk Moses, Samuel Moyn, and Elliot Neaman, 162–182 (New York: Berghahn Books, 2008).

Chapter two originally published as "Recent French Discourses on Stalinism, Nazism, and 'Exorbitant' Jewish Memory," *History and Memory* 18 (2006): 43–85.

Both chapters have been expanded and revised in this volume.

Aversion and Erasure

INTRODUCTION

Victims, Suffering, Identity

These days, it is indelicate to speak of the concentration camps. You risk
being accused of posing as a victim, or of harboring a gratuitous love for the
macabre in the best of cases: in the worst, of telling lies pure and simple, or
even of offending public morality.

PRIMO LEVI (1955)

In the past the Jews were envied because of their money, qualifications,
positions, and international contacts—today they are envied because of the
crematoria in which they were burned.

WITOLD KULA (1996)

In 2004, several French newspaper articles focused on Marie L., a young
woman who, while traveling on the Paris metro with a baby, marked herself with swastikas and then blamed French men of Arab and African
descent for having done so. This incident precipitated first a round of national soul-searching about renewed anti-Semitism in France and then,
when the police discovered that Marie L. had pulled off a hoax, another

Epigraphs: Primo Levi, "Deportati. Anniversario," *Torino* 31, 4 (1955): 53–54, reprinted in
Primo Levi, *L'asimmetria e la vita: Articoli e saggi 1955–1987,* ed. Marco Belpoliti (Turin: Einaudi,
2002), 5–7 (citation p. 5); Witold Kula, *Rozdzialki* (Warsaw, 1996), 216, quoted in *The Neighbors
Respond: The Controversy over the Jedwabne Massacre in Poland,* ed. Anthony Polonsky and Joanna
B. Michlic (Princeton: Princeton University Press, 2004), 9.

set of denunciations, this time of a society "obsessed with" victims, and in which victimhood had become a form of prestige.[1]

This incident weaves together a series of increasingly pervasive concerns in the United States and Europe about how victims rather than heroes are now celebrated, about the prestige and social recognition putatively afforded victims, and about the conviction that Jews take pride of place in the grand pantheon of victims because they were targeted for extermination and nearly annihilated during the Second World War. This assumption about the iconic status of the Holocaust and the peculiar privilege accorded to Jews appears to have led non-Jews like Marie L. to appropriate Jewish identity and the special victim status she imagined it conferred.

According to a vast array of European and American critical voices, both Jewish and not, Jews experience victimization as a surrogate identity. Walter Benn Michaels and Michel Feher insist that Jews have forsaken their history and culture and replaced it with Holocaust trauma as a substitute for collective identity.[2] Tzevtan Todorov and Ian Buruma both argue that the so-called desire to be a victim represents the perceived narcissism of Jewish and minority groups' claims to public recognition: Jews in particular are overinvested in an identity linked to having been excluded, and obsessed with Holocaust memory.[3] Peter Novick maintains that the peculiar status accorded Jewish suffering has something to do with a culture in which "the status of the victim has come to be prized."[4] He thus identifies American Jews' so-called wish to be or to have been victims

1. Among others, see "On se légitime par le malheur que l'on subit," *Le Monde,* August 21, 2004; "L'affaire Marie L. révèle une société obsédée pas ses victimes," *Le Monde,* August 24, 2004. In 2009, this incident inspired a film by André Téchiné, *La fille du RER* (*The Girl on the Train*).

2. Walter Benn Michaels, "'You Who Never Was There': Slavery and the New Historicism—Deconstruction and the Holocaust," in *The Americanization of the Holocaust,* ed. H. Flanzbaum (Baltimore: Johns Hopkins University Press, 1999), 195; Michel Feher, "1967–1992: Sur quelques recompositions de la gauche américaine," *Esprit* 187 (1992): 75.

3. Tzvetan Todorov, "In Search of Lost Crime," *New Republic,* January 29, 2001, 26; Ian Buruma, "The Joys and Perils of Victimhood," *New York Review of Books,* April 8, 1999, 4–9.

4. Peter Novick, *The Holocaust in American Life* (New York: Mariner Books, 2000), 121. For a different, French version of the same claim based on an analysis of the memory of Vichy France, see Henry Rousso, *The Haunting Past: History, Memory, and Justice in Contemporary France* (Philadelphia: University of Pennsylvania Press, 2002), 12–13. See also Rony Brauman and Alain Finkielkraut, *La Discorde: Israël-Palestine, les Juifs, la France; Conversations avec Élisabeth Lévy* (Paris: Mille et une Nuits, 2006), 227–69.

with a widespread and prevalent cultural phenomenon in which victims are privileged and envied.

Can it then be a coincidence that Marie L. pretended to have been the victim of anti-Semitism, or that Novick suggests that the allegedly elevated status of victims is somehow related to the belated cultural recognition of the Holocaust? Todorov and Buruma's criticisms are directed against a so-called surfeit of Jewish memory. In their construction of this surfeit, Jewish memory and its demands exceed an imagined universal capacity for empathy in which each group is allocated a just proportion of fellow-feeling. In the 1980s identity politics too involved constant comparisons with the seemingly unrelated Holocaust of European Jewry: African Americans claimed that slavery was a Holocaust too; gay men and lesbians declared that AIDS was a new Holocaust; other cultural commentators, including journalists and public intellectuals, referred to a "competition of victims"; and a few scholars involved in comparing the Holocaust and slavery coined the term "Holocaust envy" to describe so-called Black attitudes toward the cultural and political capital invested in the Jewish Holocaust.[5] Annette Wieviorka refers to two young French men who identified with Jewish victims but were themselves disabled and gay, respectively: they understood little about the extermination of Jews or about Auschwitz, only that the Nazis had discriminated against and sometimes killed the disabled and gays. In these young men's minds, Auschwitz had become a symbol of their own suffering.[6] As is well known, these invocations reach beyond identity politics. Anti-abortion activists in the United States have called abortion a "holocaust," and the actress and animal-rights advocate Brigitte Bardot has invoked the term to describe the abandonment of animals during summer vacations in France. She has also called the head of the French Federation of Hunters "Himmler."[7] It cannot also be a coincidence that French philosopher Jean Baudrillard compares the effects of television ("the...process

5. Antonio de Figueiredo, "'Holocaust Envy' or a Better Deal for Africa?" *New African* 409 (2002): 8–9. Peter Novick also uses the expression in quotation marks but without appellation, in Novick, *The Holocaust in American Life,* 192.

6. Annette Wieviorka, *Auschwitz: La mémoire d'un lieu* (Paris: Pluriel, 2005), 14–15.

7. These examples are discussed in Esther Benbassa, *La souffrance comme identité* (Paris: Fayard, 2007), 224. Some animal rights groups have compared the industrialized slaughter of animals to the slaughter of Jews in the Holocaust.

of forgetting, of liquidation...the same absorption without a trace") to the extermination of Jews at Auschwitz.[8]

One does not have to look far for references to the Holocaust of European Jewry not only as an icon of 'evil in our time,' but also as the origin of the postmodern traumatic and of the privileging of traumatic wounds. Andreas Huyssen insists that commemoration of the Holocaust and the voluminous literature it spawned gave way to assertions of a "hypertrophy of memory" with its "melancholy fixations" and "privileging of the traumatic."[9] Some historians have argued not only that "memory studies have thrived on catastrophes and trauma," but also that "the Holocaust is still the primary, archetypal topic in memory studies."[10] After noting that "the Holocaust...is also at the heart of much concern with memory," another historian adds that "there can indeed be little doubt that the Holocaust has been crucial in the shift from a 'history of the victors'...to a 'history of the victims,'"[11] but provides little evidence other than a footnote to Friedrich Nietzsche and Walter Benjamin for this important historical claim, as if it were self-evident. And Eric Santner has argued that "where the Jews were once blamed for the traumas of modernity, the Holocaust now seems to figure as the irritating signifier of the traumas and disorientations of postmodernity."[12]

---

8. Jean Baudrillard, *The Evil Demon of Images* (Sydney: Power Institute of Fine Arts, University of Sydney, 1987), 24.

9. Andreas Huyssen, *Present Pasts: Urban Palimpsests and the Politics of Memory* (Stanford: Stanford University Press, 2003), 6. On the rise of a "memory industry" in the most sweeping terms, see Gavriel D. Rosenfeld, "A Looming Crash or a Soft Landing? Forecasting the Future of the Memory 'Industry,'" *Journal of Modern History* 81 (2009): 122–58. Rosenfeld rightly draws our attention to the importance of resurgent nationalism in the turn to "memory," but never notes that the idea of a "memory industry" is linked primarily to the Holocaust and its aftermath. In another vein Gabrielle Spiegel argues suggestively that experience and memory of the Holocaust are among the unrecognized causes of the "epistemological crisis" which led to the linguistic turn in historiography. Gabrielle M. Speigel, "Revising the Past/Revisiting the Present: How Change Happens in Historiography," *History and Theory* 46 (2007): 1–19.

10. Richard Ned Lebow, Wulf Kansteiner, and Claudio Fogu, eds., *The Politics of Memory in Postwar Europe* (Durham: Duke University Press, 2006), 286. On the universalization of the Holocaust, see Jeffrey Alexander, *Remembering the Holocaust: A Debate* (Oxford: Oxford University Press, 2009).

11. Jan-Werner Müller, *Memory and Power in Post-war Europe: Studies in the Presence of the Past* (Cambridge: Cambridge University Press, 2002), 14.

12. Eric Santner, *Stranded Objects: Mourning, Memory, and Film in Postwar Germany* (Ithaca: Cornell University Press, 1990), 51. This view is also expressed by Elizabeth J. Bellamy, *Affective Genealogies: Psychoanalysis, Postmodernism, and the "Jewish Question" after Auschwitz*

Some critics bemoan the allegedly widespread generalization of all violent events into traumas by scholars in various disciplines, which at least
one commentator asserts has created the stance of being a victim "and its
entitlements as a mark of the everyday."[13] This 'turn to trauma' has been
aptly diagnosed as a manner in which some poststructuralist and other theorists responded to criticism that deconstruction and postmodernism were
forms of nihilism by focusing in their own way on 'things that matter': on
injury, victims, and collective suffering. In a recent book on the Holocaust
and the production of trauma, Karyn Ball argues that there is a "tendency
among scholars to turn to trauma as moral capital that establishes them as
responsible and caring critics."[14]

This turn to trauma is now also increasingly criticized as a symptom of
too much interest in victims, in part perhaps because it tends to conflate
victims of all sorts with the more specific kinds of victimization identified with the extreme violence generated by torture, war, and catastrophic
loss.[15] Indeed, Amos Goldberg believes that the victim's voice now merely
allows for "pleasurable identification" with suffering so familiar that it
does not wrench us out of our comfortable lives to confront the pain of
others, but has become a source of entertainment. The victim's voice is

(Lincoln: University of Nebraska Press, 1997), 31. She argues that Jews have become "tropes or
signifiers for the decentered...postmodern subject" in French thought that "fetishizes" them and
is problematically philosemitic. See also the compelling discussion of the political and cultural
consequences of the Holocaust's role as the summa of suffering in Naomi Mandel, *Against the Unspeakable: Complicity, the Holocaust, and Slavery in America* (Charlottesville: University of Virginia
Press, 2006).

13. Wulf Kansteiner, "Genealogy of a Category Mistake: A Critical Intellectual History of
the Cultural Trauma Metaphor," *Rethinking History* 8 (2004): 214. See, among others, Mark Selt-
zer, "Wound Culture: Trauma in the Pathological Public Sphere," *October* 80 (1997): 3–26; Kirby
Farrell, *Post-Traumatic Culture: Injury and Interpretation in the Nineties* (Baltimore: Johns Hopkins
University Press, 1998); and Karyn Ball, on the institutionalization, as she sees it, of trauma discourse, in "Trauma and Its Institutional Destinies," *Cultural Critique* 46 (2000): 1–44.

14. Karyn Ball, *Disciplining the Holocaust* (Albany: State University of New York Press,
2008), 191.

15. Michael S. Roth, "The Art of Losing Oneself," *Raritan* 3 (2008): 161. See also Roger Luckhurst, *The Trauma Question* (New York: Routledge, 2008), 118. Luckhurst calls the turn to ethics
the "pressure of the real": "Whether the real was invoked in a posttheoretical concern for a more
ethical criticism or a pre-critical assertion of great authenticity, the memoir boom was situated in
this matrix of concerns, its value bound to its allegedly greater proximity to the traumatic real." It
is important, however, to note that many renditions of victims' suffering use trauma as a stand-in
for having been victimized, and the notion that we live in a 'wound culture' or a 'trauma culture'
merely reiterates this presumption as if it required no further examination.

thus emblematic of our melodramatic age. "It is in this context," Goldberg writes, "that one can understand the popularity of the victim in recent Holocaust representations: the flood of survivors' memoirs published by the dozen each year; the popularity and centrality of video archives; the newly erected museums such as the new Yad Vashem museum, the Berlin memorial, and the recently inaugurated Bergen-Belsen site, which all draw very heavily on the victim's voice and testimony."[16] In Roger Luckhurst's view, the "success of the trauma memoir" is not simply "symptomatic of a culture of mass narcissism." It is rather a sign of the "affective transmissibility of trauma" across a dizzying range of discourses, and the intensified fashioning of selves through the (secondary) experience of trauma that has come to define identity in our wound culture.[17]

This book discusses the now pervasive discourse about the inextricable relationship between suffering, traumatic suffering, and identity in mostly French and American debates about Jewish victims of the Holocaust. This discourse comes in many forms which are hardly monolithic. They are the product of a shifting historical terrain, are often acute, brash, and polemical, and constitutive of some of the most significant cultural

16. Amos Goldberg, "The Victim's Voice and Melodramatic Aesthetics in History," *History and Theory* 48 (2009): 233.

17. Luckhurst, *The Trauma Question*, 119. Luckhurst's is a fascinating discussion of how avant-garde work, psychiatry, and low culture embraced trauma as a guarantor of subjectivity. For an interesting and more optimistic but insufficiently historicized conception of the effects of "prosthetic memory" in which 'we' can experience historical traumas we have not lived, see Alison Landsberg, *Prosthetic Memory: The Transformation of American Remembrance in the Age of Mass Culture* (New York: Columbia University Press, 2004). Landsberg seeks admirably to defend mass culture media and historicizes memory to the extent that it can be generated now across varied collective identifications in an era of globalization. But whether the Holocaust and slavery are memories experienced in their profundity by those who are not Jewish or African American remains to be seen. The idea that the Holocaust paradigm at least makes trauma accessible as a way of thinking about crimes committed more directly by the United States' government is a good one, but it is not at all clear if such connections have occurred or with what consequences. A similar claim is made by Michael Rothberg, *Multidirectional Memory: Remembering the Holocaust in the Age of Decolonization* (Stanford: Stanford University Press, 2009), 6. Rothberg's compelling book seeks to repudiate the idea of a clear relation between memory and identity (that which contributes to a 'competition of victims,' about which more later) and to replace it with "multidirectional memory": the latter recognizes the far more complex grids through which memory (and thus identity) is constituted, including how Holocaust memory is articulated in and through a whole literature on decolonization. This argument is persuasive on its own terms, but I would suggest that any discussion of the relationship between memory and identity has to take account of the role now played by victim discourse in defining both memory and identity itself.

presuppositions of our time. They also allow us to engage in critical historical work on what is now a pervasive discussion about victims, Jewish or not, because the iconic status of the Holocaust is inextricable from the emergence of this discussion. I focus on how reflections on Jewish memory shape the most mainstream, public, and apparently self-evident discourse on victimization: the effort to distinguish between so-called real victims of catastrophic events and those who choose to play victim, embrace injury, or wish they had been victims.

The American incarnation of this discourse has been trenchantly analyzed by Alyson M. Cole, who calls it "the cult of true victimhood": 'real' victims are defined by such narrow juridical standards of blamelessness, powerlessness, and innocence that victimization is hard to prove. As she puts it, "when charges of social injustice are recast within notions of blamelessness and guilt that emanate from the courtroom, members of marginal groups must provide the equivalent of forensic evidence to demonstrate that they are in fact disadvantaged."[18] Cole notes that in the United States after the 1970s, the "Holocaust survivor [became] a model for grappling with adversity,"[19] but otherwise only speculates about the various reasons for the rise of so-called victim culture. She argues that 'real' victims allegedly suffer with dignity and refuse to proclaim their wounds too publicly.[20]

Most of the critics I discuss participate indirectly in legitimating this kind of "anti-victimism," to use Cole's term. This anti-victimism unfolds on multiple levels of discussion in both Europe and the United States. Indeed, by virtue of what has become its dominance, putative self-evidence, and sheer pervasiveness, this discourse on injury undergirds the revision of new normative frameworks within which the limits and potential of human agency and responsibility are now being reconsidered, including how we distinguish innocent from guilty victims as well as the deserving from the undeserving.

I inquire into four overlapping French and American debates about Jewish victims and victims' memory linked by their emphasis on suspicion and exaggeration regarding victims and their suffering which cannot be

18. Alyson M. Cole, *The Cult of True Victimhood: From the War on Welfare to the War on Terror* (Stanford: Stanford University Press, 2007), 6.
19. Cole, *The Cult of True Victimhood,* 16.
20. Cole, *The Cult of True Victimhood,* 5.

neatly divided up into chapters but unfold differently over the work that follows: that Jewish victims are obsessively and pathologically remembered; that Jews who were not victims long to have been victims themselves; that credible Jewish victims represent their suffering ascetically; and that efforts to define what made the industrialized murder of Jewry different from other forms of mass murder somehow deny the universal experience of suffering, the experience of having been reduced, in Michael Ignatieff's phrase, to one's "bare humanity."[21] I address these debates by treating the motifs of excess and suspicion as part of a complicated affective relationship to victims (distance, aversion, identification) that transcends context but is nonetheless fashioned by its location in particular times and places. In order to outline more effectively the phantasmatic dimension of this discourse on victims (however real the concerns it addresses), I also inquire into how victimization is inextricable from the rhetorical fashioning of the exemplary victim. I examine critics' failure to evaluate their own responses to victims: how do critics participate in victims' erasure, or on what terms does the recognition of their injuries now take place?[22]

The critics with whom I am concerned suggest implicitly that the structure of grievance in democratic societies is being transformed and contested by the power of a public display of wounds in the face of which rational debate goes mute. In this view, the real pain and perhaps trauma of the sufferer may be a false or distorted claim, as if victimization conferred desperately longed-for recognition that we will purchase at any price. This need for recognition, moreover, indicates the social deficiency of an implicitly feminized citizenry who prefers to construct its identity as a passive object of untold torment rather than as an active agent of will and resolve.[23] And finally, this criticism

21. Michael Ignatieff, *The Needs of Strangers* (London: Hogarth Press, 1984), 28–30, 51–52. I do not suggest that the Holocaust was unique in the sense that it is incomparable or transcendent, but rather that it is different by virtue of the specific historical circumstances that converged to make it happen and distinguish it from other genocides.

22. Didier Fassin and Richard Rechtman, *L'empire du traumatisme: Enquête sur la condition de victime* (Paris: Flammarion, 2007), 33–37.

23. This view is implicit in a wide variety of works. See, among others, Robert Hughes, *Culture of Complaint: The Fraying of America* (Oxford: Oxford University Press, 1993); Daniel Farber and Suzanna Sherry, eds. *Beyond All Reason* (Oxford: Oxford University Press, 1999); and G. Eric Hansen, *The Culture of Strangers: Globalization, Localization, and the Phenomenon of Exchange* (New York: University Press of America, 2002). The first is a sophisticated but highly ideological and polemical book; the last two are thoughtful interventions in debates about

of a purported culture of victims challenges the frequent claim that traumatic experience is re-lived by future generations removed from the direct experience of suffering. It asks about the tenacity of the literature on the transmission of trauma, and suggests that the idea of transmission represents not only the narcissistic appropriation of the pain of others, but also the collapse of empathy. Those who empathize do not feel for sufferers but take their place.

My aim is to explore the very constitution of a culture of victims and ask what ideological and affective investments the insistence on such a culture reveals. In particular, I wish to analyze the investment in the victim's mastery of his or her experience such that it can be described lucidly and objectively and interpreted as something past. I will insist that lucidity takes other forms than objectivity and try to understand how the affect associated with confusion and helplessness may often be the most sensitive and truthful rendition of having suffered.

From Heroes to Victims, from Memory to a Surfeit of Memory

Western historical and journalistic accounts of catastrophes since the end of the Second World War have ceased gradually to focus on brave or cowardly victims. Instead, they have revised and secularized an older association of victims with sacrifice as the redemptive discourses of the Great War were eventually outmoded by the extermination of European Jewry.[24] In his discussion of the often tense relationship between French non-Jewish resistance fighters and the Jewish victims of the Holocaust, Donald Reid

---

multiculturalism and their consequences for those who seek inclusion in the United States' democracy under that rubric.

24. Discussion about how sacrifice performatively binds communities (as articulated differently by Freud, Mauss, and Durkheim and reinterpreted since) is voluminous. The social and cultural function of the sacrificial victim, however, is not my focus here, though it would be useful to take up the meaning of sacrifice in this discursive context, as Dominick LaCapra has done explicitly and implicitly in much of his work: *Representing the Holocaust: History, Theory, Trauma* (Ithaca: Cornell University Press, 1994); *History in Transit: Experience, Identity, Critical Theory* (Ithaca: Cornell University Press, 2004); and *History and Its Limits: Human, Animal, Violence* (Ithaca: Cornell University Press, 2009). See also Fatima Naqvi, *The Rhetoric of Victimhood: Western Europe, 1970–2005* (New York: Palgrave Macmillan, 2007). Naqvi discusses victimhood in the context of wounded identity conceived as a surrogate form of connection in societies now radically atomized. She quite usefully analyzes "victimhood" as it emerges in films and novels in contemporary Austria, Germany, and, to a lesser extent, France.

argues, "The shared extermination narrative secures the place of camps like Ravensbrück [where partisans and Jews were both interned] even as the determining element in accounts of the camps has shifted from resistance to victimhood."[25] His argument is that now the fate of European Jews, who were sent for the most part to extermination camps and directed to gas chambers upon arrival, has in the eyes of many French resisters obscured concentration camps like Ravensbrück that were crucial to Nazi political and economic goals: hard labor for the war effort ensured the slow and agonizing deaths of the partisans, political dissidents, criminals, homosexuals, Jehovah's witnesses, and prisoners-of-war interned in them. After the war a patriotic narrative of national resistance enfolded Jewish victims without acknowledging the particularity of their experience as the only group other than Roma and Sinti marked exclusively for death.

The great resistance figure Germaine Tillion insisted that since Ravensbrück and Auschwitz both had gas chambers, the difference between them was a matter of orders of magnitude. They were not, she argued, fundamentally different phenomena.[26] Now, however, as Reid implies, resisters have to be more 'like Jews' if they wish to be acknowledged.[27] Like other historians since the late 1980s, Reid conceives challenges to the mythical memory of the French resistance as a symptom of the resurgent memory of Jewish victimization. The idea that one narrative merely replaced the other may be oversimplified given the multiplicity of stories heard and not heard about Jewish experience after the war. There was far more tension, overlap, and even public debate than is generally remembered (at least in France) between the universalizing patriotic and the particularizing Jewish narratives about the "camp universe" or *univers concentrationnaire*—a term coined by camp prisoner David Rousset in his famous 1946 work of the same name.[28]

---

25. Donald Reid, "Germaine Tillion and Resistance to the Vichy Syndrome," *History and Memory* 15 (2003): 55. See also Olga Wormser-Migot, *Le rétour des déportés* (Paris: Éditions Complexes, 1985).

26. Reid, "Germaine Tillion," 45.

27. Resisters felt this way in spite of their victory in securing status as targets of crimes against humanity in the Nazi Klaus Barbie's 1987 trial for the murder of Jewish children. Barbie was also the murderer of the great gentile resistance fighter Jean Moulin.

28. David Rousset, *L'univers concentrationnaire* (Paris: Minuit, 1965). Emma Kuby argues that in the immediate postwar period Rousset introduced the experience of suffering in the camps in place of resistance as quintessential, though inserted it into a narrative of heroic sacrifice applicable to all victims, including Jews, whose distinctive experience he did not fully appreciate. Kuby,

The belated memory of the Jewish Holocaust, in short, did not alone make the shift away from narratives of patriotic mourning, sacrifice, redemption, and thus ultimately tragic heroism conceivable, but ultimately revised the meaning of the Second World War through the prism of Jewish suffering.

We might argue that this struggle between Jewish memory and the memory of the French partisans is one more example of wearisome current struggles over whose memory counts. But we might also argue that the struggles over memory are embedded in and constituted by (indeed inexplicable without) the emergence of more recent cultural concepts of how humans should behave under duress, and the problems of recognition and self-recognition they express. Thus to put the emergence of new narratives about victims in the West in the broadest possible historical perspective, these narratives might be located in the brutality of Nazi occupation and its legacy, in which the frameworks of resistance were so constrained, especially in Eastern Europe, that they left little room for heroism. Clearly a minority of extraordinary men and women resisted fascism and Nazism, and their heroism was framed in the language of great men, grand gestures, and often patriotic martyrdom. But all over Europe the creation of an enormous and yet amorphous category of "victims of fascism" quietly began to replace both the image of the individuated, heroic soldier who dies for his country and the homefront of civilians whose suffering and tears redeem patriotic sacrifice, however powerfully nation-states—France in particular—clung to traditional heroic commemoration of the dead. The necessity of patriotic recovery after the war undermined differences between various targets of persecution such as partisans and Jews, now reduced to generalized categories such as victims of fascism, which allowed for the reintegration of all those deported into a redemptive narrative of national resistance in Belgium, France, and the Netherlands.[29] In Russia

Between Humanism and Terror: The Problem of Political Violence in Postwar France, 1944–1962, Ph.D. thesis, Department of History, Cornell University, 2010. Samuel Moyn has demonstrated that in France, what he has dubbed the "Treblinka Affair" in 1966 (a controversy about a fictionalized representation of Treblinka that engaged questions of Jewish heroism and passivity) challenged the narrative of patriotic resistance, and that the recognition of Jewish particularity was acknowledged far earlier than is normally believed, and shaped the reception of Hannah Arendt's work on Eichmann. Moyn, *A Holocaust Controversy: The Treblinka Affair in Postwar France* (Waltham, MA: Brandeis University Press, 2005), 141–68.

29. Pieter LaGrou, *The Legacy of Nazi Occupation: Patriotic Memory and National Recovery in Western Europe, 1945–1965* (Cambridge: Cambridge University Press, 2000).

and Eastern Europe a similar narrative cultivated by Soviet leaders and occupiers held that atrocities had been committed primarily by "fascists," making no distinction, for example, between the sufferings of Catholic and Jewish Poles. As a recent section in a collection of essays about postwar Europe entitled the *Politics of Collective Memory* puts it, "No more conquerors, no more defeated, no more enemies, nothing but war victims."[30] Finally, as other historians have argued, extra-legal and even legal proceedings against collaborators immediately after the war were often part of a larger effort not only to purge political opponents, but also to place the blame for what had happened during the course of the war on a select minority of individuals, thereby transforming the vast majority of the population into victims even if many had accommodated the enemy.[31] The most infamous example of exculpation was the politically motivated Allied construction of the majority of Germans and Austrians after the war as Hitler's victims, a fiction populations were willing to oblige.[32]

Injury from natural calamity had long been a historical fact for the vast numbers of noncombatant human beings all over the world for whom suffering was ideologically meaningless even if to be mourned and regretted. Until the nineteenth century, suffering simply defined their bodily and social vulnerability to natural disasters conceived in religious or fatalistic terms. The literal and symbolic import of some injuries arose in relation to nineteenth-century modernity and its creation of industrial and environmental accidents that created victims of non-natural causes and an administrative (legal and medical) apparatus to address their needs and

30. Sophie Wachnich, Barbara Lášticová, and Andrej Findor, eds., *Politics of Collective Memory: Cultural Patterns of Commemorative Practices in Post-War Europe* (New Brunswick, NJ: Transaction, 2008), 14. This important book identifies the leveling of perpetrators and victims and the construction of heroism in new terms after the Second World War. The book does not conceptualize so much as document that this leveling happened, and does so primarily through an emphasis on the blurring of boundaries between victims and executioners.

31. See essays in István Déak, Jan T. Gross, and Tony Judt, eds., *The Politics of Retribution in Europe: World War II and Its Aftermath* (Princeton: Princeton University Press, 2000). For a brief discussion about how the memory of Communism has recently effaced the memory of Jewish suffering in East and Central Europe, see Régine Robin, *La mémoire saturée* (Paris: Stock, 2003), 121–44. On Italy, see Michele Battini, *The Missing Italian Nuremberg: Cultural Amnesia and Postwar Politics* (New York: Palgrave Macmillan, 2007).

32. For a recent compilation of essays on the topic from all perspectives and up to the present, see Bill Niven, ed., *Germans as Victims: Remembering the Past in Contemporary Germany* (New York: Palgrave Macmillan, 2006).

concerns, including the expansion of insurance.[33] Man-made massacres and slavery were ideologically sanctioned forms of hegemony defined in religious or racist terms until abolitionist movements refused to accept the violence against those sold into slavery. But abolitionist movements had little influence on the pervasive and intensified racist violence against colonized peoples all over the globe. It was not until after 1948 that the right not to suffer violence or hatred in *genocidal* form became a central component of international human rights law and applied, at least in theory, to all people. Hannah Arendt famously exposed the limits of this universal right when she argued that the Enlightenment concept of human dignity applied to citizens but not to stateless peoples. Her reference was to the treatment of refugees during the Second World War (and other categories of people before and after).[34] Critics such as Michael Ignatieff and Samantha Power have argued that since the end of the Second World War claims to having been violated are inextricably linked to a concept of humanity not defined in terms of reason or moral worth and thus dignity but, to use Ignatieff's formulation, in terms of "bare humanity" (which should be tempered by Arendt's warning that some human beings are nonetheless deemed more human than others).[35]

With the emergence of "crimes against humanity" as a legal category as well as a broader Western commitment to human rights, however fraught in practice, the concept of victim might now refer to those Jews who had experienced untold physical and emotional deprivation with no necessarily

33. It should be clear that my reference is not to the construction of victims as persons who may seek redress for or protection from perceived wrongs (hence the invention of private and public insurance or workers' compensation law), but to victims of historical catastrophes like war and genocide. It is true that natural disasters are now often inseparable from man-made calamities given environmental policies, pollution, and technology. For those victims too, however, a new legal apparatus has developed to allow reparations to be made (even if responsibility is hard to attribute). For a discussion, see Gaëlle Clavandier, "Les victimes collectives, une notion en cours d'élaboration," in *Victimes du présent, victimes du passé: Vers la sociologie des victimes,* ed. Ewa Bogalska-Martin (Paris: L'Harmattan, 2004), 97–156.

34. Hannah Arendt, *The Origins of Totalitarianism* (New York: Harcourt Brace Jovanovich, 1976 [1951]), 300–302; and *The Jew as Pariah: Jewish Identity and Politics in the Modern Age* (New York: Grove Press, 1978), 65.

35. Ignatieff, *The Needs of Strangers,* 28–30, 51–52; Samantha Power, *"A Problem from Hell": America and the Age of Genocide* (New York: Basic Books, 2002). Michael Rothberg's discussion of Arendt's treatment of colonialism in *The Origins of Totalitarianism* is particularly interesting. See Rothberg, *Multidirectional Memory,* 33–65.

redemptive or sacrificial meaning, even as redemptive discourses remained emotionally powerful and often politically necessary.[36] It is instructive to compare the narrative of the Great War with this, later, discourse: after the Great War, mainstream cultural narratives recounted dead or wounded soldiers as tragic victims of a breakdown in the judgment of political leaders, and resurrected an older language of redemption, mourning, and suffering in sacred terms.[37] But the widespread complicity of the majority population with the Nazi occupiers and thus with the extermination of European Jewry after the Second World War rendered the narrative of tragic victimization and sacred resurrection—essentially, the discourse of patriotic mourning—a far less self-evident approach to postwar healing and renewal, and impossible in Germany. Patriotic mourning was used instrumentally in France and remained available to those in resistance movements and nations like Poland particularly targeted by the Nazis. Jews and others were instrumentally and psychologically assimilated into the general category of "victims," even though they had suffered an undeniably distinct fate from their compatriots and could not therefore participate, or only uneasily, in narratives about the common and tragic fate of the nation.[38]

In France, as Olivier Wieviorka has argued, the radical differences in victims' experiences that distinguished the Second from the First World War were only reconciled by President Charles de Gaulle's imposition of a coherent narrative in which the causes of suffering mattered less than the actual suffering of French men and women. Thus the experience of war

36. In his work on Dutch Jewry during the Second World War, historian Ido de Haan writes, "The recognition of Jewish victims was only the beginning of a broader cultural shift in which groups of people were identified first and foremost as victims of society." De Haan, *Dutch Jews as Perceived by Themselves and by Others: Proceedings of the Eighth International Symposium on the History of the Jews in the Netherlands,* ed. Chaya Brasz and Yosef Kaplan (Leiden: Brill, 2001), 432.

37. Jay Winter, *Sites of Memory, Sites of Mourning: The Great War in European Cultural History* (Cambridge: Cambridge University Press, 1995), argues that the scale of collective loss necessitated the resurrection of older forms of redemptive and sacred discourses adapted to new circumstances. He notes that these forms were no longer available after the Second World War, when the "search for meaning" generated "silence" (228). Who, Winter asks, could speak of "divine justice"—as was done after the Great War—after the gas chambers (203)? Though this view is boilerplate and thus not explanatory, Winter's divide between the two wars nonetheless reflects the perceived difference between victims of the Great War and Jewish victims of Nazi extermination.

38. Leonard V. Smith, *The Embattled Self: French Soldiers' Testimony of the Great War* (Ithaca: Cornell University Press, 2007).

veterans, Jews, partisans, French non-Jewish forced laborers, and others, was assimilated into a narrative of patriotic suffering that could not ultimately be sustained in the face of a competition between these groups for recognition and the State's eventual concession to Jewish victims in particular (after having ignored them for the most part and with some notable exceptions until 1995). After the 1970s, Wieviorka argues, the "discourse of heroism gave way to that of the victim."[39]

Hero and martyr tropes hardly disappeared, but the concept of victim was increasingly universalized and homogenized and the possibility of a nonsacrificial construction of victimization rendered conceivable if not realized. Despite conventional wisdom about the silence of Jews and others in the postwar period, there was an abundance of memoirs published by deported Jews and partisans who felt compelled to convey their particular experiences, but Annette Wieviorka argues convincingly that the lack of reference to any familiar context, combined with the small number of people who had had this experience, rendered them unmarketable, in contrast to testimonies of the Great War.[40] Zoë Waxman has also claimed that the silence surrounding the Jewish experience was perhaps less dramatic than previously thought (she notes that there were 75 memoirs published by Jews between 1945 and 1949, but emphasizes that those that made the greatest impact were written by non-Jews who spoke as partisans, like David Rousset).[41]

By the 1970s, a series of events transformed the Holocaust of European Jewry into a subject that elicited massive academic and popular interest. The leveling of victims that had obscured the specificity of Jewish suffering began to dissipate in favor of the recognition of Jewish pain. These well-known events include the televised 1961 kidnapping and trial of Adolf Eichmann in Israel, during which survivors testified about their experiences in camps; Israel's military victory in the 1967 Arab-Israeli war, which generated a profound sense of Jewish pride and defined the Holocaust as an event that unfolded because Jews had no state of their own; and

39. Olivier Wieviorka, *La mémoire désunie: Le souvenir politique des années sombres, de la Libération à nos jours* (Paris: Seuil, 2010), 154–55, 186.

40. Annette Wieviorka, *Déportation et génocide: Entre la mémoire et l'oubli* (Paris: Plon, 1992), 168–90.

41. Zoë Vania Waxman, *Writing the Holocaust: Identity, Testimony, Representation* (Oxford: Oxford University Press, 2006), 100–103, 110–11.

television shows such as the 1977 Hollywood miniseries "Holocaust," which brought the Nazis' unspeakable inhumanity to mass media and a large audience. Indeed, such was the recognition of Jewish suffering after so long a silence that Andreas Huyssen suggests that the Holocaust became the central reference point for the emergence of memory discourses elsewhere in the world: "The politics of Holocaust commemoration (what to remember, how to remember, when to remember), so prominent in the global media and in the countries of the northern transatlantic since the 1980s, has functioned like a motor energizing the discourses of memory elsewhere. There is reason to wonder whether without the prominence of Holocaust memory since the 1980s, most of the memory discourses the world over would be what they are today."[42]

In a startling metamorphosis, the near annihilation of European Jews, whose early efforts to recount their experiences met mostly if not exclusively, according to Wieviorka and Waxman, with minimal interest,[43] was now something about which not enough could be said: it became a symbol of radical evil in our time, a warning to future generations, a model of catastrophes to come, and, at worst, big business.[44] As the British journalist Hannah Betts puts it, there now exists a general consensus that the "Shoah business" has become "a spectacle, an industry—a European event brought to us by American production values."[45]

Explanations now offered for the iconic status of Jewish suffering no longer seek only to explain the increased cultural interest in the Holocaust since the 1970s, about which there is a voluminous literature on both testimony and memory: today there is a pervasive discourse focused less on

42. Huyssen, *Present Pasts,* 99. This subject of the Holocaust as a benchmark in European history is repeated in Tony Judt's epilogue to *Postwar: A History of Europe since 1945* (New York: Penguin, 2005), 803–31.

43. See the collection Richard Bessell and Dirk Schumann, eds., *Life after Death: Approaches to a Social and Cultural History of Europe during the 1940s and 1950s* (Cambridge: Cambridge University Press and the German Historical Institute, 2003).

44. Annette Wieviorka notes that the Holocaust has become a "transnational memory," manifested by the modeling of other genocidal monuments on Yad Vashem. Wieviorka, "Shoah: Les étapes de la mémoire en France," in *Les guerres de mémoires: La France et son histoire; Enjeux politiques, controverses, historiques, strategies médiatiques,* ed. Pascal Blanchard and Isabelle Veyrat-Masson (Paris: La Découverte, 2008), 106.

45. Hannah Betts, "The Testament of Ghosts," *Times* (London), May 30, 2000.

memory than on how some memories get more attention than others.[46] This discourse about the *surfeit* of Jewish memory emerged most forcefully in the 1990s and focuses on the anaesthetic effects of the proliferation of media representations and memorials of the Holocaust.[47] The collapse of the Soviet Union and the end of the Cold War, the growth of NGOs, and the political uses of the media by humanitarian and other organizations to promote the cause of human rights have all led gradually to a greater emphasis internationally on restitution and on apologies by nations who had committed atrocities against Jews and colonized peoples.[48] There is no question, as Betts suggests, that these developments have occurred against a background in which the extermination of European Jewry somehow trumps the pain of others in the memory and media of human suffering in the West.

The iconic status accorded the Holocaust not only indicates that this catastrophe has been emptied of its specific historical meaning,[49] but also leads to allegations that this trauma, rather than forcing us to pay more attention to other forms of persecution, implicitly delegitimates other claims to have suffered by its magnitude, as if all 'real' suffering had to resemble extermination by gas and other forms of mass murder invented by the Nazis.[50] It is perhaps predictable not only that other groups with their own

46. Sylvie Lindeperg and Annette Wieviorka, *Univers concentrationnaire et génocide: Voir, savoir, comprendre* (Paris: Mille et une nuits, 2008), 116.

47. It is interesting to note that in 1994 Wulf Kansteiner spoke of a shift in historical scholarship away from a focus on the Holocaust's uniqueness underway in the 1970s to a general understanding of "disturbing normality," but understood what we now refer to as a surfeit of memory primarily in terms of the distinction between the sobriety of scholarly work and the popular media representations of the Holocaust. See Wulf Kansteiner, "From Exception to Exemplum: The New Approach to Nazism and the 'Final Solution,'" *History and Theory* 33 (1994): 171.

48. Mark Philip Bradley and Patrice Petro, eds., *Truth Claims: Representation and Human Rights* (New Brunswick, NJ: Rutgers University Press, 2002); and Elazar Barkan, *The Guilt of Nations: Restitution and Negotiating Historical Injustices* (Baltimore: Johns Hopkins University Press, 2000).

49. Barbie Zelizer, *Remembering to Forget: Holocaust Memory through the Camera's Eye* (Chicago: University of Chicago Press, 1998).

50. That is, while many critics decry the 'competition' between victim groups, and while others claims that the Holocaust's status at least opened the door to a consideration of other victims' claims, there is little critical literature other than Peter Novick's efforts that examines how the iconic status of the Holocaust may have generated this competition and even less on how it actually generated an interest in other human catastrophes like slavery. One might claim that it was only by its negative impact—that is, by taking pride of place in the panorama of human suffering—that the Holocaust generated interest in the suffering of others. Novick, *The Holocaust in American Life.*

tragic histories sought to find analogies between their suffering and that of European Jewry, but also that, in Germany for example, bestsellers now seek to render the victims of carpet-bombing implicitly equivalent to murdered Jews—all victims of human indifference to life rather than of particular historical moments and political decisions.[51] In 1998, the writer Martin Walser called the Holocaust a "moral cudgel" to which Germans must cease to pay deference because its memory had become so inflated and instrumentalized.[52] In France, the trial of Nazi Klaus Barbie in 1987 sparked a debate not only about whether Jews and *résistants* had suffered equally, but also about whether Nazi crimes against Jews were comparable to French crimes against Algerians. A historian of the discourse on the Holocaust in France notes that it was someone else's turn by the 1990s— Jews had been the subject of too much memory.[53] In France, as we will see in Chapter Two, there has also been a debate about whether Stalinism was as evil as Nazism. In Italy the belated 1996 trial of Nazi Erich Preibke for an infamous massacre turned Preibke into a "victim" of enraged relatives and of Jews, whose coreligionists counted among the minority (75 of 335) of those murdered. As a chronicler of the massacre and trial explains, in spite of its initial representation in the 1950s as an emblem of Italian victimization at the hands of the Nazis, by the 1990s the killings were "the private business of the Jews," setting the stage not only for assertions about exaggerated Jewish claims, but later also for revisionist assertions that all Italians suffered equally.[54] And Norman Finkelstein argues (in)famously that there is a "Holocaust industry" that uses the fate of European Jewry merely as an occasion for profiting from the interest of the public in other people's pain.[55]

In short, Jewish claims to have suffered are not denied but often deemed to be excessive. No longer, for the most part, must we establish the reality of the

51. Joerg Friedrich, *Der Brand: Deutschland im Bombenkrieg, 1940–1945* (Munich: Propylaeen, 2002).

52. For a discussion of the debate around Walser's speech in Frankfurt (upon receipt of the Peace Prize of the German Book Trade), see Niven, ed., *Germans as Victims,* 10–12, 100–102.

53. Joan Wolf, *Harnessing the Holocaust: The Politics of Memory in France* (Stanford: Stanford University Press, 2004), 42–68.

54. Alessandro Portelli, *The Order Has Been Carried Out: History, Memory, and Meaning of a Nazi Massacre in Rome* (New York: Palgrave Macmillan, 2003), 256. See also pp. 241–58.

55. Norman Finkelstein, *The Holocaust Industry: Reflections on the Exploitation of Jewish Suffering* (London: Verso, 2000).

suffering of Jews or others: that Jews were victimized does not prevent them or their heirs from at the same time being perceived through the lens of anti-Semitic prejudice and from becoming the objects of other uncontrolled projections and displacements. Oddly, fantasies of Jewish power now derive not from Jews' putative cunning and ability to adapt to and thrive parasitically in any environment, but from their recent survival of the Nazi effort to banish them from earth.[56] Thus the questions we must address in this context are not under what circumstances someone or some group might claim to have been victimized and why or why not the claim would be successful. We must move outside the conventional frameworks in which such questions are usually posed: the parameters of power politics, such as which victims are more easily dispensed with from a geopolitical perspective or which groups militate more effectively for recognition from the point of view of their political strategies and impact; and normative sentiment, such as which groups elicit more sympathy (women and children, but also those with whom we most identify).[57] All of these approaches are significant and can hardly be ignored, but they might be more explicitly framed by and embedded in other questions: How has the status of being disempowered or traumatized become central to self-definition? How is the centrality of suffering to identity related to the alleged triumph of affect over rational debate? When might affective response to victims be contrary to or more nuanced and difficult to decipher than normative sentiment and how are those responses shaped and mapped onto institutions? How, in short, have discourses about the impact of the Holocaust and its effects emerged and with what consequences to define the very meaning of victimization and to generate so much skepticism about victims?

Economies of Suffering

It is perhaps not surprising that, given the implicit or explicit discussions of constrained agency in discourses on victims, ideological investments in

56. For the notion that Jews are attached, however ambivalently, to their own exceptionalism and its consequences, see Jean Daniel, *La prison juive: Humeurs et méditations d'un témoin* (Paris: Odile Jacob, 2003). I am not interested in this discussion here.

57. For a comprehensive account of recent issues in this vein, see Barkan, *The Guilt of Nations*.

victimization and their definitions, contexts, and forms of expression are so central to addressing new concerns about the status of human choice, will, and action in the twenty-first century. Indeed, debates and discussions about victims have arguably become the primary conceptual location of an ongoing struggle to define the parameters of human will, resolve, and accountability. The knowledge that suffering can be distorted, denied, or used instrumentally for political purposes is hardly new, but because its representations are now the focus of unprecedented claims for rights and recognition, and the alleged source of so much pleasure, increasing numbers of critics insist on a clear-eyed account of when injuries are real or manufactured, and lucid criteria by which to assess different kinds of pain.

The efforts to establish clear boundaries between real and would-be victims on which we focus are related to the so-called surfeit of Jewish memory generated by the iconic suffering attributed to the Holocaust of European Jewry, about which much has been written, but most of it unsystematically. It is in keeping with these concerns that Annette Wieviorka, speaking of the publicity afforded Holocaust survivors, dubs the contemporary period the "era of the witness." She argues that Western culture has transformed victim testimony into a media spectacle and blurs boundaries between real victims of historical catastrophe and those who can tell a good story, making it impossible to discern the truth about the past.[58] Wieviorka claims that the emergence of new media replaces rational debate and interpretation with an under-scrutinized appeal to emotions, and encourages a now passive citizenry to seek recognition in victimhood rather than in deliberative action. One writer has denounced the phenomenon of Holocaust experience "stolen" by faux victims who write memoirs that instantly gain attention from those who can't get enough of suffering.[59] In an extreme version of some of this criticism of our putative obsession with victims, which discards any reference to Jewish memory, the philosopher Jean Baudrillard argues that victim identity is no longer attached to the real state of having been victimized, but to the liquidation of personhood in any meaningful sense by mass media: there is no real or false meaning because all

58. Annette Wieviorka, *The Era of the Witness,* trans. Jared Stark (Ithaca: Cornell University Press, 2006).

59. Daniel Mendelson, the writer, in an op-ed piece, "Stolen Suffering," *New York Times,* March 9, 2008.

references are now copies of copies, and their origins are no longer retrievable. He also asserts that people claim or want to be victims because to have suffered or sacrificed confers a transcendent meaning on lives rendered insignificant by late capitalism and its destruction of meaning-generating contexts and communities.[60]

French historians have attributed contemporary "memory wars" (between victims and other victims for attention and between victims' and perpetrators' versions of the same events) to new information technologies that place such conflicts in the public realm as never before. They attribute the globalization of memory to the American appropriation of the European memory of the Holocaust.[61] They also attribute memory wars to an increasing sense that as national identities founder, populations focus more narrowly on their own groups.[62] The memory of suffering and injustice, sometimes suffused with nationalist nostalgia, has thus also intensified, even if, according to one of memory discourse's most important scholars, Pierre Nora, "whoever says memory, says Shoah."[63] The social scientists and doctors Didier Fassin and Richard Rechtman have argued that the old suspicion of the victim has been replaced by a "moral economy" of trauma in which psychiatric nomenclature (specifically posttraumatic stress syndrome) has replaced an older vocabulary of "social mobilization" to fight oppression in favor of a medically legitimated cultural imperative to sal-

60. See Naqvi, *The Rhetoric of Victimhood,* which discusses Baudrillard extensively.

61. Blanchard and Veyrat-Masson, eds., *Les guerres de mémoires,* 38. The book's editors never conceptualize the relationship between various post-Holocaust memory wars in France and the fact that it is the memory of the Holocaust that appears to account for all the attention to memory, including the surfeit they decry.

62. Blanchard and Veyrat-Masson, eds., *Les guerres de mémoires,* 15–49. On the role of technology in these discourses, see Paul Frosch and Amit Pinchevski, eds., *Media Witnessing: Testimony in the Age of Mass Communication* (New York: Palgrave Macmillan, 2009). For an important corrective to the idea that minorities tend to be favored by discourses on victimization, see Joan Scott, *The Politics of the Veil* (Princeton: Princeton University Press, 2007). Scott argues that debates over Muslim schoolgirls wearing the veil (hijab) demonstrate that a majority of French people imagine themselves as victims of a foreign culture that wishes to impose its own norms on French cultural and social life. Her critique helps to explain the power of Pierre Nora's much earlier work on "sites of memory," and other work that followed it by Italian and Polish scholars: "memory studies" were also often a form of nostalgia, longing for a national past in the face of modernization and in the aftermath of the Holocaust. Pierre Nora, ed., *Realms of Memory: Rethinking the French Past,* ed. Lawrence D. Kritzman, trans. Arthur Goldhammer, 3 vols. (New York: Columbia University Press, 1996–1998).

63. Nora quoted in Müller, *Memory and Power,* 14n53.

vage the victim.[64] Fassin and Rechtman note that the Holocaust of European Jewry was the origin of this flourishing of collective trauma which was then invigorated in the 1980s by psychiatric discourses, but they barely discuss the Holocaust at all.[65]

A minority of other thinkers decry this interpretation of the centrality of suffering to identity because, they argue, it discredits claims to have been victimized and turns real victims into phantoms, or at least makes them hard to find. Wendy Brown, Lauren Berlant, and Alain Badiou bemoan the centrality of victimhood in political discourse. They seek instead to figure out how real pain might be recognized rather than negated by uncovering the ideological mechanisms by which the centrality of trauma to identity obscures structural subordination. They argue in different ways that human rights and sentimentalized politics turn social negation into the victim's very identity. The ideological configuration of politics as feeling renders the pain of others the objective and self-evident criterion of what is wrong with the nation: the stress on traumatized identity confuses what the victim has become (and thus the social processes by which she has been victimized) with who she is. In Berlant's view, feeling for the presumably traumatized victim takes the place of political action, and mourning the pain of others in this context evacuates their suffering of substance.[66] Brown conceives the victim's claims to identity-based rights founded on injury, however legitimate they may be, to obfuscate the state's role in using such claims to regulate identity itself. She argues that injury will cease to define victims' identities as they make politically empowering demands based on what they want rather than who they are.[67]

64. Fassin and Rechtman, *L'empire des traumatismes*, 237–40.

65. Fassin and Rechtman, *L'empire du traumatismes*, 33–37.

66. Lauren Berlant, "The Subject of True Feeling: Pain, Privacy, and Politics," in *Cultural Pluralism, Identity Politics, and the Law,* ed. Austin Sarat and Thomas R. Kearns (Ann Arbor: University of Michigan Press, 1999), 54–57. Michael S. Roth has also provided a nuanced but less developed if similar perspective in his "Victims, Memory, History," *Tikkun* 9 (1999): 59–95, where he notes that "outraged complaints about the 'culture of victimhood' are not a substitute for careful differentiation between claims for justice and demands for 'special treatment'" (95). See also his *The Ironist's Cage: Memory, Trauma, and the Construction of History* (New York: Columbia University Press, 1995). Roth argues, like Brown, that "the award of moral superiority [to marginalized minorities and victims] is no real substitute for justice, but it can be a powerful balm in a world of continued economic, social, and political inequality" (11).

67. Wendy Brown, *States of Injury: Politics and Freedom in Late Modernity* (Princeton: Princeton University Press, 1998).

Somewhat differently, Badiou argues that human rights discourses conceal their real contempt for victims under the guise of caring for them. To the extent that the rights of man must be afforded to those who do not yet possess them, they mark the dispossessed by definition as "being-for-death," or not-yet-human. Human rights discourses become a pretext for differentiating between the victim as animal and the human being, and thus define human beings as potential or real victims because the rights of man are exercised over "the contingency of suffering and death."[68] And human beings, he claims, are usually found on the side of the civilized West, whose intervention is required to turn victims into real human beings through the granting to them of human rights.[69] In short, being "for" victims, as Berlant and Brown also argue, masks the extent to which human rights discourses create the pretext for colonial intervention and domination of the powerful, and camouflage the very processes in which they are implicated. In Brown's work, the appropriation of traumatized identity by victims themselves constitutes a misguided concession to dominant culture's self-palliative efforts to feel in place of doing: the victim's embrace of his wounds reveals an attachment to the recognition accorded his suffering. For Badiou, even the appellation "Jew" allows the state to define one as part of a homogenous mass to be regulated and is thus an identitarian or affective attachment that should be rejected at all costs.[70]

However compelling these analyses of the anaesthetic and depoliticizing effects of mass-media appeals to human rights and victims' embrace of their own wounds, such accounts do not provide much help in explaining how victims can ever offer a genuine rather than ideologically suspect response when they are debilitated by their injuries. Or to put it differently, what if some victims find making demands traumatic, and how do others come to terms with their pain sufficiently to formulate what they want? Are not despair, disempowerment, and confusion symptoms of injury, discrimination, and marginality such that "empowerment" is a complex undertaking (even when successful)? To ask such questions is not to insist that we sustain a focus on the traumatic past, but to suggest that theorists

---

68. Alain Badiou, *Ethics: An Essay on the Understanding of Evil,* trans. Peter Hallward (London: Verso, 2001), 12.

69. Badiou, *Ethics,* 13.

70. Alain Badiou, *Circonstances 3: Portées du mot "juif"* (Clamecy: Léo Scheer, 2005), 3, 33–36.

sometimes erase the impediments to recovery that pain generates even when, as does Brown, they ask hard questions about how pain generates an attachment to itself that proves antithetical to healing.[71] The insistence that liberal capitalism generates victim identity reduces potentially traumatic symptoms to epiphenomena of often ill-defined structural factors, and identity to a psychological effect of state regulation. But trauma and its affective burdens may persist even once wrongs are rectified and surely, as Berlant recognizes implicitly in other work, cannot be reduced to a matter of state-regulated (and thus fixed) identities.[72] Badiou opines that "the modern name for necessity is, as everyone knows, 'economics,'" so that the multifaceted forms that victimization might take and the affect generated are merely diversionary and require no discussion.[73]

The debates on which we focus propose other and important normative guidelines about the ideal treatment of other human beings, but also affirmatively value different kinds of suffering and responses to it, and project obsessive memory onto some sufferers and a grasp of reality or a healthy relation to the here and now onto others.

Phantom Victims

My focus on France and the United States is not meant to suggest that these arguments about victims are not pervasive elsewhere in the West. Indeed, at least one book has been written about the rhetoric of victimhood in Austria and Germany in films and texts.[74] And the emergence of memory discourses in Central and Eastern Europe has given rise to nationalist demands of various groups to be recognized as victims: Sudeten Germans expelled by the Czechs at the end of the war, for example, sought a memorial to their sufferings. The new criticism of the surfeit of Jewish

---

71. This problem appears in Fassin and Rechtman, *L'empire du traumatismes,* in another way: the inversion of social norms from hostility to the acceptance of victims tends to reiterate an opposition between heroism and human frailty that ultimately cannot explain frailty except as the other of heroism.

72. Lauren Berlant, "Hard Feelings: Stephanie Brooks," *Criticism* 49 (2007): 407–19. This essay is a brilliant discussion of minimalist affect that recognizes the complexity of unsettled identities.

73. Badiou, *Ethics,* 30.

74. Naqvi, *The Rhetoric of Victimhood.*

memory has led to assertions of equal victimhood not only in Germany and France, but also in Italy, where a new strain of revisionism calls attention to the fascist victims of partisan violence after the war.[75] This logic makes it difficult to distinguish victims from perpetrators and is thus instrumental in diminishing the dramatic contrast between the two into a more general, ahistorical message about the human potential for violence. It also tends to replace historically precise narratives about victims and perpetrators with another narrative about the human potential for acting in ways both good and evil.[76] Thus oppression is not a historical but a human tragedy in which we are all potentially heroes and victims, and all potentially wounded and capable of wounding.[77]

In France and the United States, the discussion of the surfeit of Jewish memory and its relation to the centrality of suffering to identity, as well as to the reduction of historical memory to a moral claim, is complex because these countries are home to the two largest Jewish populations

75. During the commemoration of an Italian partisan fighter in 2001, then president Carlo Azeglio Ciampi proclaimed the equivalence of fascist and partisan fighters after 1943, and asked those gathered to recall the youth who sought to carry on Mussolini's struggle in the Republic of Salò: Italian unity, he said, "was a sentiment that moved many of the young people who, back then, made different choices and did so because they believed that in so doing they were also honoring their country." *La Stampa*, October 15, 2001. A year later, on the sixtieth anniversary of the 1942 battle of El Alamein (in which Italians and Germans under the command of General Rommel were defeated), Ciampi did not insist that national reconciliation means the acknowledgment of past wrongs, or that Italians had an obligation to make restitution by preserving the memory of what happened: instead, he subtly relieved them of moral responsibility for fascism. "Not only were totalitarianisms defeated," said Ciampi, but the world [since the battle] "has changed profoundly...and it has been changed by the same generation that fought in El Alamein." *La Stampa*, October 21, 2002.

76. For a view of how states make transitions to democracy after a legacy of crime (and which refuses the viability of 'forgiveness' and implicitly rejects categories of good and evil except insofar as they affect the dispensation of justice), see Wole Soyinka, *The Burden of Memory, the Muse of Forgiveness* (Oxford: Oxford University Press, 1999).

77. In a particularly troubling yet telling example, the historian Joel Williamson, in an article about the historiography of lynching, uses images of the Holocaust diffused immediately after the war to dramatize his discussion of human cruelty: "Can this be us? It was and *is* us, of course, and our minds will not let us free of that idea. We are the gassers, and we are the gassed. How could we do this to 5 million people, and how could we allow this to be done to us?" Williamson's article makes dramatically clear how in the discussions of those trying to be sensitive to discrimination and persecution, victims become difficult to identify or have slipped out of focus so that there is absolutely no clear distinction between us and them, gassed Jews and lynched Blacks, past and present. Joel Williamson, "Wounds Not Scars: Lynching, the National Conscience, and the American Historian," *Journal of American History* 83 (1997): 1232, 1247.

outside of Israel: debates are thus a matter of both intra-Jewish discussion and gentile-Jewish dialogue. In both countries, moreover, these discourses are embedded in other struggles to address the sufferings of minority populations. In the United States, the "competition of victims" is often a commentary on the plight of other minorities, including African Americans. In France, allegations of playing victim on both the Left and the Right are routinely bound up with debates over the struggles of French Muslims for equality, the unfolding of the Israeli-Palestinian conflict as a projection of Muslim-Jewish relations in France, and Jewish intellectuals' relation to French republicanism and its secular heritage. In spite of different national articulations, however, the complexity of the American and French debates are indebted on the one hand to a substantial Jewish intellectual engagement with Holocaust commentary, and on the other to struggles over the rights of minorities, displaced onto the discussion of the Holocaust.

I take little time to discuss the broader impact and presence of these debates in other European nations with no substantial Jewish population. I have, however, sought to remind the reader that this pervasive discussion about the centrality of suffering to identity exists elsewhere by the use of occasional references and epigraphs. Contemporary cultural narratives tend to have little self-consciously to say about how we perceive victims, as if such perceptions were self-evident or so embedded in other ideological formations that they require no discussion. In the aftermath of the Holocaust, the redemptive, patriotic, and sacrificial rites of mourning performed for soldiers have been replaced by the invocation of a potentially redeemed humanity which says "never again" to the horrors of war and genocide. Modern rituals conceive contemporary war as a tragic means of providing the conditions of future genocides as much as the proving ground of heroism.[78] In so doing, they fashion a narrative about mourning victims in which rites have more to do with a message that we should be vigilant in the future than about the content of what we are mourning. "Never Again!" is the expression of those who desperately want to recognize our potential for making people into victims. Yet in the struggle to integrate

---

78. See the discussion in Emmanuel Kattan, *Penser le devoir de mémoire* (Paris: PUF, 2002), 59–69; and Georges Bensoussan, *Auschwitz en héritage: D'un bon usage de la mémoire* (Paris: Mille et une nuits, 2003), 12–13.

memory of past crimes into collective memory there are far more obstacles than the purveyors of vigilance acknowledge, including the complicity in, guilt about, identification with, and even relative indifference to the victims with whom 'we' express solidarity.

If victims' wounds are now so often conceived to be self-generated or imaginary, then our question must not be "what injuries are real?," however important this question may be, but rather, why does victimization, even when it is recognized as having happened, generate aggression as often as empathy? Do victims become objects of (repressed) aggression by virtue of their claims on the rest of us? Is envy of the so-called moral superiority of victims, to which the idea that Jewish survivors of the camps are sacred figures with secret knowledge has contributed, itself a form of repressed aggression? How do victims avoid becoming objects of these projections, evidenced by the fashioning of Jewish victimization, including the shift from an aversion to Jewish suffering to a more recent identification with victims' pain and the profusion of words and images about it?

A recent book (by a centrist French judge) on why reparations for the Holocaust, slavery, and colonialism are ill advised takes as its premise that victims who seek monetary reparation expect or hope (even unconsciously) that compensatory payments will remedy the memory or experience of "banishment" by the majority population.[79] The presumption that money will somehow reunite victims symbolically with the social world that once exiled them is so contrary to many victims' far less idealized conceptions of what money will bring (relief from poverty, a token form of vengeance, what one 'deserves,' which will not remedy what one has suffered)[80] that it

---

79. Antoine Garapon, *Peut-on réparer l'histoire? Colonization, esclavage, Shoah* (Paris: Odile Jacob, 2008), 20–21 and implicitly throughout. Garapon's book is particularly critical of the United States for initiating this form of "legalizing" political and moral problems, and offers a rather narrow (and very conservative) interpretation of U.S. constitutional law as the conflation of the rule of law and popular sovereignty (29). That he does not make clear that this is one side of a passionate debate about the place of minority rights in the Constitution rather than the definition of U.S. law enables him to argue that reparations are a form of populism. Moreover, he conceives the Nuremberg tribunal as a form of American imperialism with no sense that while it was undoubtedly a form of victor's justice, it was also a political solution to a complex set of demands made by victorious nations and concern about Germany's role in the postwar period. Finally, it is worth noting that French law has itself introduced a wide variety of rights for victims to guarantee compensation (or at least some form of redress). See Bogalska-Martin, ed., *Victimes du present*, 97–156.

80. See John Authers and Richard Wolffe, *The Victim's Fortune: Inside the Epic Battle over the Debts of the Holocaust* (New York: HarperCollins, 2002), in which the lawyers make out like

can only be interpreted primarily as a projection about victims' expectations that implicitly paints them as unrealistic even as it condescends to feel their pain. How might we interpret this otherwise well-intended effort to argue against reparations in the name of victims? The author believes that victims who accept money are weak, needy, misguided, and willing to lose their dignity in quest of fortune.

In short, the affective relationship with victims, itself mediated by the density of different historical experiences and locations, may very well determine why some victims are deemed credible when they are not, and why some victims create more or less aversion, provoke more or less shame—perhaps simply by virtue of how they make their demands. It is not at all clear, for example, why those who are victims by virtue of having perpetrated a crime (that is, guilty and tormented victims of their own reprehensible acts) are given license to behave emotionally, while Holocaust survivors appear more credible if they demonstrate emotional control, as a recent analysis of German television programs that interview German perpetrators, bystanders, and Jewish victims suggests.[81] Injury may be unquestionable and extreme and yet still be interpreted according to normative concepts of what qualities constitute a viable victim from whom we can learn and in whose testimony we have confidence. The denial of victims' wounds also derives from a denial of the structural inequities that generate the symptoms, a denial made more potent by Brown's claim that structural inequities are increasingly recast as cultural differences—as matters of different practices and beliefs—which can be resolved by the depoliticized language of "tolerance," itself a form, arguably, of repressed aggression toward those victims whose claims one cannot abide.[82]

I do not want to try and dismantle assertions that the Jewish genocide has been accorded too much memory, but rather to question the very

bandits in pursuit of reparations from Swiss banks; and Tom Segev's discussion of the 1952 "blood money" debate in Israel over German reparations in Segev, *The Seventh Million: The Israelis and the Holocaust,* trans. Haim Watzman (New York: Henry Holt, 1991), 189–252.

81. See the discussion in Judith Keilbach, *Geschichtsbilder und Zeitzeugen: Zur Darstellung des Nationalsozialismus im bundesdeutschen Fernsehen* (Münster: Lit, 2008), 162–236. I thank Robin Curtis for this reference. See also Bensoussan, *Auschwitz,* 140, who discusses how perpetrators become victims of their own acts, and how this transformation usually serves an apologetic function.

82. Wendy Brown, *Regulating Aversion: Tolerance in the Age of Identity and Empire* (Princeton: Princeton University Press, 2006).

concept of a surfeit of memory, as if responses to catastrophic events could be allocated proper emotional parameters and memory could be apportioned in some just and measurable fashion. I have no wish to deny that the Holocaust has been used politically in order to settle scores and often to legitimate violent actions and discriminatory policies against Palestinians by the Israeli government. And I do not wish to argue that all claims are true and comparable and should never be subject to inquiry. Instead, I want to focus on how 'too much' attention to victims is given meaning and with what consequences.

This sort of analysis demonstrates how references to a naturalized view of human weakness, indifference, complacency, or even evil against which we are urged to be vigilant are inadequate to address the problems posed by social suffering because our ways of denying suffering people recognition are rhetorically and historically constituted, not simply failures of will or manifestations of all-too-human negligence. And while the representation of injury is always culturally mediated in some fashion, we should still pay attention to the ideological investments in such mediations and their impact on victims. After all, a "competition of victims" is an ideological construct that diminishes or negates the actual effects of suffering, displacing them onto another socio-psychological and at worst pathological struggle to have suffered more.

Thus legitimate concerns over the preeminence of emotion in politics, for example, and specifically about sophisticated political appeals to feeling at the expense of critical thinking can lead to the interpretation of victims' feelings as self-indulgent exercises.[83] Suspicion of feeling has a long history which appears in the most unlikely places; in the past it was most often manifested by those who envisioned women, ethnic and racial minorities, or colonized peoples as its primary repositories. But suspicion of claims to have suffered, and thus of victims' sometimes invisible wounds, crosses the political and philosophical spectrum in discourses about the centrality of suffering to identity, and appears to be part of a broader cultural effort to respond to postmodern declarations of and anxieties about the

---

83. Perhaps the best-known criticism of emotion in the public sphere is Hannah Arendt, *On Revolution* (New York: Penguin, 1977 [1963]).

contingency of meaning.[84] In particular, the conflation of suffering and identity underscores radical challenges to how humans make and control meaning through acts of will and determination. How we judge the plight of wounded people and interpret their injuries dramatically highlights the problem of compromised choice. Traumatized disempowerment and its restrictions on human freedom, will, and ability to act evoke attitudes to powerlessness from pity to aversion that should not be bemoaned as evidence that we are lost in a sea of feeling, but explored.

Perpetrators disappear in this discourse, their actions and accountability rhetorically diminished. Since it constructs victims implicitly as those who make excessive demands and thus as aggressors, structural differences dissipate into a level playing field and it is difficult to imagine a 'real' victim. Part of my task is not only to discuss how we discern real victims but also to outline the making of an aggressive, phantom victim who stands in for nothing less than threats to the rational apportioning of justice, the subsequent impossibility of disinterested indignation, and the collapse of empathic relations to others. The post-Holocaust, post-1960s construction of the victim's ostensible entitlements and its challenges to the legacy of enlightenment political culture is the phenomenon this book traces, identifies, and assesses. It uses critical inquiry to evaluate the impact of the iconic status of the Holocaust stripped of its complexity as a historical phenomenon, and thus maps what happens when critics focus more pointedly on the moral rather than historical content of suffering. It asks why this concern with victims has emerged recently and attributes it to the relatively underexplored shift away from the plethora of memory discourses on the Holocaust to the allegedly noxious consequences of that plethora, including memory overload and its anaesthetic effects. It focuses not on how the Holocaust received iconic status as the most radical evil of our time, but on how that status impacts and shapes the meaning of having been victimized and cultural responses to it. Finally, it addresses the fashioning of exemplary and less exemplary victims and how a focus on Jewish victimhood has become synonymous with blindness to the injurious treatment of others in our midst.

---

84. For years now, along with but also beyond Michel Foucault's *oeuvre,* concepts of the meaning-conferring self have been slowly replaced by a concept of knowledge and self-knowledge as a series of yet-to-be understood interconnections between shards of meaning that are mappable onto textual and visual evidence and the human brain, but not always readable and coherent.

1

THE SURFEIT OF JEWISH MEMORY

Anti-Semitism creates a 'Semitism' that is radical, full of hubris,
and often myopic and intolerant.

SERGIO ROMANO (1997)

Some sixty years after the Holocaust there now exists a voluminous testimonial literature, an array of theological, autobiographical, and philosophical debates, and theoretical discussions of "postmemory." Over the
last few decades, and particularly since the 1990s, as I have already argued,
those discussions have increasingly focused not on how and what we remember but on accusations of an alleged "surplus of talk"—companion
to the "surfeit of memory"—that the philosopher Berel Lang argues now
characterizes attitudes toward Holocaust representation.[1] At its best this
discourse thoughtfully asks how Jews and others can most substantively
engage the past in the context of 'too much' memory; at its worst, it ac-

Epigraph: Sergio Romano, *Lettera a un amico ebreo* (Milan: Longanesi, 1997), 83.

1. Berel Lang, *Post-Holocaust: Interpretation, Misinterpretation, and the Claims of History*
(Bloomington: Indiana University Press, 2005), ix. The phrase "surfeit of memory" was first used
by Charles S. Maier in "A Surfeit of Memory? Reflections on History, Melancholy, and Denial,"
History and Memory 5 (1993): 136–52.

cuses Jewish organizations of fostering a "Holocaust industry" to exploit the memory of Jewish victimization.[2] But the so-called surfeit of Jewish memory is now articulated primarily as an argument about how Jewish memory exemplifies a pathological cultural attachment to having been or being a victim. It assesses the so-called surfeit in terms of the discrepancy between fantasmic concepts of 'too much' and the right amount of identification with victims, an apparently rational calculus that has gone awry. Critics thus argue that Jewish memory voids the substance of history and the value of empathy in pursuit of identification with Holocaust victims that narcissistically appropriates victims' suffering and focuses on Jews' victimization at the expense of others.

This argument may at first appear peculiar, since concern over the legacy of anti-Semitism should not by definition preclude concern about the persecution of others. Moreover, it is deeply at odds with the initial reception of Holocaust victims and their experiences. As is now well documented, many Jewish victims of genocide feared being doubted, and their experiences were often not acknowledged. Some, as Aharon Appelfeld reminds us, wanted desperately to speak and still others to erase all memory of painful pasts.[3] But now, the dubious sacralization of survivors and the iconic status of the Holocaust have created a consensus about the ostensibly narcissistic appropriation of Jewish suffering, its consequences and impact.[4] These concerns, while manifest all over Europe, are most debated rather than simply asserted in the United States and France, and are particularly powerful in the United States as a matter of intra-Jewish debate. Influential scholars and journalists who otherwise hold a variety of political views, including Peter Novick, Esther Benbassa, Michael André Bernstein, Alain Finkielkraut, Gabriel Schoenfeld, and Zygmunt Bauman,

2. Norman Finkelstein's *The Holocaust Industry: Reflections on the Exploitation of Jewish Suffering* (London: Verso, 2000) exemplifies this perspective.
3. Aharon Appelfeld, *The Story of a Life,* trans. Aloma Halter (New York: Schocken Books, 2004).
4. Moreover, the transformation of abjection and trauma in the Holocaust into a discourse on the sublime in the works of prominent literary critics such as Shoshana Felman and Giorgio Agamben has surely been important in calling attention to the weakness of certain poststructuralist theoretical tendencies to which many mainstream critics already had serious objections. Shoshana Felman and Dori Laub, *Testimony: Crises of Witnessing in Literature, Psychoanalysis, and History* (New York: Routledge, 1992); Giorgio Agamben, *Remnants of Auschwitz: The Witness and the Archive* (New York: Zone Books, 1999).

have all recently interpreted Jewish memory of the Holocaust by reference to a vast commentary in the United States and later in France on "victimology," "victimhood," and "victim culture" that first developed in the United States and Europe during the 1940s and '50s.[5]

"Victimology" was coined originally in 1947, when the Romanian-born Israeli lawyer Benjamin Mendelsohn delivered a paper to the Psychiatric Society of Bucharest in which he argued for the creation of a new field, "victimology." It is perhaps not a coincidence that it was a Jewish refugee from Romanian anti-Semitism who, in the immediate aftermath of the Holocaust, sought to conceive the victim of criminal acts as a complicated social and psychological figure with specific propensities and sufferings not always acknowledged. Indeed, he was the first scholar to study victims as complex cultural constructions at a time when scholarship focused only on the criminals, by whose acts victims were created. In Mendelsohn's earliest work he stressed the importance of the unconscious desire to be a victim and referenced the potential complicity of rape and sexual abuse victims in their own victimization. But he also referred to the role "insufficient national, religious, economic cohesion" might play in the creation of collective victims—a reference perhaps to the role he believed the absence of a strong Jewish state played in the genocide of European Jewry.[6]

Most research in the field of victimology until the mid-1970s emphasized how victims contributed to crimes perpetrated against them, and still focused largely on women and rape.[7] It was not until then that victimologists' focus moved from "victims' complicity in the crimes they suffered to the material and psychological needs of victims."[8] And yet, as Alyson M. Cole argues, new therapeutic discourses that developed encouraged victims

5. See Robert Elias, *The Politics of Victimization: Victims, Victimology, and Human Rights* (Oxford: Oxford University Press, 1986), 17–21.
6. Benjamin Mendelsohn, "Une nouvelle branche de la science bio-psycho-sociale: la victimologie," *Revue internationale de criminologie et de police technique* 11 (1956): 96.
7. On the history of victimology in the United States, see Alyson M. Cole, *The Cult of True Victimhood: From the War on Welfare to the War on Terror* (Stanford: Stanford University Press, 2007), 123–43.
8. Cole, *The Cult of True Victimhood,* 126. In keeping with this trend, Mendelsohn in 1969 turned away from an emphasis on the unconscious desire to be a victim. He claimed that those who unconsciously wish to be victims are a small minority among victims, but receive attention because their behavior is "spectacular." He sought to codify genocide as a crime in far more detail than "crimes against humanity," and reiterated in a series of articles his commitment to understanding victims' experience in its entirety. See Benjamin Mendelsohn, "Le rapport entre la

to take responsibility for and pride in themselves, and were often critical of those victims who made their pain public by blaming others for their plight. In so doing, they articulated another version of victim-blaming.[9]

On another level, in the 1980s, identity politics in the United States—group-based identities asserted by a wide variety of groups including Blacks and women—shared this insistence on pride but also sought recognition for past wounds. This sought-for recognition coincided with the so-called memory boom, including not only the belated recognition of the Holocaust, but also many colonial powers' recognition of past crimes and national soul-searching in the West about its own past. In France, the same attention to memory and past crimes refers more specifically to criticism of the belated and presumably excessive recognition of the Vichy government's anti-Semitism and was also an attack on American multiculturalism, whose pluralism many critics feared threatened the abstract French citizen and thus French republicanism at a time when women, gays and lesbians, and eventually French Muslims were demanding rights not as individuals but on the basis of their membership in groups which had been structurally devalued.

In short, though critics use victimology and victim culture promiscuously and without precise references, the attacks on so-called victim culture and the surfeit of memory developed initially as a critique of identity politics and multiculturalism and appear indebted to earlier motifs of victim-blaming.[10] Critics like the Bulgarian-born French literary theorist Tzvetan Todorov draw on three decades of rhetoric that insists that victimization now confers social recognition, and they argue that the desire to have been a victim is now so pervasive that the enlightened imperative to care for others, even if they do not belong to our own group, has collapsed.[11] Others, like the conservative critic Gabriel Schoenfeld, asked why the "Holocaust exert[s] such great fascination these days outside the Jewish community. And why are its images being abused by those who purport

---

victimologie et le problem du genocide: Schema d'un Code du Génocide," *Études internationales de psycho-sociologie criminelle* 16 (1956): 96.

9. Cole, *The Cult of True Victimhood*, 128–34.

10. In the United States, such attacks often emerged in the context of the oft-denounced commercialization of the Holocaust in Hollywood films and in various museums. See Robert Alter, "Deformations of the Holocaust," *Commentary* 71, 2 (1981): 49.

11. Tzvetan Todorov, "In Search of Lost Crime," *New Republic,* January 29, 2001, 25.

to be custodians of its memory?" In his view, the answer to both questions undoubtedly lies at least in part in the "rising culture of victimhood, visible in our society at large…As the ultimate in victimization, the Holocaust is simply assuming pride of place."[12] In 2006 the editor and historian Pierre Nora referred to the belated French memory of the Vichy period and the ostensible transformation of victims' suffering into the violence of their demands for recognition: "I have elsewhere evoked a 'tyranny of memory'," he said, but "it would be necessary today to speak of its terrorism. So much so that we are less sensitive to the suffering that it expresses than to the violence that wants to make itself heard."[13]

When such prominent intellectuals identify the surfeit of Jewish memory of genocide as the most visible symptom of new rhetorical constructions of victimhood, they do not only seek an antidote to perceptions of exaggerated claims, even though they wish to preserve the historical record from distortion. They are not obviously fearful of the vengeful intentions victims presumably harbor—the scenario imagined by the "counterrevolutionary" who knows what moral damage he has wrought and hopes to stave off the consequences.[14] Instead, for example, in Alvin Rosenfeld's view, the reduction of Holocaust memory to a "meaningless abstraction, 'man's inhumanity to man,'" is encouraged "within those segments of American culture intent on developing a politics of identity based on victim status and the grievances that come with it."[15] The Holocaust becomes a universal symbol of human evil devoid of specific historical content, and therefore one more particularly exemplary incident in the long history of human malfeasance. For Dagmar Barnouw, Holocaust remembrance has suffocated under the "seemingly irresistible appeal of memory stories of victimization, the more

12. Gabriel Schoenfeld, "Death Camps as Kitsch," *New York Times,* March 18, 1999.
13. Pierre Nora, quoted in Michael Rothberg, *Multidirectional Memory: Remembering the Holocaust in the Age of Decolonization* (Stanford: Stanford University Press, 2009), 269. The quotation is from a 2006 article in *Le Monde.* Nora is, Rothberg surmises, responding not only to the surfeit of memory of Vichy, but to the demand that the French state remember its accountability for crimes committed against Algerians, specifically the 1961 massacre in Paris.
14. As described by Robert Meister, "Human Rights and the Politics of Victimhood," *Ethics and International Affairs* 16 (2002): 94.
15. Alvin H. Rosenfeld, "The Americanization of the Holocaust," *Commentary* 99, 6 (1995): 36.

'incredible' the better."[16] And Efraim Sicher asserts that post-Holocaust generation Jews "internalize the status of victim...[to] create an alternate Jewishness out of a legacy of suffering," so that trauma founds identity and substitutes for a history we have not lived.[17] Or more radically, this narcissism substitutes the psychological for the social dimensions of oppression so completely that only the subject's psychic wounds guarantee his existence as such.

Because according to these critics everyone wants to or believes himself to be a victim, the problem is not the political task of reconciliation with and compensation for those whose victimization we acknowledge. The task set by most writers who allege the existence of a universal quest for victimhood is not to find cultural criteria to distinguish good from bad victims, such as those who behaved bravely or those whom we judge to be more 'innocent' than others. It is instead to separate 'real' victims from others who proclaim to have been injured, identify vicariously with the injured, or become overly and thus pathologically so attached to their wounds that they unwittingly obscure their own social oppression or justify that of others.

Such critics' task is nothing less than to refine and clarify the putatively privileged category of victim, a task that exceeds the merely empirical verification that someone has suffered or not. Rather, that task requires that we determine what constitutes reliable memory of suffering at a historical moment when by the critics' own account the appellation 'victim' has become promiscuous. Charges about attachment to victim status emerge with particular intensity when Jewish sufferers, their heirs, and often Jews more generally transform violated innocence into righteous rhetoric and demands for recognition for suffering that they often did not witness. They also emerge when those whose histories of persecution have barely

---

16. Dagmar Barnouw, "The Certainties of Evil: Memory Discourses of the Holocaust," *Monatshefte* 93 (2001): 106.

17. Efraim Sicher, "The Future of the Past: Countermemory and Postmemory in Contemporary American Post-Holocaust Narratives," *History and Memory* 12 (2001): 61–63. On pilgrimages to death camps in which Jews are encouraged to see themselves as Holocaust victims, see Jack Kugelmass, "Missions to the Past: Poland in Contemporary Thought and Deed," in *Tense Past: Cultural Essays in Trauma and Memory,* ed. Paul Antze and Michael Lambek (New York: Routledge, 1996), 202, 205.

been remembered make similar claims for restitution, as if all claims to injury were intrinsically insatiable and grandiloquent demands.

Identity Theft

Whatever the claims of various victim groups, the very act of making claims now raises questions about the extent to which such demands participate in the allegedly pervasive condition of wanting to have been or to be a victim. The notion that there are many people who wish to be victims both testifies to the pervasiveness of victimhood as a new and crucial category of being and seeks to address the conundrum of victims who become 'too' attached to their wounds. The narcissism and displacement that characterize a presumed relation to Jewish suffering has been examined extensively in the now voluminous literature on the "second generation"—the children of Holocaust survivors—some of which has expressed negative or ambivalent views about the impact of psychiatry in defining the nature of victims' wounds.[18] Undoubtedly for some critics, the unwillingness to engage medical or psychoanalytic literature on trauma is partly a repudiation of the "psychotraumas" or pathologies attached to survivors. For the historian Ido de Haan, the reduction of Jewish persecution to a "psychotrauma" set up Jewish survivors as "original victim[s] against which [*sic*] all other forms of victimization would be measured. But it also implied that various categories of victims were grouped under the common denominator of a psychotrauma, even if the events that caused these traumata differed dramatically."[19] Recourse to psychiatry originated in survivors having to prove themselves mentally afflicted by their experience in order to quality

18. Helen Epstein, *Children of the Holocaust: Conversations with Sons and Daughters of Survivors* (New York: G. P. Putnam's Sons, 1979), 101–9.
19. Ido de Haan, "The Postwar Jewish Community and the Memory of the Persecution in the Netherlands," in *Dutch Jews as Perceived by Themselves and by Others: Proceedings of the Eighth International Symposium on the History of the Jews in the Netherlands,* ed. Chaya Brasz and Yosef Kaplan (Leiden: Brill, 2001), 432. From the point of view of psychologists who work with survivors, however, the tendency to reduce survivors to pure victims or heroes is primarily related to our own narcissism, voyeurism, sadism, and, above all, the need to displace our own rage or shame when confronted with those who have been brutally victimized. See the essays in John P. Wilson, Zev Harel, and Boaz Khana, eds., *Human Adaptation to Extreme Stress: From the Holocaust to Vietnam* (New York: Plenum Press, 1988).

for German restitution after 1953, when West German indemnification laws allowed them to seek damages related to Nazi persecution—hence the invention of "survivor syndrome," among other medically defined psychological conditions affecting former camp inmates.[20]

However sensitive this second generation of Jews was to the plight of their parents, or perhaps because they were, some of their work self-consciously cannot seem to escape what Ruth Franklin has termed "identity theft":[21] from the symbolically charged but admittedly boundary-blurring definition of the second generation as "children of the Holocaust," to Eva Hoffman's fear that in adult children of survivors "awe" of the Holocaust "may be...an element of that strange envy we felt towards our survivor parents. Authenticity of experience, in our period, is often conflated with catastrophe, with those traumatic histories with which we are so eager to identify."[22] Hoffman goes so far as to conclude that all the preoccupation with the "memory of the Holocaust" may have something to do with this generation's "feeling of being, in relation to this history, subsidiary; secondary."[23]

Critics of 'victim culture' tend problematically not to attend to post-traumatic symptoms of the sort articulated by de Haan and Hoffman, but conceive them instead as part of the presumably excessive affect attached to

20. See Ruth Leys's discussion in *From Guilt to Shame: Auschwitz and After* (Princeton: Princeton University Press, 2007), 24–32. The term "survivor syndrome" was coined by William G. Niederland in 1961, and was classified as "Delayed Stress Syndrome" in the DSM-III (Leys, *From Guilt to Shame,* 27n18). On the history of the meager postwar German restitution (and the debate in Israel over German "blood money" in 1952), see Suzanne Schrafstetter, "The Diplomacy of *Wiedergutmachung:* Memory, the Cold War, and the Western European Victims of Nazism, 1956–1964," *Holocaust and Genocide Studies* 17 (2003): 459–79; and Michael J. Bazyler, "The Holocaust Restitution Movement in Comparative Perspective," *Berkeley Journal of International Law* 20 (2002): 11–44. For the ambivalence of those who escaped the Nazis toward their own status as victims, see Jeremy Popkin, "Holocaust Memories, Historians' Memoirs: First-Person Narrative and the Memory of the Holocaust," *History and Memory* 15 (2003): 49–84.

21. The phrase is in the essay from which I borrow the title of this section of this chapter: Ruth Franklin, "Identity Theft: True Memory, False Memory, and the Holocaust," *New Republic,* May 31, 2004, 31–37.

22. Eva Hoffman, *After Such Knowledge: Memory, History, and the Legacy of the Holocaust* (New York: PublicAffairs, 2004), 175. Froma Zeitlin has reflected on some of the more complicated expressions of "identity theft" in such a way as to render it inescapable but ultimately undesirable. Froma I. Zeitlin, "The Vicarious Witness: Belated Memory and Authorial Presence in Recent Holocaust Literature," *History and Memory* 10 (1998): 5–42.

23. Hoffman, *After Such Knowledge,* 176.

victims that voids historical understanding. In so doing, they do not reject the reality of injury itself but treat traumatic symptoms and their potential transmission over time as if they were instrumental or self-indulgent responses unbefitting the dignity of those who have really suffered. Thus the second generation's struggle with a sense of displaced identity, with how to relate to the sufferings of parents or murdered relatives, perhaps best epitomized by Henri Raczymow's character Esther, who feels she should have died in a Nazi camp and dies by her own hand, is recast not as a tormenting psychological struggle but as narcissistic self-indulgence.[24]

The literary theorist Walter Benn Michaels uses the figure of the ghost, taken from Toni Morrison's novel about slavery, *Beloved,* as an allegory for a process of remembering what we have never lived through—in this case, slavery and the Holocaust. He argues that when the rhetorical device of the "deconstructive performative" is used, that is, when the text performatively enacts a gap in understanding that, like trauma, is an experience transmitted but not conceptualized or worked through, the "prohibition against understanding the Holocaust is at the same time formulated as the requirement that it be experienced instead of understood, and this requirement…makes it possible to define the Jew…as someone who, having experienced the Holocaust, can, even if he or she was never there, acknowledge it as part of his or her own history."[25] And this transmission of conceptually unassimilable experience becomes the defining feature of Jewish identity—an identity now shorn of any references to real Jewish persons or religious practices, referring only to Jewish culture. Benn Michaels's acerbic criticism of any intergenerational transmission of trauma (what Hoffman refers to not as memory but as "something more potent and less lucid; something closer to enactment of experience, to emanations or sometimes nearly embodiments of psychic matter")[26] rightly undermines the narcissistic appropriation of others' traumatic experiences and the emptying out of History (as does Hoffman). But Benn Michaels also denies entirely the possibility that trauma may impact anyone other than

24. Henri Raczymow, *Writing the Book of Esther,* trans. Dori Katz (New York: Holmes and Meier, 1995). The book was originally published as *Cri sans voix* (Paris: Gallimard, 1985).

25. Walter Benn Michaels, "'You Who Never Was There': Slavery and the New Historicism—Deconstruction and the Holocaust," in *The Americanization of the Holocaust,* ed. Hilene Flanzbaum (Baltimore: Johns Hopkins University Press, 1999), 195.

26. Hoffman, *After Such Knowledge,* 7.

those 'who were there.' Cultural memory replaces History, phantom-Jews replace real ones, and the performative enactment of the Holocaust in certain texts allows us, who were not there, to survive it.

Zygmut Bauman offers a primarily psychocultural explanation about Jewish latter-day "martyrs," arguing that "hereditary victimization" is a peg on which other forms of anxiety hang themselves.[27] He too allegorizes the Holocaust as a "ghost" who inhabits the would-be victims' bodies, makes their own relative comfort indistinguishable from survivors' trauma, and gives them license to feel "unequivocally wronged": it appears invisibly and unexpectedly in the symptoms exhibited by children of survivors, and has been "issued an official permission of domicile, recognized as the lawful plenipotentiary of the 'real thing,' and so...the troublesome and worrying distinction between the 'real' and 'virtual' reality has been declared null and void."[28]

According to this logic, 'we' find ourselves in the peculiar position of experiencing a Holocaust we have not lived, or may even feel that this memory that we have not had is more painful than the real suffering of the victims. Bauman and Benn Michaels repudiate Eric Santner's nuanced discussion of the "ghosts" inherited by second- and third-generation Germans. In Santner's work, Germans' identification as Hitler's victims becomes, for the perpetrators and their heirs, a narcissistic defense against one's own (or one's parents') complicity with National Socialism and a haunting, inherited repression that perpetuates the "inability to mourn."[29] Instead, for Benn Michaels, overidentification appropriates the Holocaust itself as a lived-historical experience, as if "ghosts" might not be complicated traces of identifications that should be explored, but stand-ins for an instrumentally conceived demand for attention. For Benn Michaels, the Jewish overidentification with victims cannot be a narcissistic defense against guilt: instead, to the extent that Jews feel guilty, they narcissistically appropriate victims' experience, putting themselves scandalously in their

27. Zygmunt Bauman, "Hereditary Victimhood: The Holocaust's Life as a Ghost," *Tikkun* 13, 4 (1998): 35–36.
28. Bauman, "Hereditary Victimhood," 35.
29. Eric Santner, *Stranded Objects: Mourning, Memory, and Film in Postwar Germany* (Ithaca: Cornell University Press, 1990), 35. Santner refers to the famous argument by Alexander Mitscherlich and Margarete Mitscherlich, *The Inability to Mourn: Principles of Collective Behavior,* trans. Beverly R. Placzek (New York: Grove Press, 1975).

place. Thus Benn Michaels decontextualizes and equates the memory of slavery with the memory of the Holocaust, as if the two generated exactly the same symptoms in a culture in which having been a victim is the only way to achieve recognition or to have experienced historical trauma is the only way to have historical experience—in which traumatic and historical experience have thus been entirely conflated.

Jews have long been a specific kind of victim-object whose sufferings have since the late 1960s become problematically iconic of 'evil in our time' (a position many scholars reject and others embrace). Hannah Arendt already anticipated the problem of a cult of victimization among Jews in 1946. Since all Jews, from the "newborn child" to the "repulsive usurer," were innocent in proportion to Nazi crimes against them, "we Jews are burdened by millions of innocents, by reason of which every Jew alive today can see himself as innocence personified.... We are simply not equipped to deal," she wrote to Karl Jaspers, "with a guilt that is beyond crime and an innocence that is beyond goodness or virtue."[30] Arendt worried that the burden of Jewish innocence—the inconceivable discrepancy between the conduct of the victims and the death to which they were condemned— would eventually transform itself into a necessarily insatiable demand for compensation and recognition. Since innocence can never be avenged and the guilty never sufficiently punished, Jews will forever renew demands for the recognition of betrayed innocence: each will see himself as "innocence personified" because he has suffered or belongs to a group that once did. The alleged centrality of trauma and victimization to Jewish identity allows us to explore more generally the rhetorical and political consequences Arendt feared: if Jews are pathologically attached to being victims, the Holocaust is no longer an icon only of human tragedy but also of the potential for the distortion and exploitation of human tragedy and even for the victimization of others. If all Jews overidentify with Holocaust victims, the Holocaust no longer represents only a culturally privileged image of inhumanity, but also the anaesthetic effects generated by the proliferation of media representations and memorials. And if Jewish trauma, to go beyond Arendt to current extrapolations, not only stands in for Jewish history, but

---

30. Letter to Karl Jaspers, August 17, 1946, in Lotte Kolher and Hans Saner, eds., *Hannah Arendt–Karl Jaspers, Correspondence 1926–1969*, trans. Robert Kimber and Rita Kimber (New York: Harcourt Brace Jovanovich, 1992), 54.

is also a paradigm of a now socially privileged condition of victimization tout court, then trauma becomes a privileged marker of identity rather than sets of symptoms from which one might ideally recover.

Identity is not, then, developed over time, shaped by long- and short-term events, effects, and particularities that define a specific relation to past and present, but is a wound that does not heal. 'Wounded identity' thus has an origin but no chronological limits or spatial boundaries: time collapses into media-saturated space, and history folds into a memory-screen onto which we publicly project private desires. The desire to be a victim blots out the victim's real suffering, and the surfeit of memory about the Holocaust is shorthand not only for the narcissistic appropriation of suffering, but also for the presumption of (traumatized) identity. The French historian Esther Benbassa denounces what she conceives as the overidentification with victimization among French Jews and an offensive "competition between victims" mobilized in France by both Jews and Blacks (by which she means French citizens of African or Caribbean origin), in which the contest to have suffered more leads to an obsession with identity as suffering and death. She also bemoans to what degree the "memory of the past and of the Shoah has been imposed on us to the point, sometimes, of suffocating life—to the point of legitimating a surprising tendency to victimization."[31] In Italy, the historian Ariel Toaff issued a *J'accuse* condemning Jewish scholars' blinding attachment to the Holocaust for their criticism of his work that sought to prove against all available evidence that medieval Jews may have engaged in the ritual murder of Christian children. This attachment, according to Toaff, is characteristic of all Jews in the diaspora, whose guilty relation to Israel precludes an impartial treatment of Jewish history.[32] Heirs to Holocaust memory insist that Jewish suffering is no longer discussable in the language reserved for garden-variety

31. Esther Benbassa, "La Shoah comme religion: Les bien-pensants, juifs ou non, expient en ranimant la flamme du souvenir face aux descendants de l'Holocauste," *Libération,* September 11, 2001. She refers to a specific incident involving the French satirist Dieudonné, originally from the Antilles, who staged anti-Semitic skits that enraged the French Jewish community and initiated a discussion about so-called victim competition. See also Benbassa, *La souffrance comme identité* (Paris: Fayard, 2007), for a synthesis of these views in France, and, for a polemical assessment of the Dieudonné scandal, Anne-Sophie Mercier, *Dieudonné Démasqué: L'enquête qu'il a voulu interdire* (Paris: Seuil, 2005).

32. Ariel Toaff, *Ebraismo virtuale* (Milan: Rizzoli, 2008), esp. 10–11. The book that elicited the critical response is Toaff, *Pasque di sangue* (Bologna: Il Mulino, 2007).

agony because victims' "innocence beyond goodness or virtue" has no worldly equivalent save for the hushed tones of the memorial service (identification with victims presumably compensates for "guilt" about not immigrating to Israel). Thus the "tendency to victimization" expresses the worship of survivors and the obsession with death, manifests the narcissistic identification with the pain of those one imagines suffered most unbearably, and relieves the guilt of diaspora Jews!

Ian Buruma describes the alleged and culturally pervasive identification with victims as a masochistic attraction to injury which has no substance other than its own oddly comforting self-gratification and thus dissolution into nothingness and forgetfulness.[33] He argues that historically victimized groups began to demand recognition in the 1970s and '80s, when younger generations proclaimed what their parents had refused to say too loudly: that their parents had been victims. In so doing, Buruma claims, they seek some form of identity in an increasingly globalized world. The infamous silence about and of Jewish victims after the Second World War, the silence of Chinese victims of the Nanking massacre, that of the Korean 'comfort women,' as well as the repression of their voices by governments with bigger or other fish to fry have recently given way to demands for recognition of past wrongs. Buruma implicitly seconds Todorov's interpretation, in which so-called victim culture is the unpredictable symptom of the otherwise commendable diffusion of human rights. In Buruma's view, the elite younger generation, now globally oriented by choice and opportunity, watches *Seinfeld,* eats Chinese take-out, and asserts a special relation to suffering because their parents' sufferings were not recognized.

The French philosophers Michel Feher and Alain Finkielkraut both insist that Jewish nonconformists of yesteryear now derive their identity from the "suffering of their parents." Feher warns of the dangers of seeking a coherent identity based on victimization. He associates the American Left's multiculturalism with Jews' refusal of the "cosmopolitanism" with which they are "inevitably associated." Jews now abandon a "cosmopolitan sensibility" wary of grand commemorations in favor of an empty solidarity founded on shared suffering. In other words, for both French critics, multiculturalism is monological, conceives identity in terms of

33. Ian Buruma, "The Joys and Perils of Victimhood," *New York Review of Books,* April 8, 1999, 6.

injury, and worships "grand" memorials that in reality are surrogate social bonds.[34] For her part, Esther Benbassa distinguishes between the United States, where the "legitimacy of multiculturalism" at least permits a debate about victims' claims, and France, where, she argues, the refusal of multiculturalism in favor of republican universalism tends to obscure the real debate, or at least the recognition that universalism is often a stand-in for all citizens when it really represents white, Catholic men.[35] One might note that any so-called competition of victims still contemptuously displaces the recognition of suffering onto a contest over who-has-suffered-more organized around the icon of the Holocaust of European Jewry. It is nonetheless true that the greater comfort felt by American Jewish intellectuals in denouncing the surfeit of Holocaust memory derives from Benbassa's observation that in the United States, minority rights, if not equally recognized, compete in the public sphere and are not therefore refused recognition by a universalism that claims to represent all citizens. This observation may help explain why Benbassa herself is an unusual if not lone voice among French Jewish critics who defend Palestinian rights: most French Jewish intellectuals have been forced to choose between express support for French republicanism or for Israel, symbolic of the incompatible allegiance (in French cultural and political terms) between a universalist order and a so-called particularist interest in the rights of a minority group.

But Benbassa too is impatient with grandiloquent representations of Jewish suffering because they render it too familiar and encourage a narcissistic or sublime identification with suffering not your own that imparts no meaningful knowledge of genocide. Jews' allegedly pathological attachment to victimization is thus a cultural manifestation of too much Jewish memory and of the inflated prestige therefore accorded to Jewish wounds. As the Left-wing French essayist Pascal Bruckner quipped in 1995, "The whole world wants to be Jewish."[36] The dubiousness, not to mention plain silliness, of his assertion brings into relief the current perception of Jewish

34. Michel Feher, "1967–1992: Sur quelques recompositions de la gauche américaine," *Esprit* 187 (1992): 75. See also Alain Finkielkraut, *The Imaginary Jew,* trans. Kevin O'Neil and David Suchoff (Lincoln: University of Nebraska Press, 1994).

35. Benbassa, *La souffrance,* 233–34.

36. Pascal Bruckner, *La tentation de l'innocence* (Paris: Grasset, 1995), 131–32.

trauma as an exaggerated attachment to one's wounds that stands in for the desires of all victims, who do not merely want recognition, but implicitly want to be acknowledged to be the most victimized of all.

One of the most infamous expressions of this peculiar identification with Jewish victims is Binjamin Wilkomirski's 'child survivor' memoir, *Fragments: Memories of a Wartime Childhood.* Wilkomirski's memoir transformed its author into a revered international hero and tragic figure until it turned out to be the story not of Binjamin Wilkomirski, but of Bruno Dössekker [Grosjean], a young Swiss boy given up ambivalently by his mother and adopted by parents he did not love and who showed him little affection. Dössekker rewrote his own childhood as the story of a young Jewish child who survived the camps. Until his fraud was exposed beyond a doubt, Dössekker held fast to his story, and was supported by Jewish organizations as well as groups of Holocaust survivors as he toured European and American cities as an authentic survivor. Critics spilled a lot of ink discussing the success of *Fragments* once it was revealed to be a fake (though suspicions, largely ignored, were raised immediately upon its publication in 1995 because of the unlikely survival of a very young child in death camps).[37] In a particularly interesting view articulated by the historian and writer Régine Robin, Wilkomirski's fiction is a larger symptom of what she calls "simulated memory": Wilkomirski is the "real witness"— the "meta-witness" of postmodernity, testimony no longer to the confusion of fact and fiction but to a fantasy that is factual, to the dissolution of the "real" and the "imaginary" rather than to the eruption of fantasy into the realm of fact. She bemoans rather than explores this "transferential space" in which projections collapse the distance between fact and fiction and presumably allowed Wilkomirski to believe he had been a Jewish child, and notes ironically that such witnesses have emerged just as witnesses to the events we call the Holocaust are in danger of disappearing.[38]

Many other critics attributed all the attention Wilkomirski received to the public's uncritical embrace of suffering. When everyone wants to be a victim, and a Jewish victim of the Holocaust brings the highest price, talk of Nazi criminality is cheapened, and there is no telling the difference

---

37. For an investigation into Wilkomirski's fable, see Stefan Maechler, *The Wilkomirski Affair: A Study in Biographical Truth,* trans. John E. Woods (New York: Schocken Books, 2001).
38. Régine Robin, *La mémoire saturée* (Paris: Stock, 2003), 240–42.

between what really happened and mere dramatization. According to Wilkomirski's critics, it is the dubious fascination with Holocaust victims that has contributed to this sorry state of affairs: the appeal of victims' stories, the fear of appearing insensitive to a victim of genocide, our illusion that we know their suffering better if we figure out how vicariously to feel it. Or, as Dagmar Barnouw sees it, the alleged triumph of emotion in public life is related to "the explosive growth of Holocaust memory stories," which are themselves "linked to current Western ideological multiculturalism that supports multiple, often mutually exclusive monological public memories and histories of identity on the basis of former persecution."[39]

History, Memory, Identity

Surely quests for clear lines between better and worse ways of remembering, between respectful, bounded memory and the self-indulgent appropriation of memory, and even between real and fraudulent victims that have been obscured by culturally sanctioned, narcissistic investments in suffering constitute important critical ventures. They take on kitsch renderings of Jewish experience wrought by "identity politics." And they underline the problematic sacralization of survivors, which makes it difficult to ask hard questions about victims' veracity. But these criticisms of the centrality of suffering to identity do not merely assert that real victims are those who were in the most literal sense there. They also seek to define the meaning of reliable memory and thus how we best remember. For all their emphasis on the contrast between empirical facts and the so-called surfeit of memory, these critics do not conceive empirical facts alone as sufficient to establish the veracity of memory. They seek instead to recover the history of injury undistorted by wounded attachments by designating what rhetorical relation to suffering represents reliable—insightful, useful, historically accurate, and ethically valid—memory, and what relation to suffering represents unreliable memory. For reliable memory of the past can counter the distortions generated by wounded identity and its various affirmations, whether illusions that one has survived a Holocaust that

39. Barnouw, "The Certainties of Evil," 105.

one has never experienced or the appearance of somatic symptoms resembling those of survivors. In so doing, reliable memory distinguishes clearly between 'real' and would-be victims. At the same time, these critics conflate traumatic memory so entirely with the pathological inflation of pain that they not only beg the question of how and when memory becomes traumatic, but also render trauma itself inconceivable except as an overwrought and potentially unreliable experience of suffering.[40] This is to say simply that the construction of 'victim culture' offers a significant and yet problematic interpretation of how best to remember Jewish suffering, and thus how insights into and information about the past can be gleaned reliably, and from whom.

What then is the proper relationship to the past suffering of one's group and to suffering humanity more generally? When does the relation to suffering become a self-indulgent, narcissistic projection? Michael A. Bernstein argues that the idea that victimhood should "endow one with special claims and rights" is part of an ideology in which extreme suffering underlines previously invisible worthiness and thus accords victims a special standing. Those who use the rhetoric of victimization fail to realize that "victim" is a historically mutable category that must be pinned down: after the Great War, many Germans saw themselves primarily as victims, and elected Hitler to restore their lost honor.[41] Some historians have argued similarly that the fluidity of victim identity accounts for the perpetuation of modern war: the use of sophisticated media, propaganda, and technology combined with impersonally waged warfare (because soldiers since the Great War for the most part do not literally see their enemy) constructs national, ethnic, or religious enemies as perpetrators and one's group as victims regardless of their actual status.[42] In this context, the rhetoric of victimization becomes a means of mastering social crises by projecting responsibility for them onto enemy others who violate the nation's

40. For a recent example of this kind of conceptual failure (in an otherwise thought-provoking book), see Gary Weissman, *Fantasies of Witnessing: Postwar Efforts to Experience the Holocaust* (Ithaca: Cornell University Press, 2004), 21. On the general problems created by the insistence on a clear binary division between history and memory, see Dominick LaCapra, *History in Transit: Experience, Identity, Critical Theory* (Ithaca: Cornell University Press, 2004), 112–18.

41. Michael André Bernstein, *Foregone Conclusions: Against Apocalyptic History* (Berkeley: University of California Press, 1994), 91, 87.

42. Omer Bartov, *Mirrors of Destruction: War, Genocide, and Modern Identity* (Oxford: Oxford University Press, 2000).

innocence, itself often embodied by women and children. War or a mental state of siege accompanies the construction of victimhood as a form of identity, since wounded national or religious aspirations by definition must be avenged or healed.

This intimate relation between the fluidity of the victim's role and the potential violence it generates also constitutes one of the main arguments against victim culture, since our perception of ourselves as a group besieged leads inevitably to the prevalence of violent self-defense as the only way to sustain group identity. As Zygmunt Bauman argues, "The thesis of hostility to the Jews being the prime mover of the Holocaust is sacralisation's principal, and most effective, instrument. Sacralisation sets the Jews as the sole bearers of the Holocaust memory, apart from the rest of the world incurably saturated with Jew-hatred, the site of the past holocaust and the hotbed of holocausts to come."[43] In the discourses of would-be victims—in this case, Jews who overidentify with Holocaust memory—the "sacralised hostility" that is deeply felt but not examined threatens to define the memory of the Holocaust itself.[44]

The putatively excessive attention to the Holocaust is thus no longer merely about the event's commercialization, but also about how Holocaust memory is increasingly framed by an unbearable collective injury whose would-be victims inflate their agony. The French historian Henry Rousso and the journalist Éric Conan note that such distortion—in their view most contemporary Jews believe in the perpetual resurgence of anti-Semitism in spite of evidence to the contrary—occurs now because "everyone wants his own genocide,"[45] including Jews who did not live through the Holocaust. Rousso famously outlined the collective symptoms of a

---

43. Zygmunt Bauman, "Categorial Murder, Or: How to Remember the Holocaust," in *Re-Presenting the Shoah for the Twenty-First Century,* ed. Ronit Lentin (New York: Berghahn Books, 2004), 31.

44. The literary theorist David Carroll writes, "The Shoah is for many the sign that no people can trust any other people...and that aggressive 'self-defense' at all costs must be the political principle of the post-Shoah era." Carroll quoted in Alan Milchman and Alan Rosenberg, "The Problematics of Memory: A Hermeneutical Inquiry into the Holocaust," in *The Uses and Abuses of Knowledge: Proceedings of the 23rd Annual Scholars' Conference on the Holocaust and the German Church Struggle, March 7–9, 1993, Tulsa, Oklahoma,* ed. Henry F. Knight and Marcia S. Littell (Lanham, MD: University Press of America, 1997), 45.

45. Éric Conan and Henry Rousso, *Vichy: An Ever-Present Past,* trans. Nathan Bracher (Hanover, NH: University of New England Press, 1998), 202.

nation, France, which had not worked through its relation to its collabo-rationist past. He later denounced the stubborn persistence of one of those symptoms, too much memory, and noted that the surfeit of memory about the Vichy period had become increasingly "Judeocentric."[46] He maintains that this "Judeocentrism" is a problem, because it "seeks to reread the en-tire history of the [Nazi] Occupation [of France] throught [*sic*] the prism of anti-Semitism: While in our eyes, the anti-Jewish policy is a major aspect of the Occupation, it was at the time of the Occupation only one among many others, since the Jews were victims just like the others who had been persecuted or condemned. The fact that it may shock our conscience is one thing, but the notion that it should lead us to remake history is another; the anachronism consists of confusing the morality of posterity with the reality of the past."[47] Conan and Rousso stress that in spite of popular perception, after the war Jews "had refused at all cost to appear as victims distinct from the other victims of the Nazis."[48]

More forcefully, the historian Peter Novick, whose contentious and most in-depth response to this question from the Left, *The Holocaust in American Life,* garnered much attention, argues that the rise of "identity politics" and a "culture of victimization" enabled, though they did not cause, Jews to "embrace a victim identity based on the Holocaust." Though his is a long and detailed historical study of the Holocaust's increasing pre-eminence in American Jewish culture, his general argument is that the sacrosanct status of the Holocaust in American life is a pretext for the as-sumption of victim status, a surrogate identity in a Jewish world shorn of more traditional forms of affirmation and in which "faltering Jewish identity produced so much anxiety about Jewish survival."[49] For Novick, this surfeit of memory is bound up with a new cultural status accorded victimization in which Jews suffer most of all. He rightly notes that the du-biously privileged status of Jews as the most victimized group problemati-cally transforms them into objects of identification and envy or even icons of mysterious and sacred suffering. But his argument that Jews' irrational

46. Conan and Rousso, *Vichy,* 51, 198. He puts the word in quotation marks, indicating a de-sire to distance himself from the concept even as he employs it.

47. Conan and Rousso, *Vichy,* 199.

48. Conan and Rousso, *Vichy,* 51–52.

49. Peter Novick, *The Holocaust in American Life* (New York: Houghton Mifflin, 2000), 189–90.

and anxious embrace of the iconic status accorded Jewish pain *explains* the pathological attachment to wounds simply asserts tautologically that victim culture accounts for why Jews enthusiastically embrace some form of victimization. That is, for Novick, Jewish pathology is clearly bound up with a broader cultural pathology in which the desire to be a victim is best symbolized by Jewish narcissism: the gap between empirically verifiable anti-Semitism and Jews' perception of their own vulnerability is, according to Novick, enormous, rendering Jewish perceptions particularly distorted and troubling. Ultimately, in his view, Jewish pain must stand in for everyone's, so that all claims for restitution and recognition turn into a "competition of victims," a battle of cultural one-upmanship in which terms such as "holocaust envy" are rhetorical cannon fodder.[50] In other words, today's self-appointed Jewish victims as well as those who claim that Jews have always been victims have a distorted memory of the past.

When the construction of the victim is located historically, when moral judgment can be reliably linked to a clear conception of who has been violated and who has not, when the heirs of sufferers do not confuse history and memory but rationally assess the level of hostility toward them rather than projecting their own anxieties onto others, victims' heirs might establish a healthy relationship to reality. Arguments on the political Left contend that the embrace of victimization leads paradoxically to a rationalization of Israel's treatment of Palestinians. But those on the political Right, like Gabriel Schoenfeld, denounce the way in which victim culture leads Jews to an emotional identification with suffering so devoid of content that a victim is a victim and it is not at all clear what makes Jewish victimization specific and meaningful. For both Left and Right, the fluidity of victim identity threatens Jewish identity and even the survival of Israel.

In this context the refusal to succumb to emotions, to vengeance,[51] and to paranoia characterizes a healthy relationship to past suffering and allows for a proper assessment of the boundary between memory and history. The mastery of disorientation is essential to preserving those boundaries, and the loss of such mastery is also crucial to defining when a particular relation

---

50. Antonio de Figueiredo, "'Holocaust Envy' or a Better Deal for Africa?" *New African* 409 (2002): 8–9.

51. David Carroll quoted in Milchman and Rosenberg, "The Problematics of Memory," 44–45.

to past suffering will generate surplus memory that entirely absorbs history in the guise of recalling it. Those who have criticized the surfeit of memory have in this way sought to expose our investment in Jewish victimization as charged and problematic: we have attributed "revelatory virtues"[52] to catastrophe; we are obsessed by victims' traumas; and we confuse trauma and historical experience. They believe that victimization now trumps heroism in conferring identity and prestige, and that public discourse is dominated by minority groups that demand public recognition, including recognition of their own memories. They wish to ensure a clear distinction between history and memory, and recoil from an emphasis on the unspeakableness of victims' suffering and from arguments about the traumatic nature of the event in favor of an emphasis on the virtues of the ordinary.

Real Victims

These arguments tend to situate truth and clear-sightedness on the side of history, and opacity and trauma on the side of memory far too simplistically. Rousso's and Conan's insistence on French universalism, their insistence, that is, that Jews wished to be treated like others (which may have been true in some cases and not in others), appears to return to the period before the particularity of Jewish suffering under Nazism was recognized, as if universalism did not have a complicated history that erased Jewish experience in the war's aftermath. In particular, they attribute postwar Jews with not wanting to be victims or with refusing to demand a particular space for themselves in the pantheon of the various interest groups that demanded recognition either for their contribution to France's liberation or as French citizens who had suffered at the hands of the Nazis. They characterize the so-called surfeit of memory as a matter of finding the right equilibrium between too much and too little Jewish memory rather than as an opportunity to examine the ideological investments in the erasure *or* the alleged surfeit of Jewish memory, and thus to examine the historical construction of Jewish victims or even the context in which Jews might have felt uncomfortable making particular demands. In the same vein, many

---

52. Michael André Bernstein, "Homage to the Extreme: The Shoah and the Rhetoric of Catastrophe," *Times Literary Supplement,* March 6, 1998, 6–8.

critics' restriction of discussions about victims to nationalist or patriotic contexts long after the globalization of the concept has complicated if not rendered obsolete such usage, appears to be a response to the idealization of Israel as the only guarantee of Jewish memory (or the emptying of that guarantee through recourse to glib forms of commemoration). In the name of rescuing history from the platitudinous excess of memory, these critics too reiterate a restricted and unexamined history of the term "victim" even as their arguments about the dangers of patriotic usage ring true. In so doing, they never analyze the historical phenomenon of the secularized centrality of suffering to identity except in the context of patriotic resurrection and mutual national destruction. They thus do not consider accusations of victim culture as a potentially defensive response to the pain of others. In their view, that phenomenon is always and dangerously about self-pity.

This lack of historical self-consciousness in the name of recovering 'history' facilitates a particular rhetorical formulation of victimization as a trajectory from trauma to recovery accomplished by force of ordinary virtues and a strenuous coming-to-terms. By this trajectory I mean that these critics militate against the "misconceived selfishness" that constitutes the "sacralisation"[53] of Jewish victims by stressing the virtues of the ordinary, the known, and the human dimension of catastrophic events: they do not merely affirm empiricist concepts of historical causation and accountability, but also link the moral project intrinsic in the historian's efforts to preserve 'what happened' with having persevered in the face of too much memory. Indeed, they articulate a tendency within many post-Holocaust discourses to struggle against the hyperbole associated with contested claims that the Holocaust is unique, unspeakable, and therefore that its victims have suffered uniquely and unspeakably.

The premises of this discourse against victim culture are not reducible to any particular philosophical approach. Many critics insist along with Michael Bernstein that "the reserve of writers like Dan Pagis or Primo Levi may be invoked and held up as exemplary in numerous discourses, but, in fact, their suspicion of the sonorous and grandiloquent has been conspicuously *un*influential. Their rhetorical austerity has been praised

---

53. Bauman, "Categorial Murder," 30.

precisely in order to be replaced by later critics' self-regardingly ornate and often explicitly rivalrous formulations."[54] This homage to the ordinary also shares the late historian Sybil Milton's impatience with what she called the "universal willingness to commemorate suffering experienced rather than suffering caused"[55]—to identify with victims' suffering while not inquiring too deeply into the historical conditions that made it possible, rendering uncritical, self-indulgent, and untroubled identification with those who suffered possible. The homage to the ordinary emphasizes quiet meditation and a neutral tone, and in particular references Primo Levi rather than Charlotte Delbo, a minimalist style over an ornate one.

Again and again, Levi's modesty and his embrace of ordinary virtues stand in for the veracity of memory. Since Levi has long been a symbol of quiet humanism and universalism, the identification with him is not surprisingly a frequent referent of those who denounce our alleged attachment to injury. Thus Gary Weissman contrasts Levi's testimony with those of "secondary" and other witnesses in order to demonstrate that real witnesses rarely claim to have been victims, and secondary witnesses often wish they had been victims of the Holocaust. Weissman claims that several generations of mostly Jewish intellectuals now vie to be "witnesses" to the Holocaust's horror. He believes that survivors were victims but also, as he says, finds "value in the distinction [Ruth Kluger] makes between survivor stories and victim stories."[56] In Weissman's view, real victims are either dead or refuse to be labeled as victims. Paradoxically, it is the victims who refuse to embrace victimization that Weissman represents as the most reliable witnesses. They are more reliable not only because they were there, but also because being there apparently dictates a sense of proportion and measured response to events absent among those who can only fantasize having been there: respect for the memory of the dead and a dramatic refusal to put themselves in the place of the dead victims.

When Dössekker alias Wilkomirski proved uncooperative once questions about the veracity of his story finally became a chorus of demands for proof, the Swiss historian Stefan Maechler was asked by Dössekker's

54. Bernstein, "Homage to the Extreme," 7.

55. Sybil Milton, cited in Edward T. Linenthal, *Preserving Memory: The Struggle to Create America's Holocaust Museum* (New York: Viking, 1995), 199.

56. Weissman, *Fantasies of Witnessing,* 118, 75.

literary agent to get to the bottom of things, and wrote the definitive exposé of Wilkomirski's lies. Maechler's exemplary detective work and evenhandedness notwithstanding, his account of Dössekker's deception depicts most of Dössekker's defenders as hoodwinked because they wanted to believe in or identified with his suffering. Though he blames Dössekker for manipulating his audience, the book is nonetheless a far broader indictment of a culture so hungry for victims' stories that it has produced professional victims—in this case a woman who masqueraded as a child survivor and a victim of Satanic ritual abuse and shares the stage with Wilkomirski at one of his readings. Maechler records the refusal of many who were skeptical of Wilkomirski's story to raise their voices, including some survivors. He is also careful to attribute some survivors' desire to believe Dössekker to their fear of victimizing him all over again by questioning his veracity. But what prevails above all is the grotesque spectacle of would-be victims wooing audiences with dramatic tales of atrocity, and a noisy parade of psychoanalysts, psychiatrists, and survivors' organizations all making claims on the victims' behalf.

This is not to cast an uncritical eye on Dössekker's fraud, but rather to put Maechler's interpretation of it in the context of recent critical frameworks within which real victims have become increasingly indistinct from fraudulent or would-be claimants, and in which claims to having been victimized are ever more inseparable from the narcissistic appropriation of suffering. My point is not that these arguments deny the extraordinary nature of the Holocaust, but rather, that in seeking to be loyal to memory, they paradoxically figure symptoms not only of trauma, but also of resentment, anger, and the desire for vengeance as an unassimilable residue of that event—as feelings that should ideally have already been mastered. Indeed, in this rhetorical context it is impossible to imagine any means of claiming to have been or to be a victim that might be legitimate other than by having already resolved one's relationship to that experience. The traumatized Jewish victim thus figures the memory of a history that cannot be assimilated or reconciled to any normative pattern. Oddly, the historical and psychological experience of some Jews is erased or diminished in the high-stakes effort to distinguish between history and memory, true and false claims to having been victimized, and measured and hyberbolic renderings of what actually happened. To the extent that this homage to the ordinary uses the idea that victims are a privileged cultural category and a stand-in for an implicitly or explicitly hyperbolic, pathological memory that always exceeds its referent, a certain kind of unrestrained relationship to victimization stands in for the perils of memory against history. Trauma, if unresolved, may figure the wrong sort of victim, one overly attached to her victimization. In the worst cases, the traumatized victim may be conceived as not a real one.

Victims, in a culture that now casts suspicion on all those who claim to be victims or to have been victimized, become the repository of unconstrained affect and thus of experience not sufficiently worked through. Would-be victims are symptoms of democratic rationality gone awry: rational consensus building has apparently lost its bearings in a sea of feeling and thus of false claims. Moreover, critics believe that empowered victimhood has replaced the disinterested indignation that permits the proper evaluation of grievances in democracies, so that the judicious examination of claims is swept away by the rhetorical force of the victim's "fearless" voice.[57] The grievance structure of rational, democratic contestation is replaced by the unconstrained projection of phantasmatic wounds. The historian Charles Maier has written that "modern American politics, it might be argued, has become a competition for enshrining grievances."[58] The editor-in-chief of the German weekly *Die Zeit,* Josef Joffe, similarly bemoaned how "victimhood has become an almost universal quest throughout the Western world."[59] In the United States and Western Europe this vast commentary thus mostly shares Esther Benbassa's assertion that "in our society, to have been a victim nourishes the quest for identity and authorizes the demand for cultural recognition."[60] The would-be victim becomes a symbol less of the quest for identity than of a wounded narcissistic investment: this discourse then tells the story of how democracies fail if we are not vigilant about the dangers of imagining ourselves only as victims. But this version

57. Jonathan Simon, "Parrhesiastic Accountability: Investigatory Commissions and Executive Power in an Age of Terror," *Yale Law Journal* 114 (2005): 1421, 1450–51, 1454. Simon takes the term "fearless speech" from a translation of Michel Foucault's own invocation of an ancient Greek concept.

58. Maier, "A Surfeit of Memory?" 47.

59. Josef Joffe quoted in Andreas Tzortzsis, "World War II's Latest 'Victims'," *Christian Science Monitor,* September 23, 2003, 6.

60. Esther Benbassa, "Les Noirs, les juifs, et la victimisation," *Le Monde,* March 17, 2005.

of the story risks confusing real victims and imaginary ones, because it conceives all victims as imaginary unless proven otherwise.

The demand for clear distinctions between history and memory and history and rhetoric insists on a normative framework within which victimization might be clearly defined. Thus, for example, the strength of such a framework might expose the rhetorical sleight of hand with which Left-wing intellectuals compare Israel to Nazi Germany and the Palestinians to Jews as yet one more historical distortion appealing to a moral claim to victimization (one that again and self-consciously privileges the Holocaust as a tragic marker of persecution). And yet this discourse too demonstrates how difficult drawing such normative distinctions might actually be, however self-evident they appear to be in practice. For as I have sought to argue, it manifests deep ambivalence attending to the potential meaninglessness of suffering and the disorientation, helplessness, or fragmentation of the victim that may result in a judgment about his inability to forgive, forget, and move on.

The problem posed by that suffering, rendered so vivid by the constant struggle, in Eva Hoffman's generally self-reflexive text, between critical distance from and overidentification with survivors, marks just how profoundly difficult it is even (or especially?) for those spokespersons of the "second generation" to avoid the pitfalls of "vicarious witnessing" which Hoffman claims "tough-minded critiques" of the "Holocaust cult" underestimate and diminish.[61] She herself writes of feeling that a young woman's explicitly manifest grief at a memorial in a death camp was somehow inappropriate to the setting. And yet, as Ruth Franklin notes, might not such grief be appropriate? On the one hand, Hoffman suggests that perhaps Aharon Appelfeld's antidote to trauma—using ordinary language in its accessibility and humility—may not always be adequate, and on the other, she embraces her parents' trauma protectively in the guise of what one almost hesitates to call bourgeois propriety—one doesn't grieve so unabashedly in public. We might ask if efforts to define victims rhetorically and culturally as those who have already mastered disorientation characteristic even of the most sensitive critical voices, if efforts to define victims as those who have refused to succumb to the traumatic or other effects

61. Hoffman, *After Such Knowledge*, 177.

of events, are not rather a defense against the never quite reliable and yet uncanny memory of those who have lived through them. We might ask if, aside from the surely appropriate criticism of masochistic attraction to injury and the persuasive critiques of identity politics, allegations of 'victim culture' also manifest perhaps predictable discomfort with and, at worst, distaste for the seemingly unrestrained claims of certain kinds of victims and those who claim to speak on their behalf. However predictable they may be, such attitudes should be the subject of consistent critical scrutiny that they generally do not receive.

If "everyone wants to be Jewish," or in another variant on the theme, everyone wants to be a victim, has any credibility, it can only be because victims have become an object of conscience while other desires to remember have been somehow delegitimated or obliterated. Thus the academic mandate to focus only on the memory of once traumatized peoples, asserted by Eelco Runia in a mostly self-reflexive and ironic text, only reinforces the sense that scholars really want to engage in deeply felt commemoration of a variety of experiences with which they might identify, but feel confined to muse only on legitimate objects of memory.[62] The question here is not whether this is true, but why the idea that victims have become a fetish object is so pervasive and with what consequences. For every questionable sort of identification such as that manifested by Wilkomirski, there are just as many denials or distortions of victims' assertions about their victimization, some in the interest merely of forgetting. What might it mean to say, as Runia does, that commemoration is now the "self-exploration" of our time? Whose commemoration, and thus whose self-exploration? Perhaps this difficulty in seeing victims clearly has something to do with the way discomfort with victims usually appears to be indirect, unconscious, and frequently articulated in otherwise rational and often persuasive arguments. Indeed, the violence it is our burden to identify is rhetorical rather than literal (but no less real), and it is as nuanced and indirect as commentators' own conscious or unconscious relation to their subjects. And this complicity may be informed by more complex and often negative attitudes toward victims reduced to their bare humanity, attitudes remarked upon so often by victims themselves.

---

62. Eelco Runia, "Burying the Dead, Creating the Past," *History and Theory* 46 (2007): 322.

French Discourses on Exorbitant Jewish Memory

> This surfeit of memory that engulfs us today could well be nothing but a figure of forgetting. Because the "new age" of the past is that of saturation... Saturation by a return to pasts placed back to back, by the equivalence afforded to Nazi and Communist demons, by a lack of distinction between events, an absence of classification and of a hierarchy of evils, as in those discourses which, in Italy or in Spain, demonize equally the Resistance and Mussolini, Franco and the Republicans.
>
> RÉGINE ROBIN (2003)

In his preface to a 1986 work about the Terror during the French Revolution, the French historian Pierre Chaunu alluded to the similarity between the genocide of European Jewry and the massacre of the rebellious population of the Vendée who rose up against the revolutionaries' anticlerical decrees. Chaunu asked readers to recognize the repression of the uprising as "the first ideological genocide."[1] Though he made the references to Jews as well as to Stalin's gulags and the Khmer Rouge in passing, the idea that the French civil war might be conceived as "genocide" raised eyebrows. The writer Alfred Grosser argues that the polemical analogy

---

Epigraph: Régine Robin, *La mémoire saturée* (Paris: Stock, 2003), 19.

1. Pierre Chaunu's preface to Reynald Sécher, *Le génocide franco-français: La Vendée vengé* (Paris: Presses Universitaires de France, 1986), 24. Sécher's book asserts that Terror in the Vendée amounted to genocide. The book has been translated into English as *French Genocide: The Vendée,* trans. George Holoch (Notre Dame: University of Notre Dame Press, 2003), but without Chaunu's preface.

sought not to "diminish the weight of Auschwitz, as a Jewish journal had erroneously proclaimed... but argues that the Revolution had been as capable and guilty of horrors of the same sort [*du même ordre*] as Nazism."[2] Chaunu's reference to the equivalence of the Jewish genocide and the Terror is historically dubious and appears aligned with other efforts to minimize the significance of the Nazi extermination of European Jewry. During the 1993 bicentennial of the uprising in the Vendée, the reactionary politician Philippe de Villiers called the Jacobins' repressive measures against the Catholic population a "genocide" with its "dozens and dozens of Oradours" (a French town whose non-Jewish population was massacred by the Nazis), and also referred to the massacre as a "final solution" comparable to the extermination of Russian peasants under Stalin.[3]

Chaunu's words might be interpreted as an effort to dramatize the revolutionaries' crimes by polemically rather than substantively comparing their atrocities to those of other criminal regimes. In 1986, when former Nazi Klaus Barbie's lawyer Jacques Vergès argued that Barbie's deportation of Jewish children and torture of the resistance hero Jean Moulin were no more brutal than those of the French during the Algerian war, he too sought to level polemically different kinds of crimes.[4] And yet Chaunu's comment also forms part of a general effort among diverse and respected French intellectuals after the 1980s to define victims and the experience of victimization in a new cultural context. Among many scholars and critics in France, Jews, the particularity of whose sufferings under the Vichy regime and in the Holocaust were only belatedly recognized, have been increasingly associated with victims and a hyperbolic rhetoric of victimization. As elsewhere, the sustained attention paid in the last two decades both to Vichy's crimes against Jews and to the Holocaust itself in speeches, commemorative rituals, trials, and television shows led not only to an association of Jewish identity with collective injury, but also, as the histo-

2. Alfred Grosser, *Le crime et la mémoire* (Paris: Flammarion, 1998), 45. See Grosser's views of what he terms Jewish "intellectual terrorism" in "Les pièges de la mémoire," *Le Figaro*, November 16, 1989.

3. Philippe de Villiers quoted in Pierre Birnbaum, *The Idea of France,* trans. M. B. DeBevoise (New York: Hill & Wang, 2001), 45.

4. Chaunu is a conservative historian, but Vergès, who used the same logic, is a well-known figure on the French Left, whose views developed in the context of Left-wing anti-Zionism and as a critique of French colonialism. On the Barbie trial, see Alain Finkielkraut, *La mémoire vaine: Du crime contre l'humanité* (Paris: Gallimard, 1989).

rian Joan Wolf has argued, to a French backlash against too much Jewish memory.[5] The French journalist and writer Nicolas Weill uses the English words "Holocaust Fatigue" to describe the same phenomenon, and views it as the "probable cause" of public apathy when anti-Semitism allegedly resurged in France between 2000 and 2002.[6] The French "obsession" with the Vichy past so famously described by Henry Rousso thus now appears solely as a Jewish obsession that highlights Jewish suffering and neglects that of others.[7]

The condemnations of Vichy perpetrators for crimes against humanity in particular (Paul Touvier in 1994 and Maurice Papon in 1998)[8] mobilized debates about who qualifies as victims, whose demands for restitution should be honored, and which victims have been unjustly forgotten. They also generated newer variations on inclinations to blame the victim, including Jews who were said to have cashed in on the so-called dividends of Auschwitz, profiting by portraying themselves as the most victimized group of all.[9]

5. Joan Wolf, *Harnessing the Holocaust: The Politics of Memory in France* (Stanford: Stanford University Press, 2004), very usefully and broadly documents the association of Jews with perpetrators as well as victims in the aftermath of the 1967 Israeli war of independence. She also argues that the idea that Jewish suffering impeded the recognition of Armenian, Kurdish, and African suffering was first thematized after 1978. She offers little explanation for this development except to say that French intellectuals perceived Jews to be blind to Palestinian suffering (and that there was simply an absence of a shared understanding of the Holocaust between Jews and gentiles). Moreover, she claims that because the French recognized Jewish victimization in the Holocaust, the French discourse about this issue could not have been anti-Semitic, a dubious proposition (42–68, 74).

6. Nicolas Weill, *La République et les antisémites* (Paris: Grasset, 2004), 88.

7. Henry Rousso, *The Vichy Syndrome: History and Memory in France since 1944,* trans. Arthur Goldhammer (Cambridge: Harvard University Press, 1991). Rousso argued that the French confronted Vichy belatedly by projecting all the unspoken guilt and ambiguity about French collaboration onto political struggles in the 1970s and '80s (so that the election of Mitterrand in 1981 was played out as if it were a clear choice between collaborators and patriots, when it was nothing of the sort). Éric Conan and Henry Rousso, *Vichy: An Ever-Present Past,* trans. Nathan Bracher (Hanover, NH: University Press of New England, 1998).

8. These are the dates verdicts were delivered. The trials themselves took place over several years.

9. See Nicolas Weill, *Une histoire personelle de l'antisémitisme* (Paris: Robert Laffont, 2003), on a 1989 article in the journal *Esprit* which characterized Elie Wiesel as having profited from Auschwitz "dividends" (13). This denunciation of the 'Shoah business' is now more pervasive and the topic of Norman Finkelstein's *The Holocaust Industry: Reflections on the Exploitation of Jewish Suffering* (London: Verso, 2000). The book appeared in French in 2000 and was covered extensively in the country's major newspapers. *Avocats sans Frontières,* a group of lawyers headed by

This image of Jews who tout past suffering at the expense of other groups has intensified as other minorities with a past history of colonization and slavery do not perceive their demands for recognition (of the French state's brutal colonial past, of French racism now and then) to carry the same weight as Jewish ones. Increasing interethnic conflict poorly addressed by the state has led to assertions that a "new anti-Semitism" has appeared in France. According to various scholars, anti-Semitism now emerges not only in traditional contexts (primarily the Catholic Church and the Far Right) but also out of the interaction between local French concerns and global politics. In particular, the defense of Israel or the Palestinian cause as the Israeli-Palestinian conflict continues to unfold has become a projection of many French citizens' own ethnosocial positions or ideological convictions—Left-wing intellectuals, Muslim and non-Muslim adolescents burdened by unemployment, racism, and fears of a bleak future, Jews who fear anti-Semitic violence, and politicians wishing to appeal to different constituencies. Thus Michel Wieviorka argues that the so-called new anti-Semitism (which he claims is somewhat overblown) combines old fantasies about Jewish power and Jewish plots with more recent efforts to question and diminish Jewish suffering in the Holocaust, as well as with hostility to Israel. But he notes too that many French Muslim youth identify with the plight of the Palestinians—especially those who have direct experience of racism at home in France—but otherwise know little.[10]

Gilles William Goldnadel, sued Finkelstein for "racial defamation" and "incitement to racial hatred," and lost. The suit nonetheless generated much discussion. See the defense of Finkelstein and Goldnadel's response in *Libération*, March 8, 2001, and March 27, 2001, respectively.

10. Michel Wieviorka, *La tentation anti-sémite: Haine des Juifs dans la France d'aujourd'hui* (Paris: Robert Laffont, 2005), 38; P. A. Targuieff, *La nouvelle judéophobie* (Paris: Mille et un nuits, 2000); Gilles William Goldnadel, *Le nouveau bréviare de la haine* (Paris: Ramsay, 2001); and, for an autobiographical account, Weill, *Une histoire personelle*. Also, see the conversations between Rony Brauman and Alain Finkielkraut on the Israeli-Palestinian conflict, anti-Semitism, and Jews in France from the Left, in *La Discorde: Israël-Palestine, les Juifs, la France: Conversations avec Éliz-abeth Lévy* (Paris: Mille et une nuits, 2006). Left-wing anti-Semitism is hardly a new phenomenon (Faurisson's denials of gas chambers were published by the ultra-Left group *La Vielle Taupe*). There is also a (far less predominant) new philosemitism. See Elizabeth J. Bellamy, *Affective Genealogies: Psychoanalysis, Postmodernism, and the "Jewish Question" after Auschwitz* (Lincoln: University of Nebraska Press, 1997). On negationism (which identified its position using the scholarly term "revisionism"), see Pierre Vidal-Naquet, *Assassins of Memory: Essays on the Denial of the Holocaust,* trans. Jeffrey Mehlman (New York: Columbia University Press, 1992); and Valérie Igounet, *Histoire du négationnisme en France* (Paris: Seuil, 2000).

The singling out of Jewish memory as a threat to other kinds of memory may also be related to recent defenses of the universal republic and its commitment to abstract citizenship against particular ethnic and group identifications of all sorts (that is, against liberal pluralism, in which the interplay of individuals and collectives with diverse interests define the meaning of the state). These defenses have intensified even though or perhaps because republican solutions, especially the insistence on abstract equality and thus assimilation to some idea of unmarked "Frenchness," have proven inadequate to address the social problems posed by immigration and globalization.

Here my subject is not, however, how recent discussions about hyperbolic Jewish memory may be a symptom of French republicanism in crisis, as exemplified in struggles over the rights of Muslim girls to wear headscarves or of gay and lesbian couples for state recognition.[11] I would instead like to put Chaunu's assertion in the context of discourses that reassess Stalinism in light of Nazism.[12] While such discourses are often polemical, they are not aimed at making sure a Nazi murderer wriggles out of a life sentence, and thus do not seek to minimize Jewish suffering. Rather, they assert that if not all suffering is alike, suffering is nonetheless suffering regardless of its causes or context.[13] They constitute a conceptual and cultural landscape in which a wide variety of intellectuals believe that victimization—of which Jewish suffering during this time became emblematic—confers identity and prestige, and Jews' alleged (over)investment in having been excluded

11. For recent discussions of French republicanism "in crisis" and varied critical responses to it (especially as it impacts Jews and Muslims), see, among now countless works, Weill, *La République et les antisémites;* Esther Benbassa, *La République face ses minorités: Les Juifs hier, les Musulmans aujourd'hui* (Paris: Mille et une nuits, 2004); Pierre-André Taguieff, *La République enlisée* (Paris: Des Syrtes, 2005); and Joan Scott, *The Politics of the Veil* (Princeton: Princeton University Press, 2007).

12. Some authors insist on comparing Hitler's crimes to Communist regimes' crimes the world over or at least to those in Russia since the Bolshevik Revolution. I will use the less controversial reference to "Stalin's" crimes whenever possible, and will use "Communism" only when the authors cited do so themselves.

13. This narrative is hardly limited to France. On the moral equivalence of Jewish dead and German victims of Allied fire bombing, see Joerg Friedrich, *Der Brand: Deutschland im Bombenkrieg, 1940–1945* (Munich: Propylaeen, 2002). On Italy, see, among others, the essays in Enzo Collotti, ed., *Fascismo e antifascismo: Rimozioni, revisioni, negazioni* (Rome: Laterza, 2000).

leads to distortions of history.[14] Diverse French thinkers now perceive the moral goal of confronting genocidal crimes to be obstructed by the exorbitant demands of so-called Jewish memory conceived as monolithic and obsessively focused on the Holocaust's "uniqueness" or "singularity."[15] Indeed, these discourses mobilize the conviction that for many French people today Jewish suffering, as the writer Henri Raczymow has facetiously proclaimed, simply "takes up too much space"[16] (after having been virtually forgotten for several decades after the war ended).[17]

This chapter thus examines more specifically how, in discourses about comparative suffering, Jewish victimization comes to stand in for the perils of too much memory and thus represents the inappropriate and empirically invalid valorization of memory over history. This figuration of Jewish memory is clearly shaped by the recent notion that it is excessive, but how and with what consequences? And what exactly is 'excess' and how are its parameters defined? How, in other words, is universal memory sufficient

14. For the United States, see Peter Novick, *The Holocaust in American Life* (New York: Mariner Books, 2000), 121, 189; for France, see Henry Rousso, *The Haunting Past: History, Memory, and Justice in Contemporary France*, trans. Ralph Schoolcraft (Philadelphia: University of Pennsylvania Press, 2002), 12–13. See also Tzvetan Todorov, "In Search of Lost Crime," *New Republic*, January 29, 2001, 26.

15. Jewish intellectuals have long debated the 'uniqueness' of the Holocaust, and those debates have engaged intellectuals on both sides of the Atlantic. Most historians typically reject the idea that the Holocaust is not a comparable event. Others use the concept of the Holocaust's unrepresentability in complex and different ways that do not necessarily exclude comparability (see Karyn Ball's extremely thoughtful effort to discuss the proponents of such views—Adorno, Lyotard, and others—including their legacies and theoretical and political consequences: Karyn Ball, *Disciplining the Holocaust* [Albany: State University of New York Press, 2008]). Many of the French thinkers discussed do not seem aware of, do not engage, or are poorly acquainted with such discussions, and tend to project a hegemonic view onto Jewish opinions or just don't flesh out arguments in a rigorous way. For a typical example of the vagueness of French usage, see Jean-François Theullot, *De l'inexistence d'un devoir de mémoire* (Nantes: Pleins Feux, 2004), 53–54. The exception here is Alain Badiou, *Circonstances 3: Portées du mot "juif"* (Clamecy: Léo Scheer, 2005), who argues that singularity should be conceived not in terms of the exceptional or the inconceivable, but in the context of Nazism as a particular political form. Badiou's text, however, is marred by his almost total construction of the problem of the Holocaust and the Israeli-Palestinian conflict in vague and abstract terms that are embedded in the logic of anti-identitarianism and anticolonialism rather than in a deeply considered assessment of the historical dimension of anti-Semitism in France.

16. Henri Raczymow, "D'un detail qui masque le tableau," *Le Monde,* January 21, 1998.

17. As Olivier Wieviorka has pointed out, the idea of a "duty to remember" has only existed in France since 1995 and was the title of posthumously published conversations with Primo Levi and two Italian historians in 1983. Olivier Wieviorka, *La mémoire désunie: Le souvenir politique des années sombres, de la Libeération à nos jours* (Paris: Seuil, 2010), 258.

to remember every violation and every grievance, and how can we know that Jewish memory has 'exceeded' its allotted proportion? How does this imagined surfeit of memory about the Holocaust exclude Jewish victims and Jews from or envision them in conflict with the universal community of human sufferers by critics who concede, even insist, that Jews have suffered and suffered in singular terms? How does Jewish victimization come to stand in not only for a history of persecution, but also for the erasure of suffering and the obfuscation of historical truth? Finally, how do recent discourses of comparative suffering, which address legitimate concerns both about the reduction of Holocaust memory to an icon of 'evil in our time' and about the problematic sacralization of the Holocaust, also dramatically erode the rhetorical grounds of Jewish claims to injury? By analyzing how recent discussions comparing Nazism and Stalinism in France reduce Jewish memory of the Holocaust to Jewish narcissism and Jewish power, this chapter not only addresses how the claim of excessive Jewish memory is legitimated in highly sophisticated terms, but also aims to make visible a discourse that takes shape within a broader rhetorical context in which critics transform Jews into perpetrators rather than 'privilege' them as victims.[18]

The Discovery of "Totalitarianism"

In France, the comparison between Nazism and Stalinism and the entire debate about the legitimacy of the concept of "totalitarianism" are quite recent. As François Furet, Pierre Grémion, and others have noted, the French

18. Nicolas Weill has argued that the focus on "excess memory" may very well constitute a projection of otherwise disavowed or unself-conscious anti-Semitic beliefs: Weill, *Une histoire personnelle*, 171. Vicki Caron addresses arguments about whether or not the French at various historical moments targeted Jews specifically or only as part of a broader hostility to foreigners in "The Anti-Semitic Revival in France in the 1930s: The Socioeconomic Dimension Reconsidered," *Journal of Modern History* 70 (1998): 24–28. There is also a voluminous literature on images of 'the Jew' in France that I do not address here, and which does not discuss the discourse with which I am concerned. See, among others, Robert Wistrich, *Anti-Semitism: The Longest Hatred* (Princeton: Princeton University Press, 1991); 126–44; Seth Wolitz, "Imagining the Jew in France: From 1945 to the Present," *Yale French Studies* 85 (1994): 119–34; Lawrence D. Kritzman, ed., *Auschwitz and After: Race, Culture and the "Jewish Question" in France* (New York: Routledge, 1995); Max Silverman, "Re-Figuring 'the Jew' in France," in *Modernity, Culture, and 'the Jew,'* ed. Brian Cheyette and Laura Marcus (Stanford: Stanford University Press, 1998), 197–207.

"discovered" the concept of "totalitarianism" in the 1970s and '80s just as Anglo-American historians increasingly rejected it.[19] For most if not all of the latter the term was a relic of the Cold War or not of much conceptual use. British and American social historians have long noted that totalitarianism, as it was first employed analytically by Hannah Arendt, presumes a passive view of citizens whose agency, individualism, and privacy were destroyed under a regime of terror, marking the triumph of the social over the political.[20] In the English-speaking world, a slew of books through the 1980s and '90s sought to lay the concept to rest through rigorous comparative analysis of Nazism and Stalinism both explicitly and implicitly, in studies that debunked, for example, the myth of an omniscient Gestapo.[21]

Most striking about France, however, is the absence of any discussion about totalitarianism until the 1970s. Only the increasingly contentious actions of the French Communist Party led to belated soul-searching among French Left-wing intellectuals about Stalinism and created a climate for

19. François Furet, *The Passing of an Illusion: The Idea of Communism in the Twentieth Century,* trans. Deborah Furet (Chicago: University of Chicago Press, 1999), 495–97; Pierre Grémion, *Intelligence de l'anticommunisme: Le Congrès pour la liberté de la culture à Paris 1950–1975* (Paris: Fayard, 1995), 622.

20. Arendt's work argued essentially that totalitarianism represented the unprecedented and total destruction of political life in the context of the homogenizing tendencies of the modern, expansionist, industrialized state. Much of her discussion of the Soviet Union, scholars argued, was ill informed and perhaps overly influenced by her portrait of Nazism. Arendt's major contribution was thus not her causal or comparative conclusions but her insistence on the unprecedented nature of totalitarian governments and her magisterial analysis of both the philosophical and the political dimensions of racial hatred and industrialized mass murder. In France, Arendt's 1951 *Origins of Totalitarianism* was not translated until 1972 (in Jacques Julliard's "Politique" collection at Seuil), and then only in an abridged form.

21. Ian Kershaw and Moshe Lewin, eds., *Stalinism and Nazism: Dictatorships in Comparison* (Cambridge: Cambridge University Press, 1997). Recent works suggest that Nazi terror was not directed against a terrorized and de-individuated population, but was aided and abetted by the general populace in its hunt for Jews and other dissidents. Studies of denunciation in Russia also demonstrate the radical differences between the Soviet State—which cultivated "informers" throughout the population—and the Nazi State, which depended on a motivated population to bring nonconformists to its attention. See Ian Kershaw, *Popular Opinion and Political Dissent in the Third Reich: Bavaria, 1933–45* (New York: Oxford University Press, 1983); Robert Gellately, *The Gestapo and German Society: Enforcing Racial Policy, 1933–1945* (Oxford: Clarendon Press, 1991); Sheila Fitzpatrick and Robert Gellately, eds., *Accusatory Practices: Denunciation in Modern European History, 1789–1989* (Chicago: University of Chicago Press, 1997); and Robert Gellately, *Backing Hitler: Consent and Coercion in Nazi Germany* (Oxford: Oxford University Press, 2001). See also the essays in Henry Rousso, ed., *Stalinisme et nazisme: Histoire et mémoire comparées* (Paris: Éditions Complexes, 1999).

the positive reception of Alexander Solzhenitsyn's *Gulag Archipelago,* the translation of which appeared in 1974. The last loyal Stalinist party in Europe, the PCF had defended the Soviet Union's invasion of Hungary in 1956 and failed to attract the younger generation of 1968. Its revolutionary slogans developed not with but against Communist dogmatism and thus against the post-liberation consensus about the indispensable role of the Soviet Union in antifascist struggle.[22] Left intellectuals' concerns of the 1970s led to the translation and resurrection of non-Marxist thinkers such as Arendt and Raymond Aron, and generated a plethora of books seeking to understand or denounce Soviet totalitarianism by *gauchiste* philosophers such as Claude Lefort, André Glucksmann, and Bernard-Henri Lévy. The latter two in particular used Nazism as a touchstone of evil against which Stalinism might be judged and its own malevolence highlighted, but they did not engage in systematic comparative analysis of the two regimes.[23] During the 1970s a lively and much publicized debate took place on the Left about the nature of totalitarianism that was more or less exclusively concerned with its Russian incarnation. Its most dramatic (and self-dramatizing) spokesperson was Lévy, author of the anti-Soviet *Barbarism with a Human Face,* which sold 100,000 copies in a year alone.[24] After 1975, fearing the Socialist Party's new coalition with the PCF forged by François Mitterrand, Leftist thinkers such as Lefort and Gilles Martinet temporarily joined forces with François Furet and other neo-liberals to challenge once and for all the ideological dominance of the Soviet Union in French political and intellectual life.[25]

Other discourses on totalitarianism whose focus was the comparability and commensurability of Nazism and Stalinism, as well as the general attention afforded to each criminal regime and its victims, emerged in the aftermath of the collapse of the Soviet Union and three highly publicized trials of Nazis and their French collaborators spanning the 1980s

22. For an analysis of the emergence of 'antitotalitarianism' on the French Left (which he explains in terms of the intricacies of French domestic politics), see Michael Scott Christofferson, *French Intellectuals against the Left: The Antitotalitarian Movement of the 1970s* (New York: Berghahn Books, 2004).

23. André Glucksmann, *La cuisinère et le manguer d'hommes* (Paris: Seuil, 1975), 15, 23–26, 68–78, 148, 178–81; Bernard-Henri Lévy, *Barbarism with a Human Face,* trans. George Holoch (New York: Harper & Row, 1979), ix–xi.

24. Lévy, *Barbarism;* Enzo Traverso, *Il totalitarismo* (Milan: Mondadori, 2002), 141.

25. Grémion, *Intelligence de l'anticommunisme,* 622.

and '90s—of Klaus Barbie, Maurice Papon, and Paul Touvier. These trials not only forced French thinkers to come to terms with the Vichy government's complicity in the "final solution" and raised questions about former Communist partisans, but also brought up all sorts of questions about who could claim to have been victims of the Vichy regime and Nazi occupation and on what terms. This is not the place to discuss these trials in detail, but by raising hard questions about French complicity with Nazism, they brought long-denied recognition to Jewish victims and also prompted criticism of the trial format. Did the trials constitute vengeance or justice (given the age of the defendants, the time passed since the criminal acts were perpetrated, and the legal wrangling and circus-like atmosphere that characterized some of them)? Were Jews who had been deported and partisans who were tortured equally victims of the Nazis?[26] The trials thus transformed Jewish suffering into an object of inquiry in the context of concerns about how to establish victimization and how to punish perpetrators, and conflicts about Jewish claims more generally (were they reasonable? were they excessive?).[27]

As the Nazi past and Jewish suffering had gradually become discussable in terms of the particularity of Jewish victimization and even the subject of debate, as the Communist Party lost much of its old prestige, and as a neo-liberal challenge to Marxist paradigms that first found its voice in 1970 gained credibility, books and articles explicitly or implicitly comparing Nazism and Stalinism proliferated, and assertions that a "competition of victims" had emerged became more numerous: anyone who had suffered past wrongs sought to claim their fair share in compensation for a legacy of pain.[28]

---

26. On the trials there is a large literature, but see Richard Golsan, ed., *Memory, the Holocaust, and French Justice: The Bousquet and Touvier Affairs* (Hanover, NH: University Press of New England, 1996); Richard Golsan, ed., *Memory and Justice on Trial: The Papon Affair* (London: Routledge, 2000); and Golsan's *Vichy's Afterlife: History and Counterhistory in Postwar France* (Lincoln: University of Nebraska Press, 2000).

27. For a history of the tensions and conflicts that emerged around the recognition of the particularity of Jewish suffering in France as early as 1966, see Samuel Moyn, *A Holocaust Controversy: The Treblinka Affair in Postwar France* (Waltham, MA: Brandeis University Press, 2005).

28. Neo-liberals drawn from Right-leaning students at the Institut d'Études Politiques (Paris) who studied with Raymond Aron founded *Contrepoint* in the spring of 1970. Their primary aim was to combat the domination of post-'68 Leftist trends. They looked to Tocqueville as their patron and took a positive view of the United States. The new visibility and academic prestige of neo-liberalism in France is probably best represented by François Furet's promotion to the presidency

Some of these works merely represented historians' efforts, in the context of the potentially apologetic role of such comparisons during the coming-to-terms with the Vichy past, to offer comparative analysis of Nazism and Stalinism for French digestion.[29] Some historians offered empirically based comparisons and still others depicted parallels between Nazism and Stalinism on the level of metaphor (claims that both regimes sought to "purify," to "cleanse" and eliminate "repellent insects").[30] Others represented a new effort on the part primarily but not exclusively of Right-leaning intellectuals to expose the crimes of Stalin and of Communism more generally by brokering a comparison with Nazism. And still others deplored all genocidal crimes and used the comparison to bemoan in other terms all tendencies, particularly in the context of debates about the Holocaust's uniqueness, to make distinctions between greater and lesser victims.[31]

Other than the surely legitimate comparison between the two putative forms of totalitarianism, pervasive in many of these works was the implicit contrast between excessive—consistently evoked, obsessive—Jewish memory and the foggy, insufficient recollection of Stalinism and other instances of collective suffering. This particular contrast and its legacy were and continue to be the most visible manifestation of the assertion not only that Nazism and Stalinism were commensurable but also that our negligence of murderous crimes the world over had something to do with the attention accorded to Jewish suffering.[32] This claim is most evident in the debates over the enormously controversial *Black Book of Communism*

of the École des Hautes Études en Sciences Sociales in 1977. See the discussion in Grémion, *Intelligence de l'anticommunisme,* 571–80. On the trials and the question of Jewish victims, see among others, Rousso, *The Haunting Past;* and Finkielkraut, *La mémoire vaine.*

29. See, for example, Rousso, ed., *Stalinisme et nazisme;* Marc Ferro, ed., *Nazisme et Communisme: Deux régimes dans le siècle* (Paris: Pluriel, 1999).

30. Pierre Hassner, "Par-delà l'histoire et la mémoire," in Rousso, ed., *Stalinisme et nazisme,* 364; Krysztof Pomian, "Qu'est-ce que le totalitarisme?" in Ferro, ed., *Nazisme et communisme,* 143–66.

31. Again, many French thinkers tend to use "uniqueness" to mean "singularity." Since few discuss such debates about the Holocaust in any detail, and usually treat "Jews" as a homogeneous group, I use whatever term the writer under discussion uses rather than trying to clarify the usage of the term, which most of those texts under discussion do not themselves do.

32. Wolf, *Harnessing the Holocaust,* addresses the history of this "attention" in France since 1967.

(*Le livre noir du communisme*), first published in 1997,[33] as well as in the related discussion of a so-called competition between victims in which each group struggles shamelessly for its own piece of the imaginary pie, and thus to be recognized and compensated for past wrongs.

The Black Book of Communism is a series of historiographical essays that are also a compilation of the crimes of Communist regimes the world over, encompassing cultures and contexts as different as North Korea and the Soviet Union. By 2002 it had sold one million copies worldwide in several translations, including Russian and Chinese (Hong Kong) versions.[34] In the introduction, the editor Stéphane Courtois claimed that Communist regimes had not 6,000,000 but "100,000,000" victims' blood on their hands, a figure he determined by combining estimated death tolls from Communist regimes the world over. He noted that we must pay as much attention to Communist as to Nazi victims ("a single-minded focus on the Jewish genocide in an attempt to characterize the Holocaust as a unique atrocity has also prevented an assessment of other episodes of comparable magnitude in the Communist world");[35] and he most infamously insisted that a child dying in Stalin's artificially manufactured famine in the Ukraine was surely the moral equivalent of a child starving in the Warsaw Ghetto. The book caused a sensation in France. A discussion about its contents took place in the pages of *Esprit, Le Monde,* and elsewhere, where its critics were numerous. Daniel Lindenberg noted (in a review in *Esprit*) that the book's title, however conventional, alludes to a book of the same name by Vassili Grossman and Ilya Ehrenbourg written in 1947 under the auspices of the Soviet Jewish antifascist committee. The latter exposed Nazi crimes

33. Stéphane Courtois et al., eds., *The Black Book of Communism: Crimes, Terror, Repression,* trans. Jonathan Murphy and Mark Kramer (Cambridge: Harvard University Press, 1999). See the discussion of the Holocaust in relation to other episodes of great suffering, which touches on many of the points made in this chapter, in Robin, *La mémoire saturée,* 196–214.

34. Figures quoted in Martin Malia, "Judging Nazism and Communism," *National Interest* 69 (2002): 69. In 1998 Italy's prime minister Silvio Berlusconi gave an Italian translation of the book as a gift to those attending a conference of Alleanza Nazionale, the now mainstreamed neofascist party that formed part of the governing coalition. "Gli orrori dei regimi comunisti: 'Libro nero'," *La Stampa,* June 9, 1998.

35. Courtois, "The Crimes of Communism," in Courtois et al., eds., *The Black Book of Communism,* 23. Also note his assertion, on p. 19: "In contrast to the Jewish Holocaust, which the international Jewish community has actively commemorated, it has been impossible for victims of Communism and their legal advocates to keep the memory of the tragedy alive, and any requests for commemoration or demands for reparation are brushed aside."

against Jews in the former Soviet Union, was suppressed by Stalin after the war, and first appeared in French translation in 1995.[36] The allusion was hard to miss, as if *this* Black Book were the companion volume to *that* one, as if Nazi and Stalinist crimes were therefore commensurable.[37]

Two contributors to the collection, the historians Nicolas Werth and Jean-Louis Margolin, rejected the polemical tone of Courtois's introduction and concluding remarks, which rendered Nazism and Stalinism equivalent. In *Le Monde,* they repudiated the self-evident relationship Courtois had asserted between Communist theory and practice, as if Communism in practice was merely the unfolding of totalitarian theory. They also took issue with his claim that Nazism and Communism were fundamentally similar forms of totalitarianism. They noted that there were no extermination camps in the Soviet Union and that Stalin had eliminated people not because of who they were but because of their alleged political status as "class enemies."[38] Others, such as the historian Annette Wieviorka, accused Courtois of using the same methods of propaganda as Communists themselves by disguising a polemic in the language of social science. She also argued that his suggestion that the memory of the Jewish genocide masked "Communist criminality" did not accord with the facts, for the allegedly blinding force of Jewish memory did not become central to Western European cultural memory until the 1980s, long after Stalin's crimes had been publicly exposed.[39] The famous Jewish writer Henri Raczymow angrily derided Courtois's comment that there was no difference between a starving child in the Ukraine and a starving child in the Warsaw Ghetto.[40] And the journalist Nicolas Weill summed up all this commentary by claiming that it treated *The Black Book* as "an ideological war machine against the theory of the Shoah's uniqueness."[41]

36. Ilya Ehrenbourg and Vassili Grossman, *Le livre noir: Textes et témoinages réunis par Ilya Ehrenbourg et Vassili Grossman* (Solin: Actes Sud, 1995).

37. Daniel Lindenberg, "Remous autour du Livre noir du communisme," *Esprit* 1 (1998): 190–91.

38. Ariane Chemin, "Les divisions d'une équipe d'historiens du communism: Les coauteurs contestent la preface du *Livre noir du communisme,* un ouvrage collectif coordonné par Stéphane Courtois," *Le Monde,* October 31, 1997.

39. Annette Wieviorka, "Stéphane Courtois, en un combat douteux," *Le Monde,* November 27, 1997.

40. Raczymow, "D'un detail."

41. Nicolas Weill, "Crimes et châtiments: Pour lire *Le Livre noir du communisme* hors polémiques," *Le Monde,* January 8, 1999.

Critics of *The Black Book* claimed essentially that Courtois challenged the consensus that the Holocaust of European Jewry was unprecedented to suggest not only that Jewish memory had masked Communist criminality but that Communism was worse. Counter-claims were forthcoming: Pierre Rigoulot and Illios Yannakakis attributed historians' demand for more historical specificity (historians claimed that it would not do simply to put Cambodia, North Korea, and the Soviet Union in the same volume under the rubric of the "crimes of Communism") to the demand for "refined" analysis. They also asserted that "a concentration camp is a concentration camp: various modes of liquidating opponents—in or outside of the camps—in no way attenuate their bleak and repetitive character or the horror that seizes us."[42] Pierre Chaunu insisted that "the *Einsatzgruppen* of summer 1941 and the armed bands of 'War Communism'[the forced expropriation of grain from peasants in the years immediately after the Bolshevik Revolution] committed crimes comparable in more than one way."[43]

The assertions of *The Black Book*'s defenders are part of a larger narrative that remains for the most part unexamined in terms other than those of the book's detractors, who mostly demonstrate that Courtois is on shaky historical grounds when he replaces the particular historical meaning of genocide with an appeal to the universal struggle against evil embodied by totalitarian regimes. Such arguments against Courtois continue to be made in valuable and important historical works that contest in empirical terms the premises of *The Black Book*'s assertions about Communism.[44] The main argument against *The Black Book*'s rhetoric is thus that it substitutes a moral for a historical approach to suffering and in so doing, collapses history into memory and turns history into dogma—into a moral narrative not amenable to empirical or other forms of critical analysis. As the French historian Henry Rousso argued in his own criticism of the text, a self-conscious and intellectually rigorous policing of the porous boundary

42. Pierre Rigoulot and Illios Yannakakis, *Un pavé dans l'histoire: Le débat français sur Le livre noir du communisme* (Paris: Robert Laffont, 1998), 71–72, 167.

43. Pierre Chaunu, "Les jumeaux 'malins' du deuxième millénaire," *Commentaire* 21 (1998): 224.

44. Aside from the more polemical Jean Suret-Canale et al., eds., *Le livre noir du capitalisme* (Pantin: Le Temps des cerises, 1998), see Michel Dreyfus et al., eds., *Le siècle des communismes* (Paris: Éditions de l'Atelier/Éditions Ouvrières, 2004). Note that Communism is rendered in the plural, an important criticism of the *Black Book*'s approach.

between history and memory and history and morality can prevent the dangerously regressive, not to mention intellectually irresponsible tendencies to simplification and denial.[45] But the now common assertion in French philosophical and historical discussion that in the end gulags and death camps are two forms of the same phenomenon is not only a denial or repression of historical (rather than moral) truth or an oversimplified and politicized interpretation of historical facts. That is, historians' objections to the erasure of historical context by a theory of totalitarianism (or a general appeal to good and evil), persuasive and important as they are in combating the problematic conceptual apparatus of *The Black Book* and its polemical intentions, still leave unexamined the rhetorical construction of Jewish suffering within which Courtois's diminution of the Holocaust comes to make sense. We must draw a broader picture of the rhetorical landscape in which Jewish suffering now putatively mutes the suffering of Stalin's victims, in which Jewish victims allegedly insist that their children's suffering was worse than that of any other children.

The Opacity of Communism and the Clarity of Nazism

In his influential bestseller *The Passing of an Illusion,* published in 1995, François Furet traced the stunning political and psychological versatility of the Communist "idea" and Communist leaders. He mentioned the murder of Jews only sporadically and never sought to compare Nazism and Stalinism systematically. The book was inspired by Furet's effort to understand his own youthful membership in the Party as well as the depth of French intellectuals' commitment to the Soviet Union even after 1956. It asks how Communist intellectuals transformed the Russian Revolution into a symbol of universal justice, and focuses most profoundly on how Soviet Communism manufactured such a "false and so compelling"[46] illusion and why those intellectuals who should have known better were so easy to fool. Furet argued that the Russian Revolution inherited the French revolutionaries' conviction that human beings invent themselves. Yet the Russian revolutionaries insisted not only on human volition, but also on history's

45. Rousso, *The Haunting Past,* 50–52.
46. Furet, *The Passing of an Illusion,* 148.

objective fulfillment of that volition, so that humankind's will toward self-invention and toward the expansion of democratic individualism embodied in the promise of liberty and equality now became an objective reality toward which all of history was directed. In a series of texts and actions, he argued, Soviet leaders equated the Revolution with the triumph of social justice and therefore with the universal values so cherished by committed democrats everywhere. In particular, the war against Hitler turned Stalin into the antifascist par excellence, a pose that, in its "false simplicity," acted as a "trap" into which Western intellectuals fell.[47] Thus, Furet wrote in 1998, "Communist ideology, because it derives from a cultivated universalist tradition, constitutes a lie more dangerous than Nazi ideology, itself far more elementary and less mystifying."[48]

Pierre Chaunu used Furet's emphasis on the universalist appeal of Communism to argue similarly that Communism "is perhaps more dangerous [than Nazism] because it is less easy to confine" to a particular metaphorical and historical map. Nazism is far more particular, he wrote, to a time and place.[49] In *The Black Book,* Courtois asserted that Communism "was a particularly devious system" that used the "image of Enlightenment" to foster beliefs that it furthered humankind's progress while concealing its murderousness.[50] Even closer to Furet's contrast between Nazism's primitivism and Communism's sophistication, the late Martin Malia invoked an otherwise unarticulated difference between the performative dimension of the Soviet system and the literalness of the Nazi one. An American historian who wrote extensively in French and English on the Russian Revolution, Malia said in his preface to the English edition of *The Black Book* that "Nazis killed off their victims without ideological ceremony," whereas Communist confession—part of the elaborate ideological machinery that spun into motion to legitimate the execution of potential 'enemies'—pretended "to be virtuous."[51]

47. Furet, *The Passing of an Illusion,* 246.
48. François Furet, "La gauche est-elle antifasciste sans être antitotalitaire?" *Commentaire* 21 (1998): 247. It is important to note that Furet played an important role in encouraging research on the Holocaust. In 1982 he organized, with Raymond Aron, a conference at the École des Hautes Études en Sciences Sociales on "Nazi Germany and the Jewish Genocide."
49. Chaunu, "Les jumeaux 'malins,'" 220.
50. Courtois et al., eds., *The Black Book of Communism,* 20–21.
51. Martin Malia, Preface to Courtois et al., eds., *The Black Book of Communism,* xv.

The implication that Nazism's struggle against so-called world Jewry was a straightforward assault on a delimited target is insufficiently complex. One of the most salient features of Nazi anti-Semitism (indeed of anti-Semitism more generally) was its anxiety that Jews mutated surreptitiously and took on a wide variety of masks, evading detection and ensuring an endless quest to find them everywhere on earth. Surely Stalin's show trials were for public consumption and Nazi death camps were (for the most part) out of public view. But the claim that the Nazis' unceremonious dispatching of their victims was less deceptive and implicitly less mystifying can be borne out only if we find the organized and industrialized genocide of millions of people because they were Jewish fairly easy to grasp. This argument ignores the modern dimensions of ritualized anti-Semitic phobia. The historian Saul Friedländer refers to "redemptive anti-Semitism,"[52] by which he means a sacralized struggle against Jews that renders Nazism a quintessentially modern genocide whose motives remain opaque to researchers who seek to understand the transition from the segregation of Jews to their extermination in ideological terms.

The very presumption that Communism is more compelling and less primitive than Nazism also appears yoked to a fiction that Communism was powerful because it not only seduced workers, but also educated young intellectuals, including those who have now turned against it, while the menace of Nazism was somehow more tangible and less sophisticated in its power to seduce and mystify, even though its ranks too were full of academics, writers, doctors, lawyers, intellectuals, and at least one great philosopher. In this French discourse, Nazism is characterized by its straightforwardness, its historical constraints, and its particularity. The meaning of Communism, in contrast, curiously unlike propaganda and more like a work of great literature or criticism, must be deciphered, its power over its readers embedded in the complexity of its narratives and its ability to offer (deceptively) self-reflexive commentary.

Indeed, Communism's potential for deception appears to be so infinite, and its ideological ceremonies ultimately so ungraspable, that we will perhaps never get to the bottom of things. The "illusion," to paraphrase Furet, reconstitutes itself anew and even in its passing stubbornly refuses

---

52. Saul Friedländer, *Nazi Germany and the Jews,* vol. 1: *The Years of Persecution, 1933–1939* (New York: HarperCollins, 1997), 73–112.

to go away. According to Furet, Nazism has been discredited. But since Communism drew its power from our ever renewable demand for a new, more just society that can never be fulfilled, adherents are bound to emerge again and again.[53] Many if not all Anglo-American historians repudiated the concept of totalitarianism in part because a totalitarian state, dependent on the expansion of terror and the destruction of political life, should end, as did Nazism, catastrophically, whereas the Soviet Union did not.[54] But Communism's greatest menace in this discourse on totalitarianism is its power to adopt new political guises, to renew itself and thus to continue to 'compel' us even once we know all the facts. This power—what it inherits from the Western intellectual tradition and the French concept of democracy since the Revolution—ultimately keeps it alive in our midst and suggests that we must be particularly vigilant.

The historian Alain Besançon, an esteemed and highly regarded liberal luminary, published his 1997 inaugural lecture to the Institut de France on "memory and the forgetting of Communism" in the Right-leaning *Commentaire,* and then as a longer book.[55] Besançon had been a student of Raymond Aron and thrust himself into the intellectual limelight in 1974 with his criticism, in the liberal *Contrepoint,* of *Le Monde* and *L'Express*'s reviews of Solzhenitsyn's *Gulag Archipelago.* He asked why "the USSR's massacres, deportations (twenty-five million deaths at a minimum) and brutalization of the masses beat by far all the records of Nazi Germany, and yet continue to be called into question.... The reason is simple: there are Communists. There are no more Nazis."[56] We might note that these comments were made in the midst of a revival of neo-fascism in France and Italy, followed by the reemergence of the extreme Right in Central Europe. They seem blissfully to ignore those elements of fascism, racism, and

53. Furet, *The Passing of an Illusion,* 503.

54. For an interesting defense of totalitarianism as nonetheless a valuable heuristic concept, see Pierre Hassner, "Une notion insaisissible mais irremplaçable," in Yannis Thanassekos and Heinz Wismann, eds., *Révision de l'histoire: Totalitarismes, crimes et genocides nazis* (Paris: Du Cerf, 1990), 90. Post-revisionist historians of the Soviet Union have now developed multiple interpretations of the regime's demise that do not resort to the concept.

55. Alain Besançon, "Mémoire et oubli du communisme," *Commentaire* 20 (1997/98): 789–93. The essay was translated as "Forgotten Communism" in the American journal *Commentary* 105, 1 (1998): 24–27. See also Besançon's *Le malheur du siècle: Sur le communisme, le nazisme et l'unicité de la Shoah* (Paris: Fayard, 1998).

56. Besançon cited in Grémion, *Intelligence de l'anticommunisme,* 606.

anti-Semitism represented by the powerful role played by the neo-fascist Jean-Marie Le Pen and his successors in French politics, and clearly do not anticipate the return of executive power, deprivation of civil liberties, and torture carried out as policy by the United States. And yet, the historian Jacques Julliard wrote, "since the beginning of the world" no other regime had managed to accomplish what the Soviets did, not even Nazism, from which history has moved on.[57]

In their preface to Besançon's 1997 address, the editors of *Commentaire* note that *The Black Book* had productively and provocatively raised questions about how we have forgotten Communist crimes (a dubious assertion beyond French boundaries outdone only by the even more surprising assertion that there are no more Nazis). They go on to claim that the debate over Courtois's text demonstrates how lively the debate about Communism remained in France, where "amnesia has triumphed."[58] In his essay and in a more elaborate book on the topic, Besançon, who has written extensively about Soviet Communism, concedes the so-called uniqueness of the Jewish genocide, but also asserts that French intellectuals are nonetheless saturated with the "surfeit of memory [*hypermnésie*] of Nazism" while they suffer "amnesia [*amnésie*] about Communism."[59] Each of those critics invited to comment on the text in the next issue of the journal, including the founder of the center-Left magazine *Le Nouvel Observateur*, Jean Daniel, treats this assertion as self-evident, and some dramatize it. Thus Pierre Chaunu notes his enthusiasm about the essay but adds that the scope of "surfeit memory" extends throughout "the West, in France, in Germany, and paradoxically in the United States (at least in intellectual milieux) with different inflections if surely for similar reasons."[60] The conservative intellectual Jean-François Revel simply notes that it is not clear why "negationism [Holocaust denial] and the contestation of crimes against humanity are legally punished when it is a matter of Nazi crimes and not when they

57. Jacques Julliard quoted in Alain de Benoist, *Communisme et nazisme: 25 Réflexions sur le totalitarisme au XXe siècle (1917–1989)* (Paris: La Labyrinthe, 1998), 17n4.

58. Editors' preface to Besançon, "Mémoire et oubli," 789.

59. Besançon, "Mémoire et oubli," 793.

60. Chaunu, "Les jumeaux 'malins,'" 221. I assume he says "paradoxically" in reference to the United States because the Holocaust did not take place on American territory and is not directly part of the American historical experience.

concern Communist crimes."[61] Alfred Grosser adds less polemically that many intellectuals' fears of diminishing the horror of Nazism led tragically to "the non-examination of the shadows, the Soviet darkness."[62] Though Jean Daniel takes issue with any argument that Hitler and Stalin are the same, and says he feels fear when he reads critics who assert that "Stalin was worse," he nevertheless concedes that "Nazism and Communism's unequal treatment in historical memory is irrefutable. I even share the idea that this inequality is in no way justified."[63]

Besançon's own explanation of why we remember Nazi crimes and forget Communist ones is both predictable and interesting. Predictable perhaps are his arguments that Nazism is "better known" than Communism; that the "Jewish people" have admirably devoted all their energies to conserving the memory of the Shoah; that those people capable of doing the same for Communism are few and far between; and that the debate about Communism has always been so polarized between Right and Left that polemic overwhelmed frank discussion. And taking up the famous arguments developed by Furet, Besançon also insists that Stalin's antifascism "weakened Western immune systems against the Communist idea," and that Communism's own ideological power over its adherents helped sustain factually untenable contrasts between itself and other forms of authoritarianism and totalitarianism.[64]

More interesting, however, is the argument that underlies these various points and aligns the historian like so many others closely with Furet: the contrast between Communism's opacity and Nazism's "less mystifying" nature. It is not only that Communism was a compelling idea with cunning practitioners, but also that Nazism in theory and practice was far more straightforward. Besançon contrasts Nazism's "simple secret" with the "thick ideological fog" that characterized Stalinism.[65] The gas chambers were isolated, witnesses (the *Sonderkommando*) executed, and bonds of secrecy established between the perpetrators. In contrast, the existence

61. Jean-François Revel, "L'essentielle identité du fascisme rouge et du fascisme noir," *Commentaire* 21 (1998): 232.

62. Grosser, *Le crime et la mémoire*, 83.

63. Jean Daniel and François Furet, "La gauche, le communisme et le nazisme," *Commentaire* 21 (1998): 248; and in the same issue, Jean Daniel, "Sur un text d'Alain Besançon," 227.

64. Besançon, "Mémoire et oubli," 791–93.

65. Besançon, *Le malheur du siècle*, 18.

of camps within the Soviet Union was masked not by efficiently enforced secrecy, but by the incredulous attitude toward them by true believers. Communism is "more dangerous [than Nazism] because Communist education is insidious...and disguises the evil acts it commits as good ones. It is also more dangerous because less predictable for its future victims. [Under Communism] everyone at one moment or another can take on the enemy role, while Nazism designates its enemies in advance. It depicts them in fantastic terms with no relation to reality, but behind the man designated as inferior [*le sous-homme*] is a real Jew." Moreover, "universalism, which is...the great advantage of Communism over Nazi exclusivity, becomes, once in power, a universal menace"—Nazism targets only Jews and others it deems inferior, Communism potentially everyone.[66] Thus Nazism, regardless of its deeds, is less dangerous because its secrecy had a clear rationale liable to lucid interpretation, and implicitly its adherents know that the acts they commit are evil. Hitler's victims knew who they were, and even Nazi fantasies were finally confined 'only' to Jews.

According to Besançon, then, we have forgotten Stalin's victims because Stalinist persecution is more difficult to account for than the Nazis' extermination of Jews. However unthinkable and unprecedented, Nazi genocide was far clearer about its aims. Our amnesia about Stalin's victims is the logical result of Stalinism's pretense to universalism, to be other than what it was, while Nazism called a spade a spade—meaning that Stalin's victims' sufferings are always suspect, always potentially legitimate or justifiable, while Hitler literalized racial prejudice, making Jewish victims' claims to innocence absolutely legitimate and, at least implicitly, an easier sell. Thus Communism is more "dangerous" than Nazism, for it fosters the illusion that it stands for democratic, universal values. The struggle against amnesia is thus a struggle to recognize that Stalin's victims were innocent too.

This task is easier said than done. Not because the victims were guilty of anything, but because Communism transformed even the most innocent person into a potentially guilty traitor persuaded of his or her own complicity. The emphasis on Communist deception, meaning its ability to win the loyalty and trust even of those who were its victims, whether one

66. Besançon, *Le malheur du siècle*, 63.

attributes deception to an illusion or not, renders Communism not only particularly sinister but also impossible to hold to account. The power of Communist ideology lies in its ability to claim that its victims were legitimately punished, however ludicrous the charges against them. Besançon argues that unlike Stalinism, Nazism "did not morally contaminate its victims or those who survived it, and required from them no adhesion to Nazism," suggesting that unlike Nazism, Stalinism polluted everyone by forcing its victims to swear allegiance to a cause in which they might or might not necessarily believe.[67] Besançon implies that because the Nazis despised their victims, Jews and others remained immune to the moral effects of being despised, and because Nazis sought to expel and to kill Jews rather than to fold them into the Party, Jews were never forced to "contaminate" themselves by virtue of their complicity. But it is not at all clear that Nazis left their victims uncontaminated in Besançon's meaning of the term. Indeed, after the war, as countless witnesses recount, to have survived was often perceived as evidence of moral contamination, and we know that survivors were tormented by guilt for having collaborated with the enemy even in coercive conditions or undermined others in order to live.[68]

The prominent philosopher Claude Lefort, the vocal Left-wing critic of Communism, does not argue that Nazism's enemies suffered greater or lesser moral contamination. But he also insists in many works that the Communist belief in equality and redemption through adhesion to its principles turned into a form not of enhanced freedom, but of collectively and self-enforced tyranny, of "despotism without a despot" that constitutes the particular enigma of Communist rule.[69] More recently he argues, pace Furet, that those Communists who betrayed the law and "confessed" were not under any illusion about the legality of their trials but felt their identities and destinies bound to the Party. Lefort thus does not identify the power of Communism as its fabrication of illusions—he insists that such a view does not hold former Communists sufficiently accountable for their convictions or the destruction they wrought. Instead, he focuses on

67. Besançon, "Mémoire et oubli," 791.

68. See, for example, Ruth Klüger's comments in *Von hoher und niedriger Literatur* (Göttingen: Wallstein Verlag, 1996), 35.

69. Claude Lefort, *Éléments d'une critique de la bureaucratie* (Paris: Gallimard, 1979), 174–75.

how legal formalism and bureaucracy, no longer merely administrative organs, destroy civil society. He analyzes the power and particularity of Soviet totalitarianism as its ability to turn all its subjects into potential accomplices by blurring the boundary between legality and illegality in the creation of a Party-State that fuses the social and the political by abolishing all modern distinctions between different spheres of society. Each person embodies the law because all citizens speak one language, become "one" in a unitary and indivisible mass, and any thoughts not aligned with the now self-policing oneness of the homogeneous body politic are already betrayals. All citizens are always potentially guilty of betrayal and always complicit with the state, and for this reason among others, he insists that the Soviet regime is far more exemplary of totalitarianism than is Nazism.[70] Finally, he states that the "Communist mode of domination is in certain respects far more enigmatic than Fascism."[71]

If all citizens are potentially traitors rather than obedient or disobedient subjects "before the law," it is impossible to determine their innocence once and for all.[72] That is why punishment was always potentially legitimate. Thus the Communist construction of citizenship leads to the end, if not of conscience, then of moral accountability. Tzvetan Todorov argues that crimes committed under totalitarian regimes in Eastern Europe and the Soviet Union, whether perpetrated in camps or outside of them (for example, spying on friends), are difficult to judge in terms of available moral categories:

> Those who ran the concentration camps were neither less logical nor more excessive than those who ran the industrial sector or the smallest communes in the country. There was a kind of arbitrariness to the appointments of some agents to the task of repression and others to political management. Neither group was less vile or malicious than the other. [...] One cannot condemn one piece of the totalitarian state and leave the others alone, because

70. Claude Lefort, *La complication: Retour sur le communisme* (Paris: Fayard, 1999), 11.

71. Lefort, *La complication,* 6. The only contrasting view I have come across is that of the philosopher Jean-Luc Ferry, who writes that he finds Nazism more enigmatic than Communism. Jean-Luc Ferry, "Les banalisations à la française," in Thanassekos and Wismann, eds., *Révision de l'histoire,* 257.

72. Lefort, *La complication,* 218–19, 221–23, 237.

they all fit together ... When the crime has multiplied to such a degree, it exceeds effective punishment.[73]

Since everyone is responsible, no one can really be held to account, so the best we can do is mourn the victims whose tormentors we cannot properly punish.[74] Moral contamination occurred on such a vast scale that everyone was both "executioner and victim."[75]

The problem with these arguments is not that they are entirely wrong about the nature of the different regimes.[76] In the mainstream historical version of this argument, the specificity of Stalinist terror was its unpredictability—it was liable to strike anyone and everyone—whereas Nazi terror was "predictable and consistent," meaning its tactics and targets were clear.[77] The difference between Stalinism and Nazism lies in Stalinism's pedagogical aims: though Stalin's regime employed extralegal measures, it also conceived of dissidents as lost souls to be 'reeducated' and brought back into the fold. Nazism, on the other hand, adhered to an older model of punishment and isolation and sought to eliminate those whom it had cast out of the *Volksgemeinschaft,* namely Jews, Roma, and the disabled.[78]

It is rather the rhetorical effect of the French discourse under discussion that is so consequential, especially its erroneous insistence that Nazism is primitive and a thing of the past, while Communisms is a mystifying, wily demon and an ever-present threat. Communism is a menace as long as

73. Tzvetan Todorov, "Communist Camps and Their Aftermath," *Representations* 49 (1995): 129.

74. This reference to the lack of any effective punishment recalls Hannah Arendt's description of Nazi crimes as those that can never really be punished because they are beyond the boundaries of any conventional conception of criminality (see Chap. 1, note 30). And yet the meanings of Todorov's and Arendt's assertions are quite different. These are not the crimes that Arendt conceived as so unthinkable that Nazi leaders could remain smug knowing that their punishments could never be commensurable with their crimes. Instead, Todorov describes how a regime transformed all of its citizens into potential criminals, rendering the real dispensation of justice an impossible task.

75. Todorov, "Communist Camps," 130.

76. For example, see the discussion of Nazism and Soviet aesthetics in Amir Weiner's study of the Russian memory of the war, *Making Sense of War: The Second World War and the Fate of the Bolshevik Revolution* (Princeton: Princeton University Press, 2001), 25.

77. See Charles S. Maier, *The Unmasterable Past: History, Holocaust, and German National Identity* (Cambridge: Harvard University Press, 1998), 81; Robert Gellately, "Rethinking the Nazi Terror System: A Historiographical Analysis," *German Studies Review* 14 (1991): 30–32.

78. See Fitzpatrick and Gellately, eds., *Accusatory Practices,* 213.

there are men and women committed to a particular univocal truth and a leveling and retributive justice, while Nazism is a tragic but temporally confined episode. Nazism's targets were innocent victims of a past crime that pales before the monstrosity of the Communist illusion, whose cunning knows no bounds and whose opacity continues to mystify. These writers do not deny the horror of Nazism, negate the suffering of its victims, or deny the singularity of gas chambers: rather, by transforming Nazi murder into a relatively straightforward if monstrous crime which put its victims to a death shorn of symbolism, they "explain" rhetorically why we have accorded Stalin's own victims so little recognition. Alain Besançon notes that "the Nazi crime," because it was physical, was "flagrant." But the Gulag is still "wrapped in fog and remains a distant object."[79]

These critics do not illuminate two different but comparable political systems, Nazism and Stalinism, but end up fashioning a conceptual difference between a narrow assertion of particular, Jewish suffering and the universal tragedy of human suffering. Stalin's crimes are by definition more universally menacing and therefore more potentially universal, contaminating everyone and anyone anywhere, so that they have global and possibly future repercussions. It is more difficult conceptually to remember Stalin's crimes than Hitler's not only because of the cunning and hence dangerous manifestation of Communism in theory and practice. Communism is also the potential fate of all those drawn to a specific, univocal vision of justice and truth embedded most specifically in the legacy of French revolutionary democracy and its faith that the world can always be made anew and changed for the better. According to Furet, the French Revolution was not an "interlude between two worlds" that led to political stability, as in the United States, but was fueled by a "passion for equality which, by definition, has no threshold of satisfaction."[80] Communism refuses to go away for this very reason, and its adherents and victims could be anyone.

The intellectuals engaged in the venture of explaining why Stalin's victims have been harder to remember do not deny the Jewish experience of extreme suffering or the significance of Auschwitz. Instead, they transform the victims of Communism into the universal repository of human tragedy and turn the Soviet Union into a surrogate for suffering humanity.

79. Besançon, "Mémoire et oubli," 791.
80. Furet, *The Passing of an Illusion,* 9. See also the discussion on pp. 32–33, 70.

In so doing, they not only invert the illusory image of the Soviet Union as the symbolic center of the triumph of universal humanist values into the symbolic center of universal human suffering. And they do not simply construct the suffering of Jewish victims rhetorically as one particular mode of agony among others (which might relieve the Holocaust of the burden of representing modern human evil from which lessons can supposedly be learned). Instead, in their discourse, Jewish particularism no longer represents the experience of Jewish suffering in the Holocaust but underscores its "particular" nature—that is to say narrow, finite, graspable, and descriptive only of a minority experience—in contrast to the now universal, expansive, infinite, and potential suffering of humanity symbolized by Communism. Besançon argues that Jewish claims to having suffered uniquely misunderstand the meaning of uniqueness, and risk "irritating" other people who have suffered in their own ways. Those people, he claims, might be "tempted to take up Shylock's protest" and ask Jews in turn "whether when wounded, do we not bleed?"[81]

From this perspective, some Jews' assertions about having been particularly victimized themselves constitute a violation of humanist ethics—they dissolve empathic connection with others, stubbornly refuse to recognize that suffering is suffering by claiming the greater intensity of their own, and cynically cloak themselves in the mantle of the most victimized people of all to ensure that their voices are heard. The notion that the Holocaust was "unique" has been long debated and the iconic status of Auschwitz as the emblem of 'evil in our time' is a complex cultural production that some Jewish intellectuals reject and others embrace. Yet Besançon's comments presume a hegemonic Jewish voice and simply repeat the old gesture whereby Jewish particularism offends *against* humanism: now, Jewish memory of the Holocaust offends against and distorts the historical truth embodied by humanist values. These critics argue implicitly that since there are more "universal" and more "particular" ways of suffering and dying, there are also different kinds of victims: those who suffer in silence, and those who proclaim their agony loudly; those whose voices are drowned out and those whose voices are heard; those who reach out to the

81. Besançon, *Le malheur du siècle,* 131.

community of suffering humanity and those who claim to have suffered uniquely.

Literal Memory, Exemplary Memory

In his book on "moral life in the concentration camps," Tzvetan Todorov sought to counter the cliché that under extreme conditions all human beings act solely in their own interest.[82] He demonstrates using varied eyewitness accounts from both Nazi and Soviet camps that this claim is not true. In that book, Todorov's own perspective is that of a once-bystander—he had lived a relatively privileged life in Communist Bulgaria before moving to Paris when he was twenty-four—who retrospectively examines a variety of human experiences in extreme circumstances. He affirms that while most of us are unlikely to be heroes, we are all capable of ordinary and willed acts of kindness and acts of indifference toward others. He asserts the moral equivalence of suffering in Gulags and Nazi camps (though he does not presume that the material suffering of victims was exactly alike) and also reiterates prevalent characterizations of differences between the two criminal regimes: the imprisonment of Communists by Communists led to "the collapse of the many victims' mental universe. If Soviet guards showed more compassion than their Nazi counterparts, they could also be more capricious. Greater misery reigned in the gulags, but the kind of order applied in the German camps was a lethal one."[83] Here he first formulates the concept that everyone in a totalitarian regime is both victim and executioner (or rather, he says that the "gray zone" in totalitarian states included more or less the entire population).[84] But the rhetoric of his argument, however close to the discourse we have thus far discussed and in which I will include him, is nevertheless marked by a sensitive discussion of the Jewish experience under Nazism, in which he asserts that the

---

82. Tzvetan Todorov, *Facing the Extreme: Moral Life in the Concentration Camps,* trans. Arthur Denner and Abigail Pollak (New York: Henry Holt, 1996 [1991]).

83. Todorov, *Facing the Extreme,* 133.

84. Todorov, *Facing the Extreme,* 182. See Todorov's interesting comments on the coerced complicity of all citizens living under a Communist regime in a series of interviews he gave to a journalist in Tzvetan Todorov, *Devoirs et délices: Une vie de passeur; Entretiens avec Catherine Portevin* (Paris: Seuil, 2002), 45.

Holocaust was "almost unique"[85] and engages survivor literature (Primo Levi earns his most unstinting admiration).

A few years later, in a 1995 essay, *The Abuses of Memory,* Todorov employs concepts of literal and exemplary memory already developed in the earlier work as abstract general categories: literal memory, as he sees it, is my own, and exemplary memory is an "instance among others of a general category," a process of analogy that makes justice possible because it generalizes from the particular.[86] Though in the book on moral life in the camps he spoke generally of "recovered memory" and its more and less productive manifestations, in *The Abuses of Memory* he seeks to examine the memory of historical injustices by exploring our desire to *have been* victimized in the past: "If no one wants to be a victim, we all nonetheless want to have been victims: we aspire to the status of having been a victim."[87] To defend this assertion, he asks why, as he sees it, Jewish groups are invested in denying the comparability of Nazism and Stalinism, or of Nazism with any other "bloody" regime. He uses the distinction between the "literal" and "exemplary" memory of an event to explain his reasoning. Literal memory, he claims, establishes continuity "between who I was and who I am now, or the past and present of my people."[88] Todorov contrasts this literal memory with the exemplary memory of those who "enter into the public sphere—I open my memory to analogy and generalization; I make of it an exemplum and I extract a lesson from it; the past thus becomes a principle from which action in the present may be derived."[89] Todorov's ideal figure of exemplary memory in *The Abuses of Memory* is David Rousset, the gentile survivor of a Nazi concentration camp who

---

85. Todorov, *Facing the Extreme,* 237.

86. Todorov, *Facing the Extreme,* 258.

87. Tzvetan Todorov, *Les abus de la mémoire* (Paris: Arléa, 1995), 56. This text was first published as a short essay "La mémoire et ses abus," *Esprit* 193 (1993): 34–44. Much of the essay was then incorporated into Tzvetan Todorov, *Hope and Memory: Lessons from the Twentieth Century,* trans. David Bellos (Princeton: Princeton University Press, 2003). See also Tzvetan Todorov, "In Search of Lost Crime," *New Republic,* January 29, 2001, 25, where he writes that "until the middle of the twentieth century, the narrative favored by the Western public attributed a heroic role to our own community. But in recent decades there has been a change of paradigm, and the favorite story is now a melancholy tale in which we play the role of the victim."

88. Todorov, *Les abus,* 30.

89. Todorov, *Les abus,* 31. We might also note that there is a Christian tradition of conceiving Jews as stubbornly literal because they refuse to see a foreshadowing of Christ in Hebrew scripture and thus remain blind to the truth of his sacrifice.

risked the wrath of the French Communist Party in 1949 by appealing to Nazi camp survivors to help those interned in Soviet camps. In contrast, Jewish memory takes the form of literal memory and "remains intransitive and cannot reach beyond itself."[90] Jewish memory thus mimics the literal memory he labels self-referential and antithetical to justice.

This difference between literal and exemplary memory explains four typical reactions to comparisons between Stalinism and Nazism. Against comparing the two systems are Hitler's Jewish victims and former Stalinists ("les bourreaux côté stalinien"). Jewish victims conceive the comparison as an apology for past crimes (Hitler was no worse than Stalin), and Stalinists conceive it as an unfair accusation (they behaved as brutally as Nazis). In favor of comparing the two systems are former Nazis ("les bourreaux côté hitlérien") and Stalin's victims. The comparison permits former Nazis to imagine that they were no worse than Stalin. And it allows Stalin's victims to hold the perpetrators truly accountable, for they were treated as poorly as Hitler treated Jews.[91] Todorov notes that this description is bound to be reductive but is nonetheless heuristic and generally legitimate, for we can more easily guess "what opinion a person will have of the comparison between Nazism and Communism if we know with which of the four groups he or she identifies."[92] Opponents of Communist regimes thus find comparing Stalinism and Nazism a self-evident exercise. Todorov cites a former president of Bulgaria who insists that if there is any difference between the two, it is "not only that fascist regimes perished earlier but that they were also established later [than Communist regimes], which proves that they are merely a pale imitation, a plagiarized version, of the true, authentic, perfect, and complete [*accompli*] totalitarian regime."[93] Moreover, Todorov writes, "the Germans, for their part, can identify with both kinds of attitudes to which Nazism gives rise and, as the recent 'historians' debate' has shown, they may stress either the sameness

---

90. Todorov, *Les abus,* 30.

91. Todorov, *Les abus,* 40.

92. Todorov, *Les abus,* 40–41.

93. Todorov, *Les abus,* 41. Note that this is the same argument made by Ernst Nolte, who infamously claimed that Nazism was provoked by, a defense against, and an imitation of the Soviet regime, provoking the *Historikerstreit* (historians' debate), the post-1986 debate among German historians, to which I have already alluded. For a summary, see Peter Baldwin, ed., *Reworking the Past: Hitler, the Holocaust, and the Historians' Debate* (Boston: Beacon Press, 1990).

of the two regimes or their difference."[94] Germans have proven willing to examine their memory critically and, depending on their social position as bystanders, dissidents, or heirs of the Nazi past, they may come to different conclusions. But Jewish victims, like Stalinist perpetrators, have little interest in opening their memory to a dialogue which might challenge its veracity, subject it to debate, or render it usable by future generations. Thus Jews get stuck in their refusal to forgive and cannot move on, and former Stalinists and their heirs stay mired in fears that they will be charged with the same crimes as Nazis.

Todorov contrasts implicitly the so-called simplicity of Nazi persecution and the mystifying quality of Stalin's crimes: Nazism is "flagrant" and Stalinism is opaque; Nazism literalizes prejudice; Stalinism makes it hard to discern; Nazism annihilates specific people; Stalinism is not particularly selective. Yet now he argues that there are distinct ways of *recalling* suffering for which different kinds of victims stand in: Stalin's victims stand in for universal human suffering (exemplary memory), while Hitler's Jewish victims stand in for particular self-referential suffering that cannot serve a universal, pedagogical function (literal memory). For reasons he does not elaborate except by reference to Jewish fears that comparisons between Nazism and Stalinism might prove apologetic (which might have led him to make an entirely different argument), "Jews" invert the Holocaust into something sacred and thus "sterile."[95] Their memory lacks multiple symbolic referents, is intransitive and stubbornly literal. Stalin's victims (and others of like mind) seek to make their suffering an exemplum, whereas Jewish victims merely seek attention. And by implication so do all victims who make similarly excessive claims, such as African Americans ["les Noirs américains"] who, while "incontestably" victims, also "desire in no way to abandon the role of victim, which assures them moral privilege."[96] Jews are just like those family members who, as Todorov sees it, inevitably play the role of victim in order to complain, protest, and make impossible demands that no one can refuse.

94. Todorov, *Les abus,* 41–42. The most comprehensive French and Belgian response to this debate appears in Thanassekos and Wismann, eds., *Révision de l'histoire.*

95. Todorov, *Les abus,* 33.

96. Todorov, *Les abus,* 56. Here Todorov refers to Louis Farrakhan as exemplary of African Americans.

Todorov thus associates 'victim culture' with the valorization of memory over history, and Jewish memory is exemplary of the sorry privilege accorded to particular over universal truth. For Todorov not only argues that specific groups' memories manifest in literal and exemplary forms, but also aligns literal and exemplary with unhealthy and healthy victims. In *Facing the Extreme,* he argues that Primo Levi remained a universalist even in his traumatized state: Levi was "beyond both hatred and resignation";[97] he believed in reason and justice and wanted to understand his former enemy so that justice could be properly dispensed. In contrast to Levi, however, the literal memory of other Jews renders their claims to having suffered regressive: they are not only particular victims but "bad" ones—unrestrained, unbounded, unhealthy, fragmented, and prone to illusion. Besançon also chided Jews for taking the material facts of gas chambers and industrialized murder to imply a more profound physical, cultural, and spiritual destruction than other peoples have faced. Jewish "uniqueness," he wrote, may lie in these material facts, but that does not make their spiritual suffering any more painful than that of others.[98] Todorov too—in a book written a few years later that recapitulates much of what he argues in *The Abuses of Memory*—insists that the Jewish Holocaust was unique because while there were equivalents of Buchenwald and Dachau in the Soviet Union, there was no Treblinka.[99] But he also concludes in terms by now familiar that:

> from a historical point of view, Communism has the central position. It lasted longer, beginning much earlier and ending much later than Nazism; it spread more widely, to almost every continent, and was not confined to the European theater; and it killed an even greater number of people. It is also more important to condemn it from our present perspective: it has a greater power to confuse and to seduce, and unmasking its imposture is more urgent. But there is an obvious imbalance in the way the two regimes are officially described. The Nazi regime is universally abhorred...whereas Communism...still enjoys wide respect. Antifascism is obligatory, whereas anti-Communism remains suspect in many European countries.[100]

97. Todorov, *Facing the Extreme,* 261–62.
98. Besançon, *Le malheur du siècle,* 130.
99. Todorov, *Hope and Memory,* 88.
100. Todorov, *Hope and Memory,* 91.

Thus claims by Jews to having suffered uniquely in the face of the global dimensions of human suffering under Communism appear ludicrously hyperbolic and incommensurate with human experience not because Hitler's crimes were so much worse than those of Stalin, but because Jews—none of them apparently "beyond hatred or resignation," as was Levi—insist that they are. Jewish claims to having suffered uniquely, according to Todorov and others, refuse to recognize the suffering of others and demonstrate that Jews are incapable of empathy and judgment, let alone the proper distribution of justice (Todorov's categories aside, we are still not told precisely who makes these claims, when, why, or how). This assault on Jews' putative hyperbole and excess thus takes the form of hyperbole and excess that presents itself on the side of humanism and truth.

Now, to follow this argument, the price for Jewish emancipation in France is that Jews relinquish the claim to having suffered uniquely (at least those who make such a claim, which remains hypothetical in the absence of citations, though we know there are those who do). If Jews wish to continue to be treated as part of the human community, they must not single themselves out as special victims and distort the historical record. The absurdity of this demand—no matter one's stance in debates about the Holocaust's uniqueness, a concept primarily if not exclusively a theological or popular rather than scholarly claim—misses the two thousand years of persecution prior to the Holocaust that accomplished just this conferring of special and marginal status onto Jews. Besançon's oddly unself-conscious reference to Shylock may indicate a rather surprising blind spot.

In his effort to explain the "competition of victims" that has festered in Belgium and France like an ugly wound, the Belgian philosopher Jean-Michel Chaumont, whose book is one of the most frequently cited of its genre, begins with the premise that Jews' insistence on what he terms the "singularity" of the Holocaust is revenge-taking for not having been initially recognized as victims.[101] Chaumont's use of "singularity," on which he writes at length and which he at least seeks to clarify, nevertheless imputes a more or less hegemonic if slightly nuanced opinion to 'Jews' since 1967, and treats American and French Jewish intellectuals interchangeably, with little regard for the different historical circumstances that shaped responses

---

101. Jean-Michel Chaumont, *La concurrence des victimes: Génocide, identité, reconnaissance* (Paris: La découvert, 2002).

to the Holocaust in different national contexts.[102] The altogether regrettable lack of postwar recognition of specifically Jewish suffering generated what Chaumont terms a "frustrated" longing among Jews for recognition. When forthcoming, recognition creates healthy human relations generated by mutual respect and appreciation of the other. But when recognition is frustrated, "a certain innocence is forever lost. That which before would have been received gratefully as a gift is now demanded as one's due. And everything happens as if the debt has in the meantime generated interest…to receive the same thing as others is to receive less since these others have enjoyed recognition for decades. All this provokes complicated and ambiguous complexes."[103]

After the war, Chaumont notes, Jewish deaths were the deaths of innocents—that is, like the "village idiot," as he puts it, they met their fate innocently and thus, unlike resistance fighters, could not claim a symbolically charged death through heroism or martyrdom.[104] Jews experienced their innocence like a stigma, and those who survived felt ashamed of their own survival; Jewish suffering was thus only whispered about and never loudly proclaimed. Chaumont insists that this nonrecognition must be attributed largely to "involuntary factors," meaning the specific kind of stigmatizing death to which Jews were subjected, rather than to anti-Semitism. For this reason, perhaps, at least one French commentator remarked that he demonstrates surprisingly little empathy for his subjects.[105] Jews have thus been driven by this frustrated recognition to turn their innocence into a badge

102. See the stinging criticisms of Pierre Bouretz, "Cette fumée-ci, pourtant, ils ne savent pas…," and Richard Marienstras, "La stupeur du monde," both in *Le Débat* 98 (1998): 156–66 and 167–76, respectively. They argue that Chaumont does not understand the Shoah's challenge to positivist constructions of historiography and thus its challenge to the divide between history and memory as articulated by historians such as Saul Friedländer; that he fails to understand debates about Jewish uniqueness within Jewish tradition; and that his tone is generally arrogant and offensive. These articles are extremely rare specimens in all the attention that Chaumont's book has received, most of it positive. The reader might also compare Chaumont's account of a discussion between Elie Wiesel, Emil Fackenheim, George Steiner, and Richard H. Popkin in New York two months before the Six Day War (99–105) with the nuanced, well-contextualized analysis of the same debate about the Holocaust's uniqueness in Michael E. Staub, *Torn at the Roots: The Crisis of Jewish Liberalism in Postwar America* (New York: Columbia University Press, 2002), 132–34.

103. Chaumont, *La concurrence des victimes*, 240. Chaumont seems to have no sense of the irony implicit in his allusion to the Jewish expectation that interest should be paid on the metaphorical "debt."

104. Chaumont, *La concurrence des victimes*, 45.

105. Bouretz, "Cette fumée-ci," 157.

of honor, to invert their stigma and wear it proudly. Jewish memory is a "retrospective illusion" and a "vain and displaced quest for prestige" that creates false conflicts among different kinds of victims and leads tragically away from "universalism"—from the ability to mourn other human beings' suffering as one would one's own.[106]

Chaumont mourns Jewish suffering and urges Jews who insist on the uniqueness of the Holocaust to come back into the fold of all sufferers. Only once the suffering of all human beings can be recognized in a healthy, undistorted manner and older normative frameworks such as patriotism for understanding retributive violence discarded, can the Holocaust help us to understand genocide more fully. Chaumont not only suggests that Jewish memory is born of a distorted and regressive collective psychology, but also that by commemorating the Holocaust as they do, Jews do to themselves what the Nazis did to them: they transform their near-slaughter into the core of their identity. He is far from such French thinkers and historians as François Bédarida, Georges Bensoussan, and Henry Rousso, who agree in principle with him that the Holocaust has lent itself to "abusive sacralizations," but not in the context of anxieties about Jewish indifference to the pain of others.[107] They argue instead that claims that the Jewish Holocaust was unique may be surrogates for a more substantive engagement with Jewish history and memory. Like Besançon and Todorov, Chaumont focuses on how Jewish assertions about their singular victimization constitute threats to the human community of sufferers. He spends most of his time not grappling with the complexities and ambiguities of post-Holocaust Jewish identity (except, like Todorov, to argue that it has taken on a pathological dimension), but demonstrating how we all prove to be

106. Chaumont, *La concurrence des victims,* 88, 13.
107. François Bédarida, "La mémoire contre l'histoire," *Esprit* 193 (1993): 9; Alain Finkielkraut, *The Imaginary Jew,* trans. Kevin O'Neill and David Suchoff (Lincoln: University of Nebraska Press, 1997); Rousso, *The Haunting Past,* 12–13, 19–22; Georges Bensoussan, "Histoire, mémoire et commemoration: Vers une religion civile," *Le Débat* 82 (1994): 90–97. The essays by Bédarida and Bensoussan were published in the context of an opening essay by Jean-Michel Chaumont, who presented in concise and less polemical form the argument he would later make in the much discussed book on the competition of victims. The conversations between Rony Brauman and Alain Finkielkraut on the Israeli-Palestinian conflict, anti-Semitism, and Jews in France also provide a dramatically different picture, but the nuances tend to be lost in the public debate in which each participates on a different side (both from the Left, but Brauman repudiates Zionism and Finkielkraut defends it): Brauman and Finkielkraut, *La discorde.*

equal members of the human community even within the metaphorical darkness of Nazi concentration camps, since we all feel shame and humiliation. Jews who continue to set themselves apart simply extend the lack of recognition that once plagued them to others who now desperately need it.

Another scholar, the Left-wing philosopher and translator Alain Brossat, argues that the memory of the Holocaust has been "paralyzed, fetishized, absolutized, particularized, and petrified, as are the pious, homogenous but no less *empty* gatherings around the memorial of Vel d'Hiv." Brossat, in long and sophisticated discussions of both Hannah Arendt and Michel Foucault, makes a case for the totalitarian implications of modern democracy. From his point of view, both thinkers share the conviction that totalitarianism in its various incarnations represents a rupture in history that has become part of the normal course of human history and hence 'historicized' ("our post-catastrophic horizon is interminably catastrophic").[108] They articulate how the literal annihilation not only of human beings but of humanity as a concept has entered the realm of normality. Moreover, according to Brossat, Arendt and Foucault believe that "catastrophe" (Brossat's term for genocide and ethnocide),[109] emblematized by the extreme conditions of totalitarian states, is part of the unfolding of the history of modern democracy that liberal democratic ideology masks. Most significant perhaps, Brossat claims that both Arendt and Foucault—though Arendt is by far more attentive to the historical specificity of totalitarian regimes and Foucault, according to Brossat, not sufficiently sensitive to the novelty of totalitarianism—conceive of Jews as a synecdoche for the fate of all humanity under modern totalitarianism.

Brossat attacks French critics of totalitarianism during the 1970s and '80s for taming the beast of Stalinism by playing up reform after the dictator's demise and therefore demonstrating a thorough misunderstanding of the normalization of terror under modern regimes.[110] And like other critics of Stalinism, he understands its particular evils in terms of its self-destructive tendencies—its assault on Soviet society and the Party itself.

---

108. Alain Brossat, *L'épreuve du désastre: Le XXᵉ siècle et les camps* (Paris: Albin Michel, 1996), 178.

109. "Catastrophe" is perhaps not coincidentally the translation of the Yiddish word "hurbyn" used originally to describe the Holocaust, as well as the translation of the Arabic "Nakba," now used by Palestinians to describe the 1948 Arab-Israeli war in which they were displaced.

110. Brossat, *L'épreuve,* 124–25.

But throughout the book Brossat saves most of his rhetorical hammering to nail Jews who claim that the Holocaust was singular and the so-called political correctness (and hence tyranny) of this view.[111] For such claims not only repudiate the murderousness of modernity itself, but seek above all to establish the memory of the Holocaust as an alibi for "inaction before contemporary catastrophes": assertions about "the 'uniqueness' of Nazi crimes [are] also an alibi...for Soviet exterminations and colonial massacres."[112] Brossat, along with Alain Badiou, absolutely rejects the appellation 'Jews' as a category and conceives this tendency as part of a genocidal logic that permits the reduction and stigmatization of a heterogeneous group of people into a singular group.[113]

Brossat's and Badiou's anti-identitarian thinking may be fruitful, but is wrenched thoroughly out of any historical context: did the Nazis invent the appellation 'Jew'? And if the 'Jews' have been forced into ghettos and into a diaspora for most of their history, if assimilation has a complex history at best, is it surprising that many Jews would seek to transform their stigmatized identity from a negative to an affirmative one, as have so many other discriminated groups? The problem, that is, is not the anti-identitarian claim, but the absolute lack of sensitivity to historical context and thus nuance that might question whether one of the most important and destructive features of Nazism is that it turned Jews into "Jews." In any case, for Brossat, claims to victim status among various groups, and among Jews in particular, reject this basic principle of resistance to extermination and take the form of empty rhetorical invocations of past suffering that have become so ritualized that their meaning is lost: the sacralization of memory thus makes a real confrontation with what Brossat calls the "actualité du totalitaire" impossible.[114]

Brossat, like Todorov and Chaumont, albeit in more extreme and explicit terms, criticizes psychological claims based on past victimization because they ultimately mask the generic nature of catastrophe in the twentieth century in favor of making refined distinctions between concentration camps and death camps, for example, that don't get us anywhere

111. Brossat, *L'épreuve*, 372.
112. Brossat, *L'épreuve*, 23.
113. Brossat, *L'épreuve*, 284–85; Badiou, *Circonstances 3*, 33–36.
114. Brossat, *L'épreuve*, 60.

ethically or conceptually (as important as he concedes such distinctions are historically, as does Todorov). But he also analyzes far more elaborately how Jewish memory has blotted out the memory of other crimes as well as dulled our response to and ability to conceptualize and confront other genocides. Jews' (and others') insistence on the singularity of the Jewish genocide, he argues, confuses the particular with the universal and history with philosophy. The notion that Auschwitz is a "universal paradigm"[115] of human suffering "paralyze[s] thought"[116] because it reduces all violence and suffering to the particular suffering of the Jews against which all other suffering is measured. "Never again" becomes "that's not it"—because a particular event is not genocide as it was perpetrated against European Jewry, it must be a more "normal" occurrence. Brossat's claim that the extermination of European Jews obfuscates other genocides is not unique. He conceives all Jewish memory as "an irresponsible and hypocritical alibi,"[117] not only for Israel's oppression of Palestinians but also for Western imperialism tout court. The Jews and the West have transformed themselves into surrogates for all of humanity and, under the guise of humanitarianism ("never again"), actually blind themselves both to the present—other oppressions, other genocides—and the past, including Stalin's crimes, which are deemed lesser evils.

This discourse on Jewish victimization has a mimetic effect. First, it mimics the perpetuation of crimes against Jews, so that Zionism—"mimetically instrumentalized victimology" which persecutes and segregates Palestinians—offends the memory of the victims. The effects of Jewish memory (what Brossat calls the "effects of the illusion" of singularity and the "continuation of politics by other means")[118] mimic the ideological form of Nazism itself: "the passage from the assertion of singularity to a situation in which elect victims are distinguished by their difference from all others produces a mental disaster that prepares the ground for yet another passage: that of the delegates designated by the victims to be more 'equal than the others' in the camps of the perpetrator."[119] It is not just that

115. Brossat, *L'épreuve*, 62.
116. Brossat, *L'épreuve*, 316.
117. Brossat, *L'épreuve*, 316, 324.
118. Brossat, *L'épreuve*, 326–37, 358.
119. Brossat, *L'épreuve*, 306.

commemoration has become empty of meaning,[120] or that the insistence on the singularity of the Jewish genocide empties all other genocides of meaning by affirming the greater victimization of some over others. Instead, and far more dramatically, Jewish memory conceived as such is itself genocidal: "All those who extract a philosophical lesson from that which is and should only ever be a historical lesson—the exorbitant particularity and irreducibility of the Evil that they [the Nazis] committed against some and not others—commit a sort of sacrilege in their very meditation on the Crime by mimetically reinstituting the representations of an irrevocable separation forged by the persecutor, in dividing and making hierarchies of the victims philosophically."[121] Brossat's admirable attention to the iconic and therefore dehistoricized status of the Holocaust leads him not to a nuanced conception of Jewish memory, but to a reductive and ahistorical construction of that memory as a figurative perpetrator indistinct from Nazism.

If we do not sufficiently attend to Stalin's crimes we collude with Stalin (the putative "forgetting" of Stalin's crimes mimics Communist terror, which makes any punishment potentially justifiable and confers on the regime's judgment an aura of legitimacy), and if we remember Jewish crimes as "unique," according to Brossat, we perpetuate the liquidation of our most cherished humanist values, meaning empathy and respect for the otherness of others. In effect, Brossat asserts that Jewish memory, reduced in his work to an insistence on the Holocaust's uniqueness, is catastrophic: it is a vehicle of modernity, of the reification and always-potential annihilation of human beings and the idea of humanity. Jewish memory is genocidal because it fails to conceive itself as one among a community of human "memories" or suffering groups that have all been or are potential targets. Because Brossat believes that totalitarianism is the universal or potentially universal experience of dehumanization inscribed in modernity, the differences between various types of regimes and degrees of suffering are ultimately part of the same general historical pattern.[122] Thus Jewish memory

---

120. Many American scholars have argued that the elevation of Auschwitz to the symbol of modern evil erases the particularity of Jewish suffering by transforming the genocide into a universal symbol of suffering. See Barbie Zelizer, *Remembering to Forget: Holocaust Memory through the Camera's Eye* (Chicago: University of Chicago Press, 1998).

121. Brossat, *L'épreuve*, 305–6.

122. Brossat, *L'épreuve*, 382.

not only represents the self-indulgence of Jews but also symbolizes the generalized amnesia of humanism about its own implications in the destruction of humanity.

All these works extend the particularist construction of Jewish suffering in discussions of Stalinism and Nazism to Jewish memory, which is part of a cover-up of human suffering more generally: recall that Jewish suffering is particular and temporally and geographically isolated, while Communism's victims are surrogates for suffering humanity. In this discourse, however, it isn't only that the murder of Jews, though singular in method, was graspable in its literality, finality, and lack of "ideological ceremony" and therefore implicitly not as renewable or as inconceivable as some Jews insist. From Todorov to Chaumont and Brossat—and these are merely the most recognizable names in a pervasive discourse—Jewish demands that we remember perversely mimic Nazi practices of dehumanization; Jewish memory itself is "petrified" and only capable of remembering "literally," that is to say of invoking again and again a particular experience of dying whose entire meaning is self-referential, narcissistic, and which views all other genocides only in the mirror of its own. Brossat, from the Left, says straightforwardly that Jewish memory of the Holocaust must be called "an ideology of genocide."[123] The philosopher Alain de Benoist, founder of the French New Right, accuses Jews who believe in the singularity of the Holocaust of repeating the Nazi conviction that some lives are unworthy of life.[124] And the humanist Todorov claims that Jewish memory impedes the remembrance of Stalinism, all the while celebrating those Jews who do not take their suffering too literally. The "universalist" Primo Levi is Todorov's hero. Hannah Arendt is Brossat's heroine because she insisted that the Jewish catastrophe be used to understand genocide more generally: Arendt sought to "universalize the experience of the camps."[125]

In this discourse, critics bemoan "Jews" so-called insistence on the spotlight and on the history of past suffering. Jews become—to cite the American historian Elazar Barkan commenting on the more general

123. Brossat, *L'épreuve*, 306.
124. de Benoist, *Communisme et nazisme*, 60–61.
125. Brossat, *L'épreuve*, 50.

phenomenon of 'victim culture'—"autistic" and "self-indulgent."[126] Jewish victims are "unique" not because the Holocaust was unique, but because Jewish memory cannot imagine it otherwise. The French discourse
is hardly isolated, but it is not identical to the more muted American coun-
terpart that we have already discussed.[127] In Ian Buruma's view, kitschy
seduction offered by sentimentalized media attention, the sacralization of
survivors, and gigantic monuments to Jewish destruction void meaning in
their pretense to provide it.[128] This sounds similar to the argument made
by Todorov, Chaumont, and Brossat according to which Jews transform
their "innocence" into a badge of honor. In Buruma's view, kitsch is the
very antithesis of dire human suffering, and culturally comforting monuments render Jewish suffering too familiar. Buruma also argues that wanting to be a victim entails putting one's self in the place of the real victim.
He speaks with dismay about a Jewish historian of China who writes about
atrocities committed by the Japanese against Chinese civilians during the
1930s. According to him, she uses that violence to think through her own
relationship to the Holocaust, which she is too young to have experienced.
Hers is a fantasy related to guilt at not having suffered. For Buruma, her
identification with victims is about taking comfort where there should
be none, and this takes the form of a regression that in his view is self-
indulgent and morally irresponsible, but it is hardly murderous.[129]

For many French critics, the overidentification with victims is also about
the negative consequences of rendering commemoration too comfortable
and self-referential. But for some of them, Jewish self-reference not only
masks and represses the discomfort caused by other genocides and is thus
not only a matter of phantasmatic projections and other mechanisms of

126. Elazar Barkan, *Guilt of Nations: Restituting and Negotiating Historical Injustices* (Baltimore: Johns Hopkins University Press, 2000), xviii. Barkan himself moves beyond this judgment
to address post–Cold War restitution claims in order to conceive the "space" of a new international
morality as the dialogue between victims and perpetrators—the race to be accountable for one's
past (that takes different forms in different national cultures and the first instance of which was
German reparations to Jewish victims of the Holocaust in 1952).

127. The American discourse for the most part is a liberal critique of minority groups' perceived turning away from enlightenment universalism toward a universalism of suffering, from
reasoned and appropriate quests for recognition to the narcissistic exploitation of that recognition
in the interests of one's own group rather than for the good of humanity. See Chap. 1.

128. Ian Buruma, "The Joys and Perils of Victimhood," *New York Review of Books,* April 8,
1999, 6.

129. Buruma, "The Joys and Perils of Victimhood."

displacement and their negative consequences (including a lack of or intensified if finally disingenuous sensitivity to the pain of others, or a narcissistic attribution of unique evil to Nazism, all of which are legitimate and
arguable positions one might take against the uniqueness thesis). Jewish
self-reference is also in its most extreme manifestation genocidal, itself a
crime that manifests as a form of infinite self-expansion and imperial con-
quest that absorbs everything else. It is not a defense against the pain of
others, or a problematic quest for identity in the form of collective and
transmissible injury. These French discourses instead hold Jewish memory
responsible for the erosion of humanity's collective memory of suffering,
for 'our' inability to recognize others as others, and thus for nothing less
than the laying to waste of empathy, dignity, and the universal values we
associate with humanism. Jews become implicitly or explicitly quintessential anti-humanists, not as those who subversively unmask humanism's
pretensions to justice and equality in the spirit of Brossat's critique of humanism, but as anti-human.

We could read this rhetorical construction of Jewish suffering as a contemporary allegory of the long history of the so-called offense Jewish particularism gives to humanism in France. For this discourse in fact offers a
series of hostile responses to the (often phantasmatic) Jewish refusal to pay
the price of emancipation. It promises assimilation as the price for emancipation, meaning that belonging to the community of human sufferers requires that Jews not insist too much on their own suffering. We might also
conceptualize this discourse as an effort to return to the universalism of the
"camp experience"—to the notion that Jews too might be enfolded in the
narrative of the tragedy that befell all of France during the Second World
War, a narrative that Jews have now rejected apparently in the interests of
loudly asserting the particularity of their own experience. But to the extent
that it also constructs the memory of Jewish victimization as implicitly or
explicitly hyperbolic or genocidal—as exceeding all conceivable forms of
human suffering—Jewish memory cannot be assimilated into a universalist narrative, and stands in for the perils of memory against history. This
discourse forges the unassimilable residue of Jewish memory, exemplary of
distortion, fragmentation, and the resentment of the 'bad' and unassimilable
citizen, into a weapon against the human community. It constructs Jewish
memory as complicit with or explanatory of current human inaction in
the face of catastrophe, and in particular of the West's refusal to confront

fully the realities of other genocides past and present. Indeed, the implicitly causal relationship between remembering Jewish suffering and forgetting the pain of others has also been one of the most persistent themes underlining an updated anti-Semitism.[130] That this remains a robust cultural assumption was summarized recently by the French philosopher Bernard Henri-Lévy's comment to the *New Yorker* magazine in 2007 in reference to the popularity of Dieudonné, an antiracist and anti-Semitic stand-up comic: "As far as being a special race [Jews], nobody believes that anymore. But anti-racist anti-Semitism—...this works. If the Jews practiced 'memorial pornography'—thus exaggerating their own suffering—they became responsible for why the world didn't care enough about the history of slavery and the suffering of blacks."[131]

However credible the arguments that some Jewish groups have instrumentalized the memory of the Holocaust, this particularly unself-conscious rhetoric of prominent intellectuals should force us to ask what is at stake in this discourse other than the legitimate criticism of the inevitably political uses of history and their consequences. Jewish suffering can never be identical with human suffering because Jewish memory cannot finally be assimilated and emblematizes a larger threat to all efforts to tell the truth about history. Jewish memory impedes our reckoning with and responsibility for current and future catastrophes. Jewish memory is excessive because it is radically incommensurable with the space and time that defines human community: Jews, like specters, do not inhabit human temporality and have no ethical obligations except to remember their own suffering.

Aside from the politically instrumental uses of Holocaust memory to which it is partly a response, the hyperbolic, phantasmatic dimensions of this argument suggest not only an underlying anti-Semitism. Its logic

---

130. Weill, *La République et les antisémites,* 88; Michel Wieviorka, *La tentation anti-Semite,* 90–93.

131. Bernard Henri-Lévy quoted in Tom Reiss, "Laugh Riots: The French Star Who Became a Demagogue," *New Yorker,* November 19, 2007, 49. The term "memorial pornography," used in reference to the Holocaust, was Dieudonné's term (see "Dieudonné s'empêtre dans l'antisémitisme au nom des Noirs," *Le Monde,* February 21, 2005). In July 2008, the comic Siné similarly became a focus of attention when he remarked, in response to the announcement that President Nicolas Sarkozy's son was converting to Judaism to marry a Jewish woman, that such conversions were a form of social climbing. He also noted that he would prefer a Muslim with a chador over a clean-shaven Jew. He was fired from the newspaper *Charlie Hebdo,* but the incident provoked a storm of controversy similar to that which surrounded Dieudonné's comments.

attributes the comparative victimology in which it is engaged not only to Jews, but also to the valorization of memory over history (and by those critics who implicitly reference their own 'memories' but treat them as if they were of another order—more real, less literal, more exemplary).

In the end, the comparison between Nazism and Stalinism reveals that in predominant French discourses, Jewish memory, however legitimate, is always compromised by its putatively intrinsic hyperbole. This argument is quite different, again, from the assertion that Jewish memory has been so sacralized that it has been transformed into an empty ritual. Instead, most French discourses of comparative suffering suggest that Jewish memory *can never have* a reliable and discernable relation to the Holocaust, and that Jewish victimization, however real, can now be conveyed only in the fantasies of overloaded and self-referential imaginations. The real victims remain glimmers in darkness, shrouded in fog, and thus figures for a truthful but ever-elusive history of human suffering already blotted out by Jewish narcissism. Moreover, some of these critics' transformation of Stalin's victims into repositories of universal suffering to be remembered and redeemed reveals a particular discomfort with the status of being a victim whose suffering is perhaps meaningless and signifies nothing other than itself. In short, in their quest to remember 'other' victims, in their projection of hyperbolic memory onto those who proclaim victim status, and indeed in their insistence on comparing suffering itself, these discourses erase the historical reality of Jewish suffering by transforming Jews into perpetrators of a crime against all of suffering humanity. They accuse Jews of using the legacy of their own pain to obscure the pain of others and thus of seeking to seize a larger portion of some phantasmatic universal memory than is accorded all other groups with grievances. The flippant notion that everyone wants to be Jewish, just as everyone wants to be a victim, should reveal not only the odd correlation of Jewish suffering with the histrionic assertion that everyone wants to be a victim, but the intellectuals' investment in obscuring the acknowledgment of Jewish suffering all the while recognizing that it exists. In what form, then, can suffering be recognized?

3

MINIMALISM AND VICTIM TESTIMONY

> Now he had come to tell his story, carefully answering questions put to him
> by the prosecutor; he spoke clearly and firmly, without embroidery, using
> a minimum of words.
>
> HANNAH ARENDT (1963), on the testimony of Zindel Grynszpan, the Jewish
> witness who most moved her at the Eichmann trial

Minimalism in its varieties is a sophisticated style characterized by aesthetic and emotive restraint. It was most prominent in postwar visual art and sculpture that emphasized the sheer contingency of the art-object by reducing it to "what you see."[1] Eventually minimalism simply described any aesthetic form marked by antisentimental austerity, and it is this now generic usage of the term to which I refer. Minimalist narratives resist hyperbole in order to avoid the potential conversion of suffering into kitsch, voyeurism, or sublimity by following a dictum the writer W. G. Sebald attributes to Walter Benjamin: "I think Benjamin at one point says that there

---

Epigraph: Hannah Arendt, *Eichmann in Jerusalem: A Report on the Banality of Evil* (New York: Penguin, 1994 [1963]), 228.

1. The phrase, now synonymous with minimalism in the arts, is attributed to the minimalist artist Frank Stella.

is no point in exaggerating that which is already horrific."[2] Even when not explicitly minimalist, some of the most nuanced Holocaust representation is antisentimental and refuses affective identification in order to undermine the restoration of the wholeness or feel-good qualities of redemptive narratives that encourage sentimental overidentification with victims or the narcissistic appropriation of their experience.[3] Experimental efforts by writers such as Charlotte Delbo and Aharon Appelfeld stress silence and use various devices to undercut affective overidentifications with victims. Delbo, for example, uses a lyrical but graphic account of the ever-incomplete effort to wash herself in Auschwitz, a passage whose elegance distances the reader sufficiently to render her experience imaginable and yet unsettling.[4]

Minimalism is not only a sophisticated style, it is also often conceived as an antidote to the alleged media exploitation of the Holocaust and insurance against the unstable and narcissistic representations of the event associated with overwrought memory.[5] Over the past three decades, a cultural consensus has emerged according to which Western European and American culture has entered the "era of the witness": we recall that Annette Wieviorka argues that the act of testifying is now a media spectacle, and injury to body and soul a source of recognition and identity in a world with few available forms of self-affirmation.[6] In this context, we know, there are already countless critics who argue that rhetorical constraint

2. Lynne Sharon Schwarz, ed., *The Emergence of Memory: Conversations with W. G. Sebald* (New York: Seven Stories Press, 2007), 86. Thanks to Dominick LaCapra for pointing me to this reference.

3. See Sidra DeKoven Ezrahi, *By Words Alone: The Holocaust in Literature* (Chicago: University of Chicago Press, 1980), 54–56, for the importance of rhetoric and style in Holocaust memoirs.

4. Charlotte Delbo, *Auschwitz and After,* trans. Rosette C. Lamont (New Haven: Yale University Press, 1995), 149–53.

5. For example, Alvin H. Rosenfeld, *A Double Dying: Reflections on Holocaust Literature* (Bloomington: Indiana University Press, 1980), testifies to the complexity of the boundary between documentary and literature in writing on the Holocaust but also deplores the commercialization and distortion with which the Holocaust has been treated in mainstream media. He discusses many texts, and William Styron's problematic *Sophie's Choice* in particular (164–65). For debates about the commercialization of the Holocaust and its treatment of the "pornography" of suffering, see Carolyn J. Dean, *The Fragility of Empathy after the Holocaust* (Ithaca: Cornell University Press, 2004), 16–42.

6. Annette Wieviorka, *The Era of the Witness,* trans. Jared Stark (Ithaca: Cornell University Press, 2006), 135–44.

avoids assigning the Holocaust any meaning other than its own 'having happened,' and thus somehow guards against false testimony in a media market in which suffering sells and no testimony is authentic or traumatic *enough.* The privilege accorded to rhetorical constraint seems often to be part of an effort to recount in conceivable terms a place, Auschwitz, which has become, in Ruth Franklin's words, "the almost platitudinous reference for the very embodiment of hell on earth."[7] In 1994, speaking of Raul Hilberg's famous work *The Destruction of the European Jews,* Hans Kellner noted that "it indeed possesses the sparse, modernist decorum now deemed suited to the event."[8] More recently, Wulf Kansteiner has argued that Saul Friedländer, the most distinguished living of all Holocaust historians, "is a master of economic understatement."[9]

We have seen that subtle critics believe that rhetorical constraint voids any concept of the Holocaust as sacrifice or punishment, pace both theological renderings of the event and secular commemoration, which have often rendered the victims sacred objects or put them on desacralizing display. Rhetorical constraint mitigates the dehistoricizing effects of one critical tendency to cast the Holocaust as commensurate with the epistemological ruptures associated with modernity and postmodernity.[10] Critics have often appropriately denounced sacred renderings of the event as distortions that transform the experience into a portent, exemplary of sin, sacrifice, or an icon of 'evil in our time.'[11]

7. Ruth Franklin, "A Thousand Darknesses: Elie Wiesel's *Night,*" in *Re-examining the Holocaust through Literature,* ed. Aukje Kluge and Benn E. Williams (Newcastle upon Tyne: Cambridge Scholars Publishing, 2009), 156.

8. Hans Kellner, "'Never Again' Is Now," *History and Theory* 33 (1994): 138.

9. Wulf Kansteiner, "Success, Truth, and Modernism in Holocaust Historiography: Reading Saul Friedländer Thirty-Five Years after the Publication of *MetaHistory,*" *History and Theory* 47 (2009): 34. I should note that in keeping with an understanding of minimalism as a transition between modernism and postmodernism (or rather, as containing elements of both), both Kellner and Kansteiner refer to Hayden White and to Friedländer's works as "modernist."

10. We should recall that there are critics who not only describe, but defend (a version of) this view in interesting if not ultimately persuasive terms. See, for example, Sara Emilie Guyer, *Romanticism after Auschwitz* (Stanford: Stanford University Press, 2007).

11. Michael André Bernstein attacks the notion that the Holocaust or any catastrophe of such magnitude is particularly revelatory. He argues that ideas about the Holocaust as *tremendum* or catastrophe themselves merit inquiry and are part of a broader tendency since the Great War to conceive extreme events as revelatory of some otherwise unfathomable truth about human nature, the Shoah being the most revelatory. Bernstein, "Homage to the Extreme: The Shoah and the Rhetoric

Such views are part of the preeminent consensus that the grievance structure of rational democratic contestation is being replaced by the unconstrained projection of the victim's phantasmatic wounds for which minimalism is an antidote. Surely the effectiveness of rhetorical constraint in Holocaust representation as an antidote to sacralization or fetishism may be fruitfully debated, and an enormous body of criticism now eloquently and nondogmatically exposes some of the troubling consequences of confusing the Holocaust and quasi-religious revelations about humankind. Indeed, this emphasis on forms of rhetorical constraint need not be at odds with the ambivalence of many survivors about their own memories and desire to represent facts knowing that they are always filtered through time or feeling. It is not necessarily at odds with sophisticated scholarly discussion on Holocaust literature, testimony, and memoirs that addresses both genre and rhetoric, including minimalism, over several generations.[12] In spite of their differences, many literary theorists focus primarily not on the fallibility and thus insufficiency of memory, but on how one might best remember given the vagaries of memory and the impact of trauma.[13]

At least one mainstream response by some scholars and public intellectuals to this recent tendency to privilege rhetorical constraint is more than simply a critique of the sort proffered by Wieviorka, discussed in Chapter One, and aimed at a clearly defined set of contemporary concerns. In a reductio ad absurdum of the argument against grandiloquence, which prefers some styles to others, some critics believe that all styles that are styles—that are self-reflexive, experimental, ornate, or exuberant—distract from the facticity and authenticity of the Holocaust victim's experience and are particularly egregious when used to represent extreme experiences of suffering and death. They presume that minimalist narrative in

---

of Catastrophe," *Times Literary Supplement,* March 6, 1998, 6–8; and *Foregone Conclusions: Against Apocalyptic History* (Berkeley: University of California Press, 1994), 91.

12. This literature is so vast that I will simply cite prominent examples where relevant.

13. As Aukje Kluge and Benn Williams note, "We, as readers, may forget the limitations of the author's memory and the mediations of language in shaping their memoirs. For these and other reasons, many current scholars are less concerned with the historical facts of the works they read than with what a literature of atrocity does accomplish." Kluge and Williams, eds., *Reexamining the Holocaust,* 9. For an attempt to theorize abstract representations of the Holocaust (e.g., Paul Celan, Anselm Kiefer, and others) as generating an unsettling "non-identification" that he labels the "holocaustal uncanny," see Eric Kligerman, *Sites of the Uncanny: Paul Celan, Specularity, and the Visual Arts* (New York: Walter de Gruyter, 2007).

its most literal incarnation as documentary or chronicle most effectively disentangles thought from aesthetic, emotional, or other disruptions which would otherwise compromise the credibility of the author.[14] In so doing, this response shapes not only a rhetorical posture in relation to Holocaust representation, but also the normative frameworks within which victims become credible and empathy for their plight conceivable. This discourse is sufficiently forceful and pervasive to warrant some exploration, in particular for the ways it reiterates and stigmatizes an 'excess' it deems measurable and restricts empathic response in an ostensible effort to render a 'healthy' or non-narcissistic form of empathy possible. I should note here that the point of this exercise is not to advocate for one style or another as the most effective means of representing atrocity (surely minimalism has been tremendously effective), but to ask about the potentially noxious consequences of the cultural privilege accorded to those victims who most effectively mimic the neutral and scientific reportage equated with the objective (rather than implicated) witness's distance from events. The argument is thus not about the most rhetorically effective strategies of representation, but about the ethical implications of a cultural practice in which credible testimony is that in which victims have mastered (or perform mastery of) their own wounds.

The Suspension of Disbelief

The suspension of disbelief is currently the preferred form of minimalist style, one that relies on accessible, bearable, unemotional narration

---

14. Though critics such as Dominick LaCapra and Hayden White have implicitly or explicitly questioned the predominance of realism and minimalism in mainstream Holocaust narratives, their views have not made much headway. LaCapra has suggested that minimalism may reduce the affect best suited to the empathic identification necessary for memory work. Hayden White has argued against a simplistic understanding of both minimalism and mimesis in historical writing on the Holocaust by underlining the continuity between realism and modernism: that is, modernist style does not represent reality any less realistically; it is merely that modernism, with its emphasis on multiple perspectives, temporal disruption, and unstable subject-positions, is more adequate to the object it seeks to represent. Dominick LaCapra, "Holocaust Testimonies," in *Catastrophe and Meaning: The Holocaust and the Twentieth Century,* ed. Moishe Postone and Eric Santner (Chicago: University of Chicago Press, 2003), 218–19; Hayden White, *Figural Realism: Studies in the Mimesis Effect* (Baltimore: Johns Hopkins University Press, 1999), 27–41.

that diminishes defensive and overly emotional responses, especially in history writing. Such responses presumably impede empathic identification by provoking suspicion that gets in the way of compassion, or by encouraging identifications with the narrator that dissipate emotional boundaries necessary to feel for the other as other rather than as a stand-in for one's own suffering. Though it may be a highly stylized (and effective) convention of minimalism or conceived merely as one among many modes of narrative restraint, the narrator's effort to suspend the listener's or reader's presumed disbelief often appears in memoirs as well as in literary and historiographical narratives of survival, sometimes among texts that resist or challenge the convention.[15]

In writing on memoirs, this tendency is perhaps most powerfully manifest in Tzvetan Todorov's work on Primo Levi, which exemplifies the conviction that rational restraint guarantees the preeminence of the tangible, the historical, and of secularized humility. Todorov implies that emotion is inevitable but that only emotional control guarantees the forcefulness and veracity of memory. Levi's words, he says, incarnate "humility: he doesn't shout, he speaks quietly, he weighs different options for and against, remembers exceptions to the rules, and seeks to understand his own reactions. He doesn't propose shattering accounts of things past, nor does he adopt the intonations of a prophet with a direct connection to the sacred: facing the extreme, he knows how to remain human, too human."[16] Michal Głowiński, a Polish literary critic whose moving memoirs were recently translated, tells us from an entirely different perspective than Todorov, since he is a survivor who spent the war in hiding, that if "literature" emerges in his account it must be "derivative, inadvertent, and unintentional," and insists that he

---

15. Several critics discuss this convention in memoirs in which the writer insists that he or she has avoided "literature" and merely documented experience. See Sem Dresden, *Persecution, Extermination, Literature,* trans. Henry G. Schogt (Toronto: University of Toronto Press, 1995), 36. Ezrahi, *By Words Alone,* points to the "interference of the literary" in documentary, but also notes that documentary art is finally a "hybrid genre" (15–23). Rosenfeld, *A Double Dying,* also insists that Holocaust representation necessarily blurs the boundaries between documentary in the most reductive sense and literature (see esp. pp. 64–65, 145). These studies by literary theorists insist that the divide between history and memory in literature is problematic because of the very nature of writing and representation.

16. Tzvetan Todorov, "Dix ans sans Primo Levi," *Esprit* 1 (1998): 135. For a different assessment of Levi's relationship to humanist thought, see Jonathan Druker, *Primo Levi and Humanism after Auschwitz: Posthumanist Reflections* (New York: Palgrave Macmillan, 2009), esp. 72–73.

writes an "authentic narrative" as devoid as possible of literary topoi. Authenticity demands an account of the "contempt and revulsion" he felt toward the Germans, but it occurs by his own description at a weak moment in which he is overpowered by feeling, and loses self-control. In spite of his efforts to speak to young Germans and to travel widely in Germany, he says, "I hold Germans in such contempt, I'm so repulsed by them, that I never again want to have anything to do with them. I never in my life want to cross paths with them, and thus I must act as if they have ceased to exist."[17]

Glowiński's hardheaded admission that there are some things one cannot get over distinguishes him from Todorov's version of Levi. Otherwise, Glowiński too is committed to a strict policing of the porous boundary between aesthetic pleasure and thought, between memory and its potential subjugation by narrative pleasure, whimsy, or traumatic aftermaths. He would probably not deny that, in Todorov's formulation, Levi is more truthful and "too human" because his style mimics the deliberations of rational thought and therefore escapes the pitfalls of literariness. But assertions that Levi manages to weigh matters judiciously in the aftermath of trauma ignore not only that he is the author of much darker works on the camps, including *The Drowned and the Saved,* in which he departs from his restrained tone, but also that he suffered from prolonged depressions (and probably committed suicide), whether or not his depression was related to his experience in Auschwitz, which he denied. Todorov acknowledges that Levi did not have the stamina to meet Albert Speer, but condescends to "understand" this lapse.[18] Indeed, in a 1976 "self-interview" (he poses himself questions and answers them), Levi seeks to undermine the idea that the lack of rancor in his work indicates forgiveness. He notes that he had not "forgiven any of the culprits," and that he abstained from explicit judgment not because he was without hatred but because he believed in reason:

> I repress hatred even within myself. I prefer justice. Precisely for this reason, when describing the tragic world of Auschwitz, I have deliberately assumed

---

17. Michal Glowiński, *The Black Seasons,* trans. Marci Shore (Evanston, IL: Northwestern University Press, 2005), 177.

18. Tzvetan Todorov, *Facing the Extreme: Moral Life in the Concentration Camps* (New York: Henry Holt, 1996), 269–70. "Getting to know a Nazi in a deep and meaningful way would have forced Levi to see him in all of his humanity, and had he done so, he would have had no weapons left to defend himself against the Nazis' intention to destroy him" (269).

the calm, sober language of the witness, neither the lamenting tones of the victim nor the irate voice of someone who seeks revenge. I thought that my account would be all the more credible and useful the more it appeared objective and the less it sounded overly emotional; only in this way does a witness in matters of justice perform his task, which is that of preparing the ground for the judge. The judges are my readers.[19]

That is, Levi deliberately chose a minimalist style in order to mimic that of an objective witness because he believed that emotional control made his testimony more effective. But this was a deliberate and crafted style he used self-consciously to repress hatred and to assume a persona he believed might more persuasively appear objective. Levi's own words go against the grain of Todorov's presumption that Levi *was* self-controlled rather than that he performed self-mastery, and make Harald Weinreich's overly literal insistence that he wrote "without hatred" appear somewhat naïve: "Primo Levi," Weinreich asserts, "writes without hatred. He wishes to be not a judge but rather a witness, and his testimony, which is based on precise observation and a trained memory, must be reliable. It *is* reliable."[20] That Glowiński appears painfully honest but feels somehow compromised by his own feelings is troubling, as if his own inability to sustain his composure reveals the tragic but inevitable impediments of memory and emotion rather than something about the nature of victimization and survival itself. Glowiński's honesty does, however, expose the investment in Levi's objectivity and absence of hatred as a projection that has little seemingly to do with Levi and a lot to do with various readers' desire that victims have mastered their experiences.

Although most literary theorists and other scholars know that Holocaust memoirs by definition can provide only mediated perspectives on the experience of their authors, the pressure on such memoirs to appear referential and unmediated is powerful. Andrés Nader describes how the view that literature occupies an imaginative register opposed

19. Primo Levi, *The Voice of Memory: Interviews 1961–1987,* ed. Marco Belpoliti and Robert Gordon, trans. Robert Gordon (New York: The New Press, 2001), 185–86.

20. Thus Weinrich translates Levi's style into a guarantor of reliable memory. Harald Weinrich, *Lethe: The Art and Critique of Forgetting,* trans. Steven Rendall (Ithaca: Cornell University Press, 2004), 193.

to the camp experience, that literature and poetry have "form" and thus reflect a human world of highly crafted culture rather than the barbarism of the camps, renders the concept of a literature or poetry of the camps oxymoronic.[21] True, the idea that "works with literary merit" may be those which best convey the event is not hotly contested as long as the focus is on the representation of emotions rather than the documentation of evidence,[22] and lots of ink has been spilled about the crucial nature of aesthetic fashioning in the representation of traumatic experience.[23] These discussions, however, neglect the dynamics of the cultural demand for a testimonial style, literary or not, that is unadorned, laconic, and as close to a performance of transparency as possible.[24] Indeed, the view that testimony ought to take this form was widespread among survivors who wrote about their experiences, including Levi, who still spoke, like

21. Andrés Nader, *Traumatic Verses: On Poetry in German from the Concentration Camps, 1933–1945* (Rochester, NY: Camden House, 2007), 39–43. Nader quotes Todorov to represent this dominant and, he believes, wrongheaded view of a divide between literature and camp literature: "Indeed, it is perhaps because Levi considered the life of the mind an ordinary virtue and not something reserved for an elite that he was able to keep faith in it and safeguard his power" (Todorov quoted, 41). In short, Levi's enjoyment of Dante in Auschwitz not only testifies to his humanism and thus his ability to sustain reason by importing the culture so foreign to the camps, but also underlines his ordinariness in the same sense—he is not, Nader remarks, like Jean Améry, full of the bitterness of the "professional intellectual" shorn of the accoutrements of culture, but uses culture to try and live, to modestly embrace its virtues, however fleeting its impact (41).

22. Susan Rubin Suleiman, *Crises of Memory and the Second World War* (Cambridge: Harvard University Press, 2006), 183–84. James E. Young has termed documentary work on the Holocaust a "rhetoric of fact," meaning that even documentary narratives work rhetorically to construct themselves as documents. He also notes that survivors' memoirs were constrained by the difficulty of language. His work is invaluable. Here, however, I am more concerned to argue how the suspicion of the literary puts pressure not only on survivors who write, but also on the reception of their works. James E. Young, *Writing and Rewriting the Holocaust: Narrative and the Consequences of Interpretation* (Bloomington: Indiana University Press, 1998), 23, 64–82.

23. For example, see Shoshana Felman and Dori Laub, *Testimony: Crises of Witnessing in Literature, Psychoanalysis, and History* (New York: Routledge, 1992).

24. When Annette Wieviorka notes the predominance of Primo Levi and Robert Antelme among survivors' testimonies, she points not to style but to the absence of the Yiddish and Polish writers from the list. Her important aim is to ask what makes the Holocaust the Holocaust for most readers: suffering in the camps or the destruction of a people? She laments the apparent absence of concern for the latter among non-Jewish writers and audiences. Hers is a more nuanced version of the common observation that Levi speaks so little about being Jewish that his work, aside from its literary merit, can be most easily universalized. Wieviorka, *The Era of the Witness*, 21–22.

Glowiński, of his fear of "falling into rhetoric,"[25] for reasons we have seen him explain.

The most devoted believer in the power of literature to convey the Holocaust, Jorge Semprun, in contrast, mocks the longing for mastery and transparency: "Certainly," he writes, "the only true witness, in fact, according to the specialists, is one who did not survive, who went to the very end of the experience and who died of it. But neither historians nor sociologists have yet succeeded in resolving this contradiction: how to invite the true witnesses, that is to say the dead, to their conferences? How to make them talk?"[26] When put this way, the insistence by many guilty survivors that the "true witnesses" are those who perished becomes a cliché appropriated by those who came later to insist on the ascetic but also potentially sacralizing idea that the truth died with the dead.[27] This demand that the living not speak for the dead is a demand for authenticity that weighs heavily on those who were there themselves, and relies on a particularly paradoxical conception of the eyewitness whose experience is by definition the most truthful and yet most incommunicable. But survivors' version of this demand is linked to their experience as survivors, and expresses their own often guilt-ridden sense of responsibility to those who died. It is less clear on what grounds those who are not themselves survivors make this claim, except to argue that even survivors don't make the kinds of overwrought claims about their experiences that others who were not there now do.

As Susan Suleiman has argued, the demand to suspend disbelief may even encourage victims to construct narratives that are false but plausible in order to enhance their credibility, meaning that the victim knows that the listener must be drawn into a narrative that feels viable in order, paradoxically, to hear the 'truth.' Suleiman has suggested that doubts surrounding the French resister Raymond Aubrac's contradictory testimony about his

25. Primo Levi quoted in Alain Parrau, *Écrire les camps* (Paris: Belin, 1995), 286. For interesting discussions aimed at reducing the sharp delineation between literature and testimony, see Michael Rinn, *Les récits du genocide: Sémiotique de l'indicible* (Lausanne: Delachaux et Niestlé, 1998); and Marie Bornand, *Témoinage et fiction: Les récits des rescapés de la littérature de langue française (1945–2000)* (Geneva: Droz, 2004). All these texts are valuable French interventions in this debate, but remain for the most part decontextualized and tend to minimize or neglect the real import of the different experiences of Jews and others.

26. Semprun quoted in Suleiman, *Crises of Memory*, 157.

27. Gary Weissman echoes this view of the "real witnesses" in his *Fantasies of Witnessing: Postwar Efforts to Experience the Holocaust* (Ithaca: Cornell University Press, 2004), 74–75.

role in the capture of Jean Moulin by the Gestapo may be derived from the listener's need for a plausible account, and Aubrac's perhaps unconscious need to fulfill that demand.[28] In spite of Semprun's sarcasm about how we mourn true victims, as if only they could clarify matters, the ascetic imperative weighs not only on self-consciously literary representation but also on written testimony with no such ambition.

"Styles of Dying," Quietly

When the topic is victims' suffering, discussions about proper style often begin with the premise that the victim who proclaims his injuries loudly may have dubious motives, implicit in the cliché that only the dead are the true witnesses.[29] This position may sometimes be legitimate: victims don't always tell the truth, and some people pretend to have or fantasize having been victimized. But the fact remains that victims in whose experience much is at stake must now overcome a particularly heavy dose of skepticism unless their claims are made in specific ways. It is not simply a matter of being vigilant about the facts, since determining the veracity of testimony exceeds the merely empirical verification that someone has suffered or not. Instead, we must determine what constitutes reliable memory of suffering at a historical moment when by their own account critics believe that injury is often phantasmatic if not false, and that claims to injury are often 'really' about the need for recognition instead of efforts to heal traumatic memories of a catastrophic event. My task is to demonstrate how some critics have rhetorically constituted the credible victim, and to show how once-victims are folded back into the quotidian of human time at the expense of their wounds.

One important argument against the increasing cultural focus on catastrophic events is that it masks and risks normalizing the now invisible everyday violence against specific groups of people, whether the social and psychic suffering generated by poverty or other forms of structural oppression. Whether or not this is true, the treatment of victims of catastrophic events themselves is not so straightforward. I would also contend

---

28. Suleiman, *Crises of Memory*, 59.
29. Michal Głowiński uses the expression "styles of dying" in *The Black Seasons*, 31.

that those critics who insist on ascetic style for the representation of suffering, who appear to believe that all literary styles betray victims, present us
with a paradox: such critics can apparently integrate victims of catastrophe
back into everyday life only once those victims have already mastered the
symptoms of suffering. Moreover, these critical efforts sometimes inadvertently expose facticity and constraint as a performance, with consequences
subversive of emotional mastery.

We should be wary of the claims made for the importance of a style which
is not one because the minimalism to which I refer often employs a mecha-
nism of displacement or repression similar to what Eric Santner has termed
"narrative fetishism."[30] In Santner's work, the expression refers to the ways
in which the narrative of an event (in his case the narrative that Germans
had been Hitler's victims) covers up or represses recognition of the real victims and contributes to an "inability to mourn" the traumatic loss one cannot
thereby acknowledge.[31] The narrative thus becomes a fetish; in his words:

> By narrative fetishism I mean the construction and deployment of a nar-
> rative consciously or unconsciously designed to expunge the traces of the
> trauma or loss that called the narrative into being in the first place...[it]
> is the way an inability to or refusal to mourn emplots traumatic events; it
> is a strategy of undoing, in fantasy, the need for mourning by simulating
> a condition of intactness, typically by situating the site and origin of loss
> elsewhere. Narrative fetishism releases one from the burden of having to re-
> constitute one's self-identity under 'posttraumatic' conditions; in narrative
> fetishism, the 'post' is indefinitely postponed.[32]

In Santner's example, the Germans cannot recognize what they have done
in Hitler's name because they believe they are his victims: they cannot engage in the work of mourning necessary to alleviate symptoms that will
continue to appear when they are confronted with questions about the past.
For Santner, those narratives in which the suffering of Germans and Jews

---

30. Eric Santner, "History beyond the Pleasure Principle: Some Thoughts on the Representation of Trauma," in *Probing the Limits of Representation: Nazism and the "Final Solution,"* ed. Saul
Friedlander (Cambridge: Harvard University Press, 1992), 143–54.

31. Santner refers to the famous argument by Alexander Mitscherlich and Margarete
Mitscherlich, *The Inability to Mourn: Principles of Collective Behavior,* trans. Beverly R. Placzek
(New York: Grove Press, 1975).

32. Santner, "History beyond the Pleasure Principle," 144.

is represented as equal represent this mode of fetishism. In reductive mini-malist style, as I will argue, traumatic loss is not denied or situated elsewhere, or not exactly: denial and displacement of the victims' own traumatic expe-riences instead take place in the form of recounting and acknowledging loss and suffering. The narratives postpone our recognition of what happened to victims not by our refusal to mourn, but through the ritual of listening to, and thereby recalling and mourning, their sufferings. If there is fetishism, it is the belief that the victims are intact and the related denial that what we hear and how we interpret it has a great deal to do with a culturally fash-ioned affective relationship to the state of being injured. This result is the opposite of that accomplished by self-consciously minimalist narratives that allow suffering to emerge in the guise of muting its impact, and thus to allow for empathic unsettlement. These narratives establish a relationship to the victim that neither denies suffering nor sacralizes it, but permits the difficult if unsettling acknowledgment of the pain of others.

In order to understand the interpretation of manifest rather than mas-tered suffering as a form of rhetorical and psychological excess (and thus of injury proclaimed as excessive), I focus on how specific texts mirror this conceptual framework, and with what consequences. Of course, there is no way of encompassing all the literature devoted to witness testimony and Holocaust representation. But I hope that by drawing a thread through vastly different approaches, I may illuminate the reductive version of the minimalist imperative. The first set of texts are historical works by distin-guished authors Saul Friedländer and Jan T. Gross, both of whom self-consciously seek to disrupt the reader's expectations of rhetorical constraint by (counterintuitively) hewing closely to the established methods of histo-riography. I will then move to the conundrums that emerge in the work of Lawrence L. Langer and Berel Lang, authors of two of the most eminent but problematic literary critical and philosophical arguments about Ho-locaust testimony and representation who, for all their differences, have much in common. In so doing I hope to address a broader discourse that seeks to ensure the legitimacy of the victim's story by presuming the de-monstrable if precarious moral coherence of the world through the logic of cause and effect, but fails in various ways.

I don't wish to rehearse arguments that pit neo-positivist and post-positivist analytic philosophers against poststructuralists and their post-poststructuralist variants in Holocaust representation, and have no interest

in demonstrating that trauma is commensurate with epistemological ruptures because it exceeds empirical frameworks and contextualization.
Rather, I wish to demonstrate how those texts that emphasize the mastery
of aesthetic and psychic disruption (even when, in Langer's case, appearing
to fetishize disruption) cannot ultimately illuminate the traumatic experiences they elaborate, even as they fashion the pain of others. Conversely,
I wish to show how historical work that seeks to disrupt readers' comfort
tends to restore it in the very style it uses to challenge readers' expectations.
The exception to this rule, Gross's work, proves the potentially subversive power of minimalist narrative in spite of the limitations imposed on
the author by the evidentiary conventions of academic historiography to
which he is fully committed.

Dominick LaCapra has already demonstrated how certain kinds of
minimalist narratives are forms of "excessive objectification." He refers explicitly to the work of Raul Hilberg, whose minimalist chronicling of and
focus on perpetrators' decisions and acts have been conceived to objectify
victims who remain passively in the background, rendering their suffering
abstract and difficult to identify with. Thus, as both LaCapra and Friedländer have argued, a certain form of minimalist chronicling may represent a
self-protective deflection: that is, it may render Jewish victims overly passive and responsible in some sense for their own fate, and allow historians
to take distance from their subject, which might otherwise be difficult to
write about. But these insights remain marginal to mainstream historiographical or philosophical reflection on Holocaust representation, which
is divided between highly specialized and highly accessible scholarship of
various sorts (psychological, historical, literary theoretical, philosophical).[33]

The historian Christopher Browning once said that only an extremely
arrogant historian would try to explain experiences which historiographical
conventions render inexplicable.[34] He argued that because historians could

33. LaCapra, "Holocaust Testimonies," 218–19; Saul Friedlander, *Memory, History, and the Extermination of the Jews of Europe* (Bloomington: Indiana University Press, 1993), 130–31. Even Berel Lang offers some commentary in this vein in his *Holocaust Representation: Art within the Limits of History and Ethics* (Baltimore: Johns Hopkins University Press, 2000), 40. I might note that in invoking minimalism, we are already challenging the realism preferred by historians because of its ability to create the illusion of reference. Historians do not interrogate how the 'fact' is situated rhetorically as such.

34. Christopher Browning, *Ordinary Men: Reserve Police Battalion 101 and the Final Solution in Poland* (New York: Harper Perennial, 1992), 188 ("The behavior of any human being is, of course,

not possibly have anything in common "experientially" with the victims, they can only unearth the evidence that they have and seek to interpret it, well aware of their limits.[35] These assumptions, tempered by a commitment to diminishing the necessary subjectivity of memoirs, find their way ambivalently into Yitzahk Arad's preface to the recently published testimony of a Lithuanian bystander to mass shootings, Kazimierz Sakowicz. Arad says that Sakowicz's minimalist chronicle of the slaughter of Jews suggests that his "diary offers 'objective' testimony from a bystander rather than from a victim, devoid of any emotional agenda that might call its credibility into question, and places it among the most important of the Holocaust testimonies."[36] This odd assertion suggests at once that objectivity is a dubious term (hence the quotation marks) and that the bystander can be 'more objective' than the victim because he has no emotional agenda that might distort the credibility of the account. Objectivity is guaranteed ambivalently by the absence of an emotional agenda, implying not that emotion is inappropriate, but that it must be controlled. And yet we might also ask why the difference between a victim and bystander—one a target of and the other a primary witness to persecution—translates into presumptions about emotional constraint which may or may not correspond to the victim's or bystander's reactions to the event. How does this difference capture the paradox of the eyewitness who sees most clearly and yet whose memory is most potentially compromised by what he or she has seen?

Victims' Voices

Two recent, touted, and compelling works of historiography—the two volumes of Saul Friedländer's magisterial study of the destruction of

a very complex phenomenon, and the historian who attempts to 'explain' it is indulging in a certain arrogance"). For a classic example of how historiographical convention defines standards of veracity in the context of testimonies, see Jean Norton Cru, *War Books: A Study in Historical Criticism,* trans. Stanley J. Pincetl Jr. (San Diego: San Diego State University Press, 1988 [1929]). Anne-Louise Shapiro brought this work to my attention. See also Leonard V. Smith, *The Embattled Self: French Soldiers' Testimony of the Great War* (Ithaca: Cornell University Press, 2007).

35. Christopher Browning, "German Memory, Judicial Interrogation, Historical Reconstruction," in *Probing the Limits,* ed. Friedlander, 27.

36. Kazimierz Sackowicz, *Ponary Diary, 1941–1943: A Bystander's Account of Murder,* ed. Yitzahk Arad, trans. Rachel Margolis (New Haven: Yale University Press, 2005), xvi.

European Jewry, *Nazi Germany and the Jews,* and Jan T. Gross's book about Polish pogroms against Jews after the Second World War, *Fear*—offer underconceptualized and yet deceptively simple narratives that repudiate the suspension of disbelief.[37] Their analyses are nonetheless wedded to the very assumptions they question. Both volumes of Friedländer's study have been feted by historians and critics alike. He was one of the first historians who sought to speak of Germans and Jews simultaneously, when the history of the Nazi extermination and the history of the Jewish experience had been written about separately, as if the Jewish experience was a peripheral chapter in the history of Hitler's war. And his narrative is masterful, interweaving individual experience, high politics, and the social history of the Jewish genocide in a vast array of nations.

One might argue that Friedländer has engaged theoretical questions, but he does not generally address these in his history writing.[38] The first volume of *Nazi Germany and the Jews* does suggest an effort, however, to approach his subject differently than have most historians of the period. The conceptual heart of the first volume, which focuses solely on Nazi Germany and the Jews, is a chapter entitled "Redemptive Anti-Semitism."[39] In an otherwise synthetic and minimalist narrative that moves forward chronologically but also weaves together various thematic concerns, this chapter sits uneasily in the middle of the volume, somewhat interrupting the narrative flow. It seeks to conceptualize outside any conventional narrative framework the peculiarity of Nazi anti-Semitism, which Friedländer defines as a sacralized if secular struggle against the Jews. He argues that under Nazism fears of racial degeneration were yoked to a belief in the redemption of Germany through the cleansing of Jews. The long legacy of Christian anti-Semitism sustained certain ideas about Jews, and the development of an explicitly racialized discourse about Jews and others in the nineteenth century folded into a sacred struggle that motivated men

---

37. Saul Friedländer, *Nazi Germany and the Jews,* vol. 1: *The Years of Persecution, 1933–1939* (New York: HarperCollins, 1997); and *Nazi Germany and the Jews 1939–1945,* vol. 2: *The Years of Extermination:* (New York: HarperCollins, 2007); and Jan T. Gross, *Fear: Anti-Semitism in Poland after Auschwitz; An Essay in Historical Interpretation* (New York: Random House, 2006).

38. See Friedländer's essays in *Memory, History, and the Extermination,* which engage trauma theory, psychoanalysis, and the work of Caruth and LaCapra, among others, none of which is ever mentioned or footnoted in his mainstream historical work.

39. Friedländer, *Nazi Germany and the Jews,* vol. 1, 73–112.

who engaged in the barbaric massacres and eventually industrialized annihilation of other human beings. Some scholars could conceive this section
as underconceptualized because Friedländer does not engage theoretical
debates about "secular religion" in the modern age (that is, whether or
not Nazism is continuous with Christian narratives rendered immanent
in the secular writing about the unfolding of human history).[40] Moreover,
this chapter is not integrated into the rest of the book primarily because it
isolates an argument about causality (why did Nazi anti-Semitism take the
form that it did?) that manifests itself in the narrative as the significance of
anti-Semitic ideology in Nazism.

Still, Friedländer seeks to explain what motivated the Nazis in terms
that most historians do not engage other than by conventional recourse to
fanaticism or "secular religion" understood in terms of Nazism's resem-
blance to religious ritual and other recognizable causes of prejudice or hatred: they do not tend to reference theoretical questions about religion and
modernity and thus the role of sacrifice and redemption in secular societies. Friedländer's point, of course, is that the Nazi clichés about Jews were
recognizable, but that the depth of the Nazis' hatred and of their desire to
annihilate Jewry everywhere on earth remains inconceivable without further conceptual elaboration. That is, however, the extent of his argument.
Though some historians comment on this chapter, which he clearly means
to frame the narrative, the majority have mostly glossed it.[41]

Alon Confino attributes this tension between causal explanation exemplified by the isolation of this chapter (among other factors) and the
narrative description that informs the rest of the book partially to the inevitable weakening of causal relations by a narrative form that emphasizes
descriptive power.[42] But most historians would readily admit that causality
is extremely difficult to prove except by the sheer weight of empirical evidence, and they often substitute contingency for causal explanation in the

40. See, most famously, Karl Löwith, *Meaning in History: The Theological Implications of the
Philosophy of History* (Chicago: University of Chicago Press, 1949); and Hans Blumenberg's criticism of secular religion in *The Legitimacy of the Modern Age* (Cambridge: MIT Press, 1983).

41. See, for example, the reviews of *The Years of Extermination* by Richard Evans, "Whose
Orders?" *New York Times,* June 24, 2007, and by Donald L. Niewyk in the *American Historical
Review* 103 (1998): 918.

42. Alon Confino, "Narrative Form and Historical Sensation," *History and Theory* 48
(2009): 199–219.

sense that the very unpredictability of what has happened or will happen always evokes a cause that may not be easily identifiable. Thus narrative history often supplies arguments about causality in the form of description, and I suspect that the infelicitous placement of a central causal argument in the first volume has little to do with the difficulty of integrating causal explanation into descriptive narrative, or, as Wulf Kansteiner argues, with an effort to disrupt historical convention.[43]

In spite of Friedländer's efforts and more in accord with critics like Confino rather than Kansteiner, most historians see little challenge to mainstream historical method in Friedländer's work, and at least one, the prominent historian Richard Evans, attributes its apparent divergence from other histories to its literary qualities. By literature Evans means the "skilled interweaving of individual testimony with the broader description of events" (but not the "unreliable testimony of memoirs"), which makes the book, as Evans views it, read like a novel. Evans means that the book has lots of subplots, unfolds dramatically, and holds one enthralled. It is hard to understand how Evans and others could miss some of the real challenges that Friedländer's work represents against Friedländer's own claims, which Evans does not discuss in any depth. I want to explore how the whole of Friedländer's study, however innovative, finally remains within the boundaries of historiographical and ideological convention, so that many historians do not recognize his effort to offer an alternative model of writing the history of Nazi Germany and the Jews.[44]

The second volume of Friedländer's study, which concerns all of Europe and the extermination of the Jews, more explicitly challenges mainstream historiography by refusing to suspend disbelief and thereby domesticate all the discomfort generated by victims' voices and the suffering they endured. Here Friedländer insists on the historian's loss of mastery at the heart of

43. In a rather unusual essay, Wulf Kansteiner transforms Friedländer's masterful synthesis into a nearly sublime postmodern work of crafted fragmentation, as if the book subverted narrative totality at every level. Kansteiner, "Success, Truth, and Modernism in Holocaust Historiography," *History and Theory* 47 (2009): 25–53. He claims that Friedländer's success among the very audience who most oppose this sort of experimental work can be attributed to the fact that both "*The Years of Extermination* and contemporary non-fiction TV aesthetics try to engage their audiences emotionally; the readers and viewers are invited to feel their way into the past and get a sense of how the events were experienced by people directly involved in them" (36). It is not clear how inviting viewers to feel their way into the past is disruptive of historiographical convention.

44. Evans, "Whose Orders?"

the most ambitious synthesis of the history of the destruction of modern European Jewry since Raul Hilberg's seemingly exhaustive work, which focused primarily on German perpetrators and the killing apparatus. He says that he will refuse to suspend belief and will tell the reader the story as it was, shorn of the redemptive story-lines that comfort (he refuses, he says, to "domesticate disbelief," to "explain it away").[45] He seeks to accomplish this goal by filling his work with the wrenching voices of victims seldom heard and here simply quoted, not interpreted or given meaning except as a form of unfiltered truth capable of disrupting historical narratives by exposing their objectivity as a mode of enforced detachment: the voices reveal what the narrative represses, which is everything it cannot wrap up neatly, at least in reference to mass extermination and mass suffering. As Friedländer puts it, "By its very nature, by dint of its humanness and freedom, an individual voice suddenly arising in the course of an ordinary historical narrative of events such as those presented here can tear through seamless interpretation and pierce the (mostly involuntary) smugness of scholarly detachment and 'objectivity.'"[46]

Throughout his well-ordered, highly readable, and richly documented narrative, Friedländer mimics narrative mastery, but his account is a mimetic adaptation that allegedly disrupts the reader's comfort and expectations by way of a seemingly subversive emphasis on victims' and perpetrators' voices that are not used as props for the larger argument. Both volumes recount hard things straightforwardly and in a spare and constrained narrative which emphasizes the "chilling normality"[47] of the words spoken by Jews, but also by non-Jews themselves about the inferiority or eventual murder of Jews. Thus a thirteen-year-old Polish boy in the occupied Eastern territories wrote a letter to a district commissar requesting the accordion of a Jewish boy he knew so that he could earn some money. Here Friedländer provides a striking example of how even the very young understood, in his words, that "no law, no rule, no measure protected a Jew."[48] All such voices are interspersed with detailed discussions of debates between high Nazi officials about the progress of the war as well

45. Friedländer, *Nazi Germany and the Jews,* vol. 2, xxvi.
46. Friedländer, *Nazi Germany and the Jews,* vol. 2, xxvi.
47. The phrase is Friedländer's, from *Nazi Germany and the Jews,* vol. 1, 5.
48. Friedländer, *Nazi Germany and the Jews,* vol. 2, 224–25.

as descriptions of the increasingly bleak situation in which European Jews of various nationalities found themselves. It is thus difficult to distinguish between narrative mastery and the refusal to suspend disbelief: how does the insistence on the reader's discomfort through the introduction of ostensibly dissonant voices both create a masterful narrative that satisfies the reader's demand for clear and objective synthesis and deny readers that very satisfaction?

Confino suggests that the book fails here because synthetic narrative domesticates the very strangeness that the introduction of the victims' voices in particular is supposed to generate.[49] But he claims nonetheless that Friedländer's narrative succeeds if we understand its aim in terms of "historical sensation" (a term coined by the historian Johan Huizinga in 1919): as the tension between causality and description undermines Friedländer's efforts to provide a satisfactory explanation of events, "historical sensation" cannot be gathered up into grand narrative and belongs instead to description of the sort that is impressionistic and can be integrated into historical narrative only by way of fragments. For Confino, Friedländer fails to recognize that sensation and "thorough historical study" involving explanation or causality are "united, comprising together historical understanding,"[50] but nonetheless shows us that they are. Confino's critique, though penetrating, still begs the question of why, if "sensation" and "causality" are united, these two levels of analysis and expression still cannot be reconciled, what it would mean to do so, and how Friedländer succeeds in doing so almost in spite of himself.

As I've noted, narrative description is hardly incompatible with argument and interpretation and indeed the historian's artistry was (and often still is) judged by his or her ability to make an argument while disguising all the untidy scholarly scaffolding necessary to making it (footnotes, the clear outline of a conceptual design, and so forth). The idea that Friedländer lets the victims'

49. As Confino puts it, "The explanation of the Holocaust as driven primarily by redemptive anti-Semitism is significant for Holocaust historiography, but in itself, I would like to argue it cannot be determinant to the making of a narrative that comingles familiarization and strangeness. There is a built-in tension between the success of this interpretation in convincing the reader and Friedländer's wish to maintain a sense of disbelief. The more convincing answer to the question 'What caused it?,' the greater the domestication of disbelief." Confino, "Narrative Form and Historical Sensation," 202.

50. Confino, "Narrative Form and Historical Sensation," 219.

voices speak for themselves is coupled with the ideological claim that they represent "freedom" and "humanness," a claim presented as self-evident (perhaps because these voices emerge in the context of an ideologically driven desire to destroy the humanity of Jews). Friedländer does not appear to consider arguments about the device of direct quotation in works of history since the ancient Greeks and, more recently, about how the "voice" is now commonly used to create or even to call attention to the fact that history writing has for a long time been not simply the experience of what originally happened, but a commentary on the difficulty of capturing unfiltered historical content. Friedländer's voices are not unfiltered in the narrative: they do not "suddenly arise," as he claims, after all, but are brilliantly integrated by the historian into the text, and they are ideologically laden. They are frail and heroic.

So what is Friedländer trying to accomplish? What does his emphasis on voices in this narrative achieve methodologically if their use is a fairly conventional technique, if the whole enterprise "aids historical understanding" so that we can feel the experience of the victims on our skin? What is subversive about voices rendered as righteous exemplars of real humanity in dark times? Why would Friedländer claim that he seeks to undermine mastery by invoking these voices that represent the triumph, in all of their frailty, of good over evil (the more tragic because they are snuffed out)? The voices are meant to exemplify a refusal to domesticate disbelief and throw the smug narrative off kilter by confronting the reader with the strangeness and opacity of horror, but they are also exemplary of pure humanness and freedom that that pierces through opacity.

Amos Goldberg has argued that the integration of victims' voices into the story does not accomplish the aim of forcing readers to hear the victims' side of the story, but is consistent with a popular, melodramatic style in which the identification with individual victims' voices provides "pleasurable suffering."[51] That is, the attempt to challenge the perpetrators' effort to normalize killing with the voices of victims only serves the current hyperbole around the Jewish narrative of genocide. The chilling normality that Friedländer seeks to re-create by punctuating the narrative with victims' voices transforms victims' suffering into melodrama

---

51. This argument is oddly consistent with, if more dramatic than Wulf Kansteiner's defense of Friedländer's ability, like "non-fiction TV aesthetics," to "engage [his] audiences emotionally." Kansteiner, "Success, Truth, and Modernism," 36.

because victims "can no longer be guardians of disbelief": in the "era of the witness" individual victims merely embody a banalized "public history" that transforms their suffering into a spectacle for popular consumption.[52] Goldberg also reiterates the trope of excess as an expression of the surfeit of Holocaust memory. In so doing, he does not refer to victims' suffering as exceeding the narrative that seeks to capture it, which is how Friedländer interprets the disruptive impact of victims' voices. He does help us to understand why Friedländer's underconceptualized use of minimalism fails to suspend disbelief or at least is consistent with the redemptive qualities of narrative synthesis (and thus with the restoration of order and comfort provided by melodrama). But the real 'excess' in Friedländer is not melodramatic, for I would contend that whatever 'excessive' role Friedländer wants these voices to play, the latter are absolutely intrinsic to the narrative and prove to be its emotional and ideological core. They may evoke suffering, but not the "pleasurable suffering" of melodrama. Instead, the voices represent a familiar story of humanity silenced but profoundly human— fearful, courageous, blind, ironic, and inventive—in adversity.

As Goldberg suggests, Friedländer rejects the heroism or idealization of victims common to the Israeli school of historiography that mostly told stories of Jewish collective resistance and heroism.[53] But he does not reject heroism altogether: he redefines it admirably as implicit in the powerlessness of voices struggling to understand what is happening to them, sometimes broken, sometimes frail, and mostly uncomprehending even as they grasp the truth that unfolds around them. Friedländer embraces victims' frailty. Indeed, perhaps it is this embrace that is subversive: at a moment when Jewish victims have been declared the object of too much memory and are still most appreciated when they appear as tragic heroes who fought back, Friedländer ennobles them all, and elevates the most naïve and unsuspecting. This gesture is admirable, not experimental, and it falls well within a discourse of humanity triumphal and an ideology of secular humanism that mobilizes the narrative. It is so familiar and ultimately

---

52. Amos Goldberg, "The Victim's Voice and Melodramatic Aesthetics in History," *History and Theory* 48 (2009): 220–37 (esp. 229–32). For more discussion of Friedländer's volume 1, see Dan Stone, *Constructing the Holocaust: A Study in Historiography* (London: Vallentine Mitchell, 2003), 164.

53. Goldberg, "The Victim's Voice," 224–26.

redemptive that it domesticates the disorientation the voices are meant to introduce.[54]

In the end, the pure mastery of synthesis sublimates the *normality* of prejudice so effectively highlighted by minimalist style. That synthesis emphasizes "historical sensation" over the uncanny, and domesticates 'excess.' Friedländer's narrative wants it (too) many ways: it wants victims' voices to remain uncanny but nonetheless integrates them into a narrative of human misery and hatred both historically specific and seemingly timeless; it wants the event we call the Holocaust to remain opaque and explicable at once. These may be his goals, but Friedländer seeks to achieve them not by challenging mainstream convention, but by insisting on the triumph of secular humanism at the heart of darkness. The grand narrative's refusal to suspend disbelief does so only by drawing us into the story, which generates discomfort and also makes us want to be better human beings. Christopher Browning identifies the tension between the argument's "evocative" and "analytical" dimensions and claims that a "single conceptual framework"— the crisis of liberalism—finally reconciles them and allows for narrative synthesis.[55] Whether or not we find his argument persuasive, Browning is surely right that synthetic mastery overcomes fragmentation. This narrative is a tale of human hatred and its consequences in a form sufficiently familiar and moving to be awarded a Pulitzer Prize.

In *Fear: Anti-Semitism in Poland after Auschwitz; An Essay in Historical Interpretation,* Gross cements his reputation not only as a great historian but also as a bête noire of Polish history. He has used his considerable detective skills to demonstrate, for example, in his controversial book *Neighbors,* that Poles in the town of Jedwabne murdered their Jewish neighbors without Nazi provocation in 1941. His work forced the Polish government to acknowledge that Poles had indeed killed Jews, dispensing with the half-century-old fiction that Poles were exclusively victims of the Nazis and

---

54. For a discussion of Friedländer as having introduced a new style in mainstream Holocaust historiography, which previously ignored the voices of victims, see Florent Brayard, "La longue fréquentation des morts: À propos de Browning, Kershaw, Friedländer—et Hilberg," *Annales HSS* 5 (2009): 1082–84. Brayard conceives Friedländer's innovation not as theoretical but as stylistic, a change necessitated by the introduction of victims' voices.

55. Christopher Browning, "Evocation, Analysis, and the 'Crisis of Liberalism,'" *History and Theory* 48 (2009): 246.

either protected Jews at considerable cost to themselves, treated them neu-
trally, or tragically, in a small minority of cases, profited from their fate.[56]
As he did in *Neighbors,* in *Fear* Gross tells a story of Poles murdering Jews,
but this time after the war, rendering the now familiar story even stranger:
why, he asks, would it be shameful for Poles to have sheltered Jews, as he
discovered from accounts of Poles who begged their Jewish friends not to
reveal who had saved them? He demonstrates that many Poles helped the
Nazis find Jews and, during and after the war, also looted or confiscated
their property, stole their belongings, and engaged in pogroms against
them, most infamously the massacre in Kielce in 1946, instigated perhaps
not inconceivably by a claim of blood libel.[57]

As he did in *Neighbors,* Gross dispenses easily with the old shibboleth
about Jews' infatuation with Communism and thus their communion
with the Russian troops (who proved to be the instrument of the Soviet
oppression of Poland) to explain Polish peasants' rage against them. He
analyzes data that demonstrate how few Jews were Communists, though
most of those still alive in 1945 undoubtedly welcomed the Soviets into
Poland as liberators. He also provides forceful empirical accounts of the
Kielce pogrom, about which much has already been written. Gross adds a
considerable level of soul-shattering detail regarding the brutality of many
Poles' treatment of Jews in a variety of anti-Semitic incidents, on trains and
in towns. He thus brings into sharp relief not only Polish anti-Semitism,
but also an apparently common indifference to Jewish suffering and a selective focus on Polish martyrdom after the war, even though murdered
Jews constituted some ten percent of Poland's prewar population. As other
historians have shown, in postwar Western Europe and more forcefully
in Eastern Europe, nation-states occupied by or complicit with the Nazis
conceived their populations rhetorically as "victims of fascism" with little
to no recognition of the particularity of Jewish suffering. Gross's books
are not simply accounts of what happened but confront the protective and
powerful self-image of Poles as "heroes and victims."[58]

56. Jan T. Gross, *Neighbors: The Destruction of the Jewish Community in Jedwabne, Poland*
(Princeton: Princeton University Press, 2001).

57. Gross, *Fear,* ix–xv.

58. Anthony Polonsky and Joanna B. Michlic, eds., *The Neighbors Respond: The Controversy
over the Jedwabne Massacre in Poland* (Princeton: Princeton University Press, 2004), 1–43; Pieter LaGrou, *The Legacy of Nazi Occupation: Patriotic Memory and National Recovery in Western*

Gross insists that he has told the tale of why Poles murdered Jews in empirically unassailable fashion. He claims to have proven that Poles killed Jews because they felt so guilty about having expropriated them that they wanted all reminders of their conduct (that is to say, the few surviving Jews who triggered their memories) expunged. The author insists that his book is nothing but an assemblage of documents that speak for themselves and should, he says, force "readers from time to time [to experience] a sense of discomfort."[59] And yet his brilliant narrative, a chronicle of events and thus the most minimalist of all styles of history writing, is a shattering, brutal assault on any attempt to deny what happened rather than a cool-headed, sober, and constrained account of things—a tone that, since *Neighbors,* has evoked a variety of comments. At least two scholars who discuss *Neighbors* argue that Gross's "hyper-empiricist strategy" and "moral outrage" undercut a serious effort to interpret why Poles did what they did, and in their view compromise his work, but also make it interesting.[60] A few critics have taken note of Gross's tone quietly, as when David Engel tells us that Gross "recoiled" before the "magnitude of the shock" as he discovered the facts.[61]

At the same time, other than some references to his emotional style (which some also credit with helping to bring his work to a popular audience), most historians indicate that *Neighbors* and *Fear* are exemplary of good history writing, although Gross's tone goes against the grain of historiographical convention. In Polish, *Fear* is even angrier, sparing nothing by using terms about Jews so violent (though actually spoken by postwar Poles) that the reader is shaken. In Polish, moreover, it is shorn of the first chapter in the English edition, a prefatory essay about the history of Poland

Europe, 1945–1965 (Cambridge: Cambridge University Press, 2000); István Déak, Jan T. Gross, and Tony Judt, eds., *The Politics of Retribution in Europe: World War II and Its Aftermath* (Princeton: Princeton University Press, 2000).

59. Gross, *Fear,* xiii.

60. Janine Holc, "Working through Jan Gross's *Neighbors,*" *Slavic Review* 61 (2002): 453–59; William W. Hagen, "A 'Potent, Devilish Mixture' of Motives: Explanatory Strategy and Assignment of Meaning in Jan Gross's *Neighbors,*" *Slavic Review* 61 (2002): 466–75. Gross was asked to respond to these and several other essays, but chose to reply only to one commentary that took issue with his treatment of sources. Most unfortunately, he offered no comment on the far more interesting discussions of his method.

61. David Engel, "Introduction to the Hebrew Edition of *Neighbors,*" in Polonsky and Michlic, *The Neighbors Respond,* 408.

meant to contextualize the events recounted for general and potentially ignorant English-language readers. The English edition thus begins the story in a more familiar, judicious fashion that helps contain the events that follow within a more conventional historiographical framework.[62] At the same time, one reviewer notes that the opening chapter is insufficient because it fails to put the Polish pogroms in context and focuses on "dry" high politics, leading to a general criticism that Gross's last two books are "underdeveloped" analytically, which is really a way of saying that they are emotionally rendered facts that have not been subjected to the sober work of objective interpretation.[63]

It is not clear why Gross believes that he has proved that Poles felt guilty about having Jewish quilts on their beds and blood on their hands, and thus not clear why this guilt might have compelled Poles to kill those Jews who remained in their midst. He documents only that Poles expropriated Jews, benefited from the spoils, and then killed them (it is perhaps this argument about guilt to which he refers by subtitling his book an "essay in historical interpretation"). Most interesting, Gross cannot tell this story using the conventions of mainstream historiography, and even his explanation of why Poles killed Jews has no foundation in empirically verifiable experience but can exist only as speculation. This, we must assume, is why critics accuse him of having failed to offer a real causal explanation of Polish violence toward Jews.

Gross, like Friedländer, chronicles events matter-of-factly, as when he uses the words spoken by Polish officials or ordinary Poles, and he too lets voices speak without making any special claims about them. But his chronicle narrows the events it recounts so hyperbolically that the abundance of detail sheds light on what happened even as it alerts readers to the difficulty of deciphering what they witness and forces them out of the role of distant observers: Gross mimics the very opacity that the murder of neighbors by neighbors continues to generate for those who seek to comprehend it in social-scientific terms. His work illuminates the power of minimalist style he believes is nothing more than standard history writing, or in his critics' terms, "hyper-empiricism." Perhaps we should not

---

62. I thank Luiza Nader of the University of Warsaw for calling my attention to these differences between the Polish and English editions and for help in deciphering them.

63. Padraic Kenney's review of Gross's book *Fear* in *Slavic Review* 66 (2007): 108–10.

be surprised that Janine Holc, speaking of *Neighbors,* believes that Gross fails to offer causal explanation (she calls his work "undisciplined" and "un-disciplinary") but then argues that his refusal to connect analytically the individual decision-making of individual Poles who murdered Jews and the collective/ethnic identity that might explain their motives except in fragmentary fashion signals "resistance to, and even prevents, a definitive choice between them." She argues further that *Neighbors* may well be a text in which a historian "works through" an event rather than simply "represent[s] it."[64] I would argue that both *Neighbors* and *Fear* are far more adequate at conveying opacity than at working through readers' relation with traumatic violence. At the same time, Holc's effort to interpret the book's so-called hyper-empiricism as doing something different that cannot be easily named or reduced to sensationalism (or "historical sensation") indicates the real complexity of Gross's undertaking and the inadequacy of hyper-empiricism to account for his accomplishment.

Unlike Friedländer's narrative, however, Gross's documentation of unpleasant truths has been deemed insufficiently objective, too empathic, and too polemical—that is to say, unconstrained, deeply identified with its subjects, and not wary about taking the victim's side.[65] Because Gross ultimately gets the facts right, most of the debate has been about how his moral outrage may prevent him from interpreting his sources accurately and thus supplying a persuasive analytical as well as empirical account of why Poles killed Jews after the war. But from Gross's point of view, establishing what happened in and of itself seems to be sufficient not only to hold the perpetrators accountable but also to explain why they did what they did. This does not mean that his critics, who accuse him of not providing causal explanations, are wrong, but that Gross undermines a conventional construction of causality (as Holc intuits) because his work is not hyper-empiricist but a sophisticated form of minimalism, one which refuses kitsch and voyeurism by presenting horror matter-of-factly, generates empathic unsettlement by refusing to domesticate traumatic violence, and demonstrates that all the interpretation in the world may still take us into a blind alley in explaining extreme events unless we develop new ways of

64. Holc, "Working through Jan Gross's *Neighbors,*" 458.
65. See in particular the essays by Polish historians and witnesses in Polonsky and Michlic, *The Neighbors Respond.*

conceptualizing traumatic material. In short, the point is not that Gross ultimately leaves us unsettled but foggy about the meaning of events, but that
his work demonstrates the limitations of conventional approaches to the
disturbingly violent material. Though his foray into the controversial topic
of Polish-Jewish relations and the Polish national self-image surely makes
him a provocative figure, his work also suggests the radical potential of an
elegantly and strategically developed constraint.

Lawrence Langer and Inconsolable Laments

The critics on whom I focus know that toneless tone may be literary and
do not for the most part seek testimony uncontaminated by literary tropes,
though Berel Lang arguably moves far in this direction. Yet for Lawrence
Langer, one of the most prominent interpreters of Holocaust testimonies,
the task of literature is not to transform the real "in a way that obscures
it," but to represent things realistically with the clarity of a wounded, anti-
redemptive vision.[66] Langer has also written sensitively about literary and
pictorial representations of the Holocaust, which he believes have a crucial pedagogical and imaginative role in conveying the experience of that
trauma: he has even criticized Lang for his suspicion of imaginative literature.[67] At the same time, he has appropriately become the target of critics
who believe that he identifies with the inconsolable mourning putatively
characteristic of survivors.[68] Indeed, by fashioning himself an opponent of
any hint of redemption or meaning in discussions of the Holocaust, he
has singled out Todorov for scathing criticism, in particular his focus on
"understanding goodness." Langer notes that "polarities, of which Todorov is unduly fond, quickly disintegrate in the atmosphere of a place like

---

66. Lawrence L. Langer, *Holocaust Testimonies: The Ruins of Memory* (New Haven: Yale University Press, 1991), 19.

67. Lawrence L. Langer, *Using and Abusing the Holocaust* (Bloomington: Indiana University
Press, 2006), 131–33.

68. See, for example, Ruth Kluger quoted in Weissman, *Fantasies of Witnessing,* 118. I should
note that Kluger spells her name without the umlaut in all her English publications and uses it
when she writes in German. I follow her usage. Weissman too respects the English usage. Michael
Rothberg, *Traumatic Realism: The Demands of Holocaust Representation* (Minneapolis: University
of Minnesota Press, 2000), 124; Nader, *Traumatic Verses,* 39.

Auschwitz." In the end, he says, Todorov seeks fundamentally to reassure his readers, "and himself."[69]

In his acclaimed *Holocaust Testimonies,* Langer criticizes the historian Martin Gilbert's insistence that modes of Jewish survival (the "passive heroism of the common Jew") partook of "the grammar of heroism and martyrdom."[70] We must admire Langer's nuanced parsing of testimonies to reveal how little heroism in the conventional sense played a role in decision making or confronting enemies: he seeks to understand a constricted world in which dying with dignity might still be a goal, and in which ideas that victims were or should have been resilient must often be our own retrospective projection, born of our refusal to confront their real helplessness.[71] But in so doing, Langer also appears to destroy any trace of a normative dialogue in which an experience may be recounted and assimilated, and thus rather breathtakingly repudiates (in the name of the victims) any notion that victims might heal.[72] He rejects utterly the notion that testimony might offer the narrator an opportunity to remake himself performatively as he recounts his story and thus reduces testimony to the mere fact of memory rescued for posterity.

Most recently, the critic Gary Weissman has taken issue with the overidentification of Jews with Holocaust victims, and among his targets is Langer, whose real *"desire,"* as Weissman puts it, to "rendez-vous with hell"[73] has been largely neglected in favor of admiring Langer's now fairly standard criticism of redemptive discourses about the Holocaust: he criticizes the idea that Holocaust experience confers meaning, that survivors should be treated as sacred objects, and so forth. Weissman does an excellent job of demonstrating a bevy of Jewish intellectuals' real attachment to and overidentification with Holocaust suffering, and his work is thus

69. Lawrence L. Langer, *Preempting the Holocaust* (New Haven: Yale University Press, 1998), 5.

70. Langer, *Holocaust Testimonies,* 163.

71. Langer, *Using and Abusing the Holocaust,* xii.

72. Langer, *Preempting the Holocaust,* 69.

73. Weissman, *Fantasies of Witnessing,* 122. Weissman speaks not only of Langer but of others, such as Elie Wiesel and George Steiner, in this vein. Weissman's book is an important and thoughtful criticism of the culture of wounded attachments to the Holocaust, but does not address some of the problems underlying this discourse, namely its problematic rhetorical constitution of wounded victims and its tendency to equate proclamations of pain with the erosion of the grievance structure of democratic contestation.

part of the discourse 'against grandiloquence' we have evaluated thus far. What interests me, however, and has received little comment as far as I know, is how Langer's desire to rendez-vous with hell is inseparable from his belief that only self-constrained, educated listeners, and himself in particular, can convey the suffering that was the Holocaust. Weissman gets at this question of how to determine why only certain people are qualified to attest to the rendez-vous when he notes that Langer divides commentary on the Holocaust into a "good" side, which refuses to sweeten the horror, and a "bad" side, which does just that.[74] This assertion nonetheless begs the question of what conceptual grounds Langer uses to make these rather dramatic distinctions and why he does not believe himself to be implicated in the "bad" side.

Langer's insistence on inconsolable mourning requires a listener, a particular kind of interlocutor he calls a "hearer." *Holocaust Testimonies* thus invokes a "hearer" of testimony who is a rational and compassionate listener and, in this early text, a stand-in for the audience. The emotionally strained, sometimes quietly and modestly delivered and sometimes tragically relived testimonies are "living dead" voices that paradoxically *guarantee authenticity because they cannot be interpreted by the hearer,* who by definition lacks the frameworks within which to make their narratives meaningful. Langer's emphasis on authenticity thus draws a bold line between the hearer and his conventional world and the groundlessness of survivors' own—its incommunicability and incomprehensibility. The survivor represents the autonomous self thrown off kilter into a world with no spatiotemporal coordinates. Yet even as he insists that survivors' speech disables critical or evaluative judgment, Langer argues that it can be authenticated. In the *New York Times* he exults, "It has been exhilarating for me, the discovery that you can bring alive such a memory.... You take the inexpressible, the unimaginable, and you take a language and don't sentimentalize it, and you can describe what happened."[75] It is as if his antisentimental exhilaration is the guarantor of a truth that Langer has brought to life, his exhilaration at hearing the truth tempered by his refusal to "sweeten" it by giving into sentiment. Or, to put it differently, Langer's

---

74. Weissman, *Fantasies of Witnessing,* 124–25.
75. Langer quoted in Weissman, *Fantasies of Witnessing,* 124.

antisentimental exhilaration somehow guarantees the authenticity of the testimony.

The problematic nature of such claims becomes particularly apparent in his more recent work, in which he repudiates the public's interest in survivors and argues that their newly attained "status" has "mesmerize[d] critical consciousness and induces an awed public to accept whatever it hears."[76] Now, in keeping with generalized anxieties about the surfeit of memory about the Holocaust, the public's inability to evaluate what it hears leads to voyeurism, hyperbole, and the distortion of an essential truth that isn't really available, if we follow Langer's other views, in the first place. Langer therefore implies that testimonies must be subjected to some rigorous criteria by which their veracity is evaluated, but which are never clearly articulated. Does testimony heard unsentimentally make experiences knowable (if not graspable) because it refuses the interruptions of the aesthetic, of narrative pleasure, or even of the hearer's own preconceptions, let alone that of an audience hungry for melodrama? If so, does the self-constraint and refusal of sentimentality guarantee the boundary between voyeurism and truth? Does self-constraint account for why some "hearers" resist the "magnetic pull" of survivor narratives while others do not?[77] What is the difference between Langer's own "exhilaration" and the voyeurism of the public other than his self-identified antisentimentalism and self-constraint when confronted with the pain and suffering of others?

We still cannot know how to guarantee that Langer's response is not infused with the elation that presumably characterizes the massified response to survivor testimony. How to determine the difference? The blinding light of survivor testimony, the conviction of irredeemable and incomprehensible damage done to human beings is signified by the dissolution of the hearer's ability to grasp testimony. But the truth of the victim's experience cannot then be known through the critical thinking that dismantles conventions. Rather, it is guaranteed by an insistence on the hearer's constrained and self-conscious refusal of voyeurism, projection, and all other conversions of horror into kitsch and, in Langer's view, into meaning, which he believes is itself kitschified. In arguing thus, Langer, who has himself been accused of fetishizing survivors, simply brackets them off as part of a world we

---

76. Langer, *Using and Abusing,* 98.
77. Langer, *Using and Abusing,* xi.

cannot understand while demanding that we take their words seriously as an "essential truth." They are not, to repeat, witnesses to the impossibility of truth as such, but to a truth that he insists must somehow be knowable and yet can never be grasped or interpreted. Such representations of survivors are luminous by virtue of their incomprehensibility.

Though Langer avoids interpreting their testimonies as grounded in the sacred and transcendental qualities of sacrifice, he also removes them—we can't understand them, after all—from the human community and thus inevitably associates victims, as they had originally been, with the sacred.[78] In so doing, Langer creates a conundrum: if survivors' testimonies cannot be mapped onto anything graspable and their traumas defy all extant narratives, how might listening to such testimonies provide an affirmation of the witnesses' story as the history of atrocity that has happened and for which perpetrators are responsible? How does the testimony avoid the structure of aporia or sublimity? It turns out that he does have an answer, implied earlier, and most rigorously developed in *Using and Abusing the Holocaust,* where the problem is no longer how to listen but how to listen well. Now we learn, over and over, that the hearer is he or she who knows enough about the Holocaust to know when a testimony is truthful or not. Thus: "When eagerness to hear about the Holocaust is combined with a failure to learn enough about it in advance, audiences have trouble separating remembered from invented reality."[79]

Langer rejects notions that Bruno Dössekker alias Binjamin Wilkomirski may have actually confused his real and invented selves, calling him a confidence man and blaming his success on "how unprepared modern audiences remain to find a niche in consciousness for the horrific substance of such narratives. In the absence of such internal locales, fake stories like Wilkomirski's, awash in feeling, are able to flourish and gain a sympathetic ear."[80] It even appears that Holocaust survivors themselves have been unconsciously infiltrated by melodramas like *Schindler's List.* Langer refers to two Auschwitz survivors who confuse gas chambers and showers in the wake of the movie, when "for anyone who knows that the gas chambers

---

78. Langer would certainly not use the word "sacred" other than descriptively because of its implications, not least its association with sacrifice.

79. Langer, *Using and Abusing,* xiii.

80. Langer, *Using and Abusing,* 54–55.

contained no plumbing, and the real showers no gas," there should have been no mystery.[81] That the Nazis represented gas chambers as showers to victims, and that victims who went to real showers worried that they might be murdered, does not seem to matter. Langer assumes that because the women knew the truth, their testimony must reflect the movie, not that the movie might have brought back a fantasy of being safe in which they can no longer entirely trust. To be fair, Langer does tell us that it is still hard to separate "what we need to believe from what is true,"[82] and does not seek to solve the problem of discerning truth other than by reference to education and to the power of mass media over minds in our "culture of fakery"—a statement that recalls George Steiner's now dated insistence that behind Nazi barbarism was the particular vulnerability of the "semi-literate."[83] Authenticity can be guaranteed only by the listener's profound knowledge of the history of the Holocaust.

However inadequate, the many functions of self-constraint and thus emotional control (as guarantors of authenticity, as a counter to mass media distortion), this time on the part of the secondary witness, make them a useful tool in establishing a boundary between history and memory, veracity and distortion, fact and interpretation that even Langer knows is hard to draw and whose ambiguity has proven at times exhilarating to the critic whose insistence on the ever-inconsolable survivor is at times inseparable from his own luminous experience of the survivor's abjection. Still, Langer knows that the exhilaration afforded by "bringing alive" memories has to be distinguished from the despair of those who lived them. The relentless advocate of anti-redemptive narratives responds, when Edith P. asks if "there is such a thing as love," that it is "inadmissible" to offer a "negative rejoinder" to the question.[84] Here he moves from his own evocation of a world in which human beings were powerless, their experiences unassimilable, to an insistence on a resolutely human world in which odds might be overcome. What remains unclear is whether the exhilaration of bringing memories alive is part of that faith in the human world, or whether it

81. Langer, *Using and Abusing*, xiii.
82. Langer, *Using and Abusing*, 94.
83. Langer, *Using and Abusing*, 54–55, 98–99; George Steiner, "Pornography and Its Consequences," *Encounter* 36 (1966): 47.
84. Langer, *Holocaust Testimonies*, 68.

is tied rather darkly to a fetishization of survivors' own: he denies these ties by insisting on a human world from which they stand apart, and at the same time asserts them by feeling exhilarated when he brings their memories alive. Indeed, the boundary between the so-called mass media exploitation of survivors and the luminosity with which they are beheld by Langer is hard to sustain even as he insists that he can determine the difference by reference to his antisentimental self-control.

Berel Lang and the Always Explicable

In perhaps his most influential and important book, *Act and Idea in the Nazi Genocide,* the philosopher Berel Lang articulates his suspicion of the literary figure.[85] In order to have the force to destroy people, Nazi language, including the term the "final solution," he argues, is not euphemistic as others would have it, but must be understood literally as a linguistic expression that manifests the self-conscious camouflage of the truth. In this way, language provides a verifiable causal link between act and idea: if the lie is but a figure of speech, it lacks the direct reference implied by Frank Stella's distillation of minimalist art, "what you see is what you see." For Stella, the object's self-evidence and putative transparency evaporated boundaries between form and content and thus had no meaning outside of its own facticity. But this meant, of course, that the object was also not self-evidently about or anchored to anything (and thereby generates unsettlement), quite the opposite of Lang's claim that poetry, drama, fiction, and so on, are all inadequate forms of representation for the Holocaust precisely because they are not directly referential. This counterintuitive argument about the nakedly causal link between language (idea) and act (genocide)—if only because language rarely if ever means what it says and is subject to misreading—draws on Lang's conviction that the reason the Nazi genocide is mostly represented in memoirs and diaries is due to the need for documentary reference and the fact that such events in drama, for example, "could be sustained only obliquely or by understatement."[86]

85. Berel Lang, *Act and Idea in the Nazi Genocide* (Chicago: University of Chicago Press, 1990).
86. Lang, *Act and Idea,* 131.

Lang's questionable distinction between the literal and figural in this context, as if the historical content of the Holocaust (or of any historical moment) could ever be apprehended unmediated by language and interpretation, has been the object of much criticism by Hans Kellner and others, who have taken him to task for his rather extreme literalism.[87] Wulf Kansteiner has written that his arguments are a form of "hyper-realism that approaches tautology."[88] Lang has been remarkably stubborn about his own position, and even dismissive of some of his critics.[89] Though the criticism of him is sufficiently known, here I would like to examine his most recent book, in which he sustains and develops these convictions more elaborately by absorbing the Holocaust ever more profoundly into a discernable logic. Lang perhaps most dramatically represents the consequences of a refusal of the figurative and allegorical, even though his grasp of what such figures may contribute to our understanding is fuller than Langer's. But his suspicion of all figuration renders his recent work a particularly interesting measure of the impact of such thinking on the rhetorical construction of victims.

Lang argues that we should not confound the genocide of European Jewry with a great rupture in history and thus with unspeakable soul shattering, but must quietly interpret it in order to expand the category of the recognizable and thinkable. Our surprise at the Nazis' violation of humanist precepts during the Holocaust derives not (pace Langer) from the intrinsic incomprehensibility of Jewish suffering or Nazi crime, but from the Nazis' contravention of a resolutely human world of predictable and well-ordered expectations. According to Lang, Primo Levi's ability to draw universal principles from particular instances renders him a crucial figure in post-Holocaust literature because he moves away from a focus on horror, the uncanny, and the unthinkable to the recognizable.

---

87. Kellner, "'Never Again' Is Now," 127–44; Robert Braun, "The Holocaust and Problems of Historical Representation," *History and Theory* 33 (1994): 172–97. See also Hayden White's seeming embrace of Lang's (one might argue problematic) version of the intransitive, which he mistakes for an argument that form and content cannot be distinct, in "Historical Emplotment and the Problem of Truth," in *Probing the Limits,* ed. Friedlander, 37–53.

88. Wulf Kansteiner, "From Exception to Exemplum: The New Approach to Nazism and the 'Final Solution'," *History and Theory* 33 (1994): 149.

89. Lang, *Holocaust Representation,* 83–92. On p. 91, he accuses Kansteiner, Kellner, and Braun of a relativism pure and simple, an accusation that is far too reductive of their positions as stated.

In keeping with a preference for constraint in our psychological responses to dramatic events and a minimalist rhetoric commensurate with
that psychology, Lang argues that Levi demonstrates that we should "learn
how to be surprised without becoming [the] victim [of surprise]."[90] Thus
Lang suggests that victims might learn to cope with the unpredictable and
unsettling, and should not respond as victims—that is to say, hyperbolically
or disproportionately, as are those confronted with radically unpredictable
or inconceivable events. In short, he narrows the boundaries of human experience so dramatically that nothing ultimately cannot be controlled, and
no person rendered utterly powerless, at least psychically. In this context,
his refusal of figuration and his admiration of Levi's insistence on the ordinary and documentary seem to be less a conviction that facts are facts and
more evidence of some anxiety that any uncontrolled or uncontrollable
response leads to helplessness, marginality, and slaughter: figuration typically marks an absence of control over the forces that seduce, betray, and
conquer. That rhetorical figures play this seductive role is an old trope and
in particular reminiscent of fears about the illusion created by theatrical
performance manifest in Jean-Jacques Rousseau's famous condemnation
of the theater's artifice. That Lang, however, should advocate linguistic
and psychological transparency as the only acceptable representation of
powerlessness suggests an effort to purge genocide of what made it oper-
able: its opacity, its mobilization of affect and surprise, its cynical manipu-
lation of hope. Moreover, his is a particularly idealized version of Levi.

Similarly, Lang has argued elsewhere, the event we call the Holocaust
was generated cumulatively by the particular intentions of individual Germans, but it could not have happened had there not been a great purpose
linking and affirming all the various instances of decision making.[91] For
him, this purpose or intention must be explained within the context of

90. Berel Lang, *Post-Holocaust: Interpretation, Misinterpretation, and the Claims of History*
(Bloomington: Indiana University Press, 2005), 113.
91. Berel Lang, *The Future of the Holocaust: Between History and Memory* (Ithaca: Cornell
University Press, 1999), 74–85. The context for this discussion was the historiographical debate between the so-called functionalists and intentionalists: functionalists believe that the Holocaust was
a series of events that culminated in extermination and had little to do with anti-Semitic intentions
or ideology. Lang, in a now common posture, took the side of the functionalists while seeking to
remind them that they could not divorce cumulative instances of the unfolding of the extermination of European Jewry from an overall purpose within which they came to make sense.

"human choice and action," and not in terms of the "indeterminacy" of
those who believe the Holocaust to be unique.[92] Thus by stringing together
a series of improbable incidents in Auschwitz, Lang argues that Levi demonstrates how even the most shocking transgressions are embedded in the
general logic of life in the camps: that people transform human beings into
things ceases to be an ungraspable horror but something about which we
can think. Our aim should be to reflect on and learn from surprise as we
would in any other context. He writes:

> I would indeed wish to claim that the Holocaust is distinctive—so much, in
> fact, that one need not step outside history or the standard patterns of histor-
> ical, reflective, and social analysis to show this to be the case. The argument
> seems to me much weightier that through *standard* patterns and categories,
> one sees more of the individual character of the Holocaust, the deliberate ef-
> fort at genocide which distinguishes it, and, behind that, the underlying will
> to violate all moral norms, than one does by projecting the features of that
> event on an extra-historical space—the tendency encouraged by claims for
> it as unique or incomprehensible.[93]

Surely the effort to locate the Holocaust's distinctiveness in historical
rather than theological or mystical terms is important. But can what we
do not yet understand about the Holocaust—indeed, about any gratuitous
act of inhumanity—only ever be understood in such terms? Lang goes a
bit further: "the distinctiveness of the Holocaust becomes most visible not
through the lenses of extra-historical categories but in the material and
moral history of everyday causality and judgment."[94] He thus puts aside
the question of how the Holocaust is both historical (it is motivated by a
set of discernable perceptions and causes) and extra-historical (it cannot, at
least, not yet, be reduced to "standard patterns" of historical experience) in
favor of a conviction that all behavior, however unfamiliar, is explicable.
The extra-historical dimension of analysis, one in which experience derives from or coincides with but cannot be entirely reduced to normative
patterns of historical understanding, becomes not an object of inquiry but

92. Lang, *The Future of the Holocaust*, 87.
93. Lang, *Post-Holocaust*, 85.
94. Lang, *Post-Holocaust*, 85.

a conceptual obstacle to productive inquiry (a "projection" that distracts from the materiality of history).

In this way, Lang writes off discussions that emphasize the traumatic and the testimonial because, he argues, they tend to replicate the problem of 'excess' posed by the Holocaust: we may want to understand the Holocaust as a traumatic event, but we should be forced to account for the event as traumatic rather than presuming tautologically that its enormity and sheer excess are proof of its authentically traumatic nature. Thus from Lang's point of view, many intellectuals and others claimed that Binjamin Wilkomirski's fraudulent autobiography of a child Holocaust survivor, *Fragments,* was authentic simply because its author had been able to imagine it.

Unlike Lawrence Langer, then, Berel Lang does not posit that Holocaust experience remains unmapped, and he refuses all recourse to an excess whose parameters remain mysterious (though he uses the term "surfeit" of memory because he envisions a moment in which the excess will be absorbed into the unfolding narrative of Holocaust history or discarded as pathological and obsessive). He does, however, similarly beg the question of how we constitute "standard patterns" of rationality. He is not simply insistent on realism at all costs, but on realism so mimetic and psychologically reductive that it can only be manifest as a persistent advocacy of an ascetic imperative. He presumes that "extremes" are always intensified versions of things otherwise recognizable (so that the extermination of Jews as it appears in some accounts that prioritize ideological anti-Semitism simply refers to "antisemitism pushed to an extreme"), and argues that we cannot understand the "final solution" if we do not understand the "larger conceptual and causal pattern" that made it thinkable.[95] Gaps in our knowledge do not result from the nature of the Holocaust qua event, but from an incompletion or inconclusiveness of understanding "that is as

---

95. Lang, *Post-Holocaust,* 4. Of course, these larger patterns cannot answer the difficult question that has so long confronted historians: how did Nazi policy shift from the exclusion and segregation of Jews to exterminating them? Larger conceptual and causal patterns can be discerned in numerous books about modernity which emphasize that sterilization, racial prejudice, eugenics, and anti-Semitism were trends hardly limited to Nazi Germany. But the transition from the medical model of the social body that informed eugenic and racist practices to outright extermination of particular populations requires that we focus not only on the larger conceptual patterns but also on the specificity of Nazi policy toward Roma and Jews.

much due to the general relation between historical events and their explanations as it is to the character of the particular event of the Holocaust."[96]
Here too a phantasmatically logical pattern uses the contingency of all historical knowledge to explain what it cannot yet account for rather than
as evidence of what we do not know. Like Langer's "hearer," this logical
pattern stands in for the boundary between memory and truth.

If Langer's "hearer" lives in a world limited to rational patterns and
is blinded by survivor testimony, Lang's historian-philosopher resolves
the problem by rendering all narratives and events reducible to rational
patterns, and things as yet unknown to the epistemological limits of historical research. That such things are rationally explicable, however, like
the boundary Langer wants to sustain between authenticity and massified
distortion, we must take on faith alone, guaranteed as it is simply by the
conviction that all things are ultimately explicable in rational terms as long
as we do not get carried away by "extremes," hyperbole, and an infatuation with trauma. That which Hannah Arendt believed to be the source
of misplaced righteousness and an infinite victim posture for Jews who inherited its legacy—the unthinkable disproportion between how Jews had
lived and Hitler's judgment that they should be exterminated, the evident
absence, that is, of any relation between cause and effect—is encompassed,
for Lang, by that which exceeds normative patterns and characterizes
Nazi policy more generally. To come full circle, Nazi policy, including extermination, is a will to violate moral norms and thus an extreme version
of something recognizable. In this sense, Lang seems to be offering a context within which to render the Holocaust thinkable and unprecedented
at once. But this context is not the history of the twentieth century, of modernity, or of modern science. Instead, the context, in keeping with Lang's
literalism, is what we already know is conceivable as a human and thus
recognizable construction of any particular act, so that the larger framework for comprehending the Holocaust is the infinite links between all
chains of human actions that have ever taken place, with no consideration
of how those actions are embedded in any specific historical construction
of their meaning. Lang domesticates hyperbole by rendering those actions
that we still cannot explain as simply exaggerated versions of those with

96. Lang, *Post-Holocaust,* 15–16.

which we are familiar. Indeed, he renders it impossible for victims to be powerless, for they should be able to anticipate, if not always succeed in triumphing over, any threat to their psychic composure.

I do not mean to suggest that genocide of any kind defies rational explication and analysis, let alone comparison, but rather, that Lang still cannot account for how it is that the recognizable will to transgress moral norms intensifies such that it leads to extermination (in this case) and mass murder. In other words, how do we account for how segregation and racism lead to genocide? Lang dismisses Friedländer's effort to understand Nazi criminality as "redemptive anti-Semitism" (we may recall that it is a sacralized but secular struggle against Jews that must be fought at all costs to salvage the national body), by implying that the concept is a more sophisticated or more comprehensive version of "garden variety of anti-Semitism pushed to an extreme."[97] In Lang's view, Friedländer focuses on the final solution as if it were the whole of the Nazi project when it was but one policy; he conflates the 'final solution' with Nazi criminality and fails to grasp the Holocaust as both fundamentally contingent and universal. Yet Friedländer tries to conceptualize in historically specific terms the dimension of anti-Semitic hatred that exceeds conventional categories of explanation and led to the genocide of European Jewry. He asks how we account for the "extreme" to which Lang claims "garden variety anti-Semitism" was pushed, insisting against Lang that extremity cannot simply be conceived as an intensified version of something otherwise recognizable (which is not therefore to say that elements of "garden variety anti-Semitism" were absent in Nazism's struggle against Jews).

Lang's work represents both a position against grandiloquence and thus for the ordinary and the recognizable, and the refusal to think beyond particular philosophical and historiographical conventions. And while Lang's account does not generate the elated dissolution of solidity one finds especially in Langer, his work on the Holocaust, however inadvertently, loses its way and becomes an infinite series of references to an "ordinary" and "recognizable" world that keeps receding. In the end, Lang's argument yokes extremes only phantasmatically to something solid.

---

97. Lang, *Post-Holocaust,* 4.

One question posed by all of these very different approaches to Holocaust testimony concerns the difference between an objectifying, aloof representation of trauma—meaning a potentially traumatized, implicated narrative—and a minimalist narrative. As I have argued, Gross uses minimalism in its most sophisticated form to sustain the difference between the two types of narrative. His "hyper-empiricist" text uses the toneless tone of the chronicle in order to disorient and "discomfort"[98] the reader: the straightforward rendering of events unsettles because constraint is represented so hyperbolically that it implicates the reader in the violence while precluding any sort of overidentification with the victims. Friedländer also uses a constrained style to expose the numbness of the traumatized narrative as the repressed expression of the overwhelming impact of events on victims. In the end, however, his use of victims' voices is absorbed into a narrative that represents their fate as the tragic consequence of denying freedom and humanity to frail and victimized persons. Those sometimes terrorized and sometimes naïve voices do, very significantly, allow us to 'hear' victims, but we also hear what the story tells us: that victims suffered, that we should embrace and seek to understand and empathize with that suffering. The tragedy, dignity, and moral righteousness with which we are left in the end doesn't profoundly disorient or discomfort us—though in individual instances we might have such feelings—because the unsettlement generated by the victims' voices is incorporated into an argument in which our role is to embrace frailty, protect the vulnerable, and to overcome evil by dint of having witnessed its consequences.

Lang and Langer are less persuasive. In different ways they seek, however implicitly, to purge the narrative of a difference between a traumatic narrative and a narrative that has already mastered the trauma (one that refuses surprise, generates the truth of trauma, and bears its weight). Both in different ways seek to sublimate the traumatic or inexplicable details that resist sublimation. For Lang, historical moments and their larger meaning are continuous and ultimately part of an explicable and coherent metadiscourse that will one day be rendered fully clear. Langer interprets the discontinuity between what we understand and what we fail to grasp ultimately as the authentic meaning of the Holocaust, which remains

---

98. Gross, *Fear,* xiii.

outside of conventional categories of understanding. And yet his own self-constraint allows him somehow to attest to the veracity of testimonies that cannot otherwise be interpreted. His self-mastery, in other words, stands in for the reliability of the witness. In the end, both critics replay the trauma in the form of a perpetual oscillation between knowing and not knowing: between an ordinary that is mastered and an extraordinary that is always deferred, always on the horizon.

In examining the writings by the four authors, I have explored uses of minimalism for better and worse, though these are particularly nuanced works that demonstrate the power of minimalist style both to convey and to displace the affect of testimony itself. To return to Santner's concept of "narrative fetishism": in its most reductive minimalist form it may repress not loss but loss of control over traumatic symptoms; it erases traumatic symptoms in the very recounting of the traumatic events; it does not defer memory and thus mourning, but short-circuits meaning-conferring affect. In its most reductive uses, however, minimalist style allegedly resolves the cultural difficulty of how to speak about having been victimized that has confronted Jewish survivors and other victims in different ways since the end of the Second World War. After the war, the cultural stigma attached to Jewish victims led many Jews to disavow that they were victims or merely rendered them silent; now, the pathologies attached to making claims to having been a victim render disavowals the most acceptable, even persuasive form of acknowledging that one was a victim. When Jewish victimhood is deemed to have garnered too much attention, a reductive form of minimalism represents victims as already having mastered the symptoms of their suffering, as already having moved on from their losses, and thus as having had an experience of victimhood that is no longer one. The opaque and difficult question about how Jews disappeared in the Holocaust is thus answered by (an almost always failed) rendition of how they have returned.

4

ERASURES

It is certain, that the same object of distress, which pleases in a tragedy, were
it really set before us, would give the most unfeigned uneasiness; though it be
the most effectual cure to languor and indolence.

DAVID HUME (1777)

Many commentators on Holocaust testimony and memoirs do not address the rhetorical construction of victims and how it generates affective
responses to survivors. Rather, they discuss survivors' experience of trauma
and how it impacts the representation of atrocity, or they assess testimony's
reliability as a chronicle of events.

Though the focus on traumatic memory and how it conveys what it
does is important, as are historians' efforts to document what happened,
the vast array of discussions about trauma by public intellectuals, historians, and literary theorists embed testimony within a set of contested rhetorical and often implicitly negative claims about victims: that suffering is
central to identity; that Auschwitz has become problematically iconic of all
identity; that victims may be objects of suspicion or sacralization. In discourses on victims, much contemporary criticism seeks to return to 'real'

Epigraph: David Hume, "Of Tragedy," in *Essays: Moral, Political, and Literary* (Indianapolis:
Liberty Classics, 1985), 218.

compassion untainted by identification and other affective responses. But to the extent critics seek to return to an empirical history of injury deemed overwhelmed by memory and advocate a mode of testimony commensurate with the mastery of symptoms, they tend to replace actual victims with their own fashioning of an exemplary victim whose symptoms are neither excessive nor overwhelming. For the most part, critics neglect questions about how affective relations to victims are mobilized, constituted, and institutionalized in the first place. They presume that the experience of Jews in the Holocaust can be stripped of its iconic status and returned to 'history' as a means of preserving what happened undistorted by memory both private and public. This phantasmatic construction of 'real' victims takes on the force of self-evidence.

In order to identify real victims, these discussions and debates often inadvertently erase victims' experiences and identities in ways great and small. Victims' memoirs say a great deal about how their authors are made to feel that they impose on others, become objects of contempt or pity by virtue of their demands, or have experiences whose painfulness is blotted out by those who care the most for them. These erasures, by which I mean 'our' usually inadvertent refusal to acknowledge fully victims' past or present suffering, are rarely discussed, and certainly not in terms of the discomfort victims arouse. Moreover, these erasures are repeated, ironically, in diverse disciplinary discourses, all of which seek to recover the survivor's experience.

When survivors write about their postwar experiences, they tend to report how well-intentioned people refused in various ways to acknowledge what victims had experienced, but scholars do not usually address this kind of testimony or discuss it as part of a narrative of what happened. The Austrian survivor Ruth Kluger recounts the contempt with which she was treated by American Jews when she settled in the United States, as if having been in a camp were a source of contamination and degradation; and Eva Hoffman tells of the overt condescension with which her Canadian benefactors treated her family when they emigrated from Poland after having survived the war.[1] Primo Levi's anxiety about others' indifference and his own isolation is perhaps the most famous expression of the fear

---

1. Ruth Klüger, *Von hoher und niedriger Literatur* (Göttingen: Wallstein Verlag, 1996), 35; Eva Hoffman, *Lost in Translation: A Life in a New Language* (New York: Penguin, 1989), 102–4.

that one's experience may not be acknowledged. In Auschwitz Levi has a recurring dream in which he tries to explain his experience to his sister, her friend, and many other people, but they remain uninterested, and his sister finally walks away.[2] Charlotte Delbo's memoir is a long testimony not only to her time in Auschwitz, but also to the difficulty of being heard: to the awkwardness she provoked in others and even to the self-protective narcissism of a friend's husband, who could not bear what his wife had suffered. In the guise of feeling for her, he takes her place and narrates her own experiences, 'remembering,' for example, the geography of Birkenau better than she does.[3]

In Anna Langfus's fictionalized memoirs, the Polish social world in which she lives is not interested in what she endured during the war. She becomes, in a quest for normalcy, the companion of a man who speaks about his own experience of the war as if it were comparable to hers, about which he never asks. He merely pities her for being so alone.[4] And though her memoir hardly exhausts a long list, Hélène Berr most vividly expresses the experience of having had her persecution entirely erased even before she herself was murdered at Bergen-Belsen. A gentile woman is horrified when she realizes that the Germans are deporting Jewish children from France, and on a visit to the Jewish Berr family rushes in to share her feelings:

> She asked Maman: "You mean to say they are deporting children?" She was horrified.
>
> It's impossible to express the pain that I felt on seeing that she had taken all this time to *understand,* and that she had only understood because it concerned someone she knew. Maman presumably felt the same thing I did and replied: "We have been telling you so for a whole year, but you would not believe us."

2. Primo Levi, *Survival in Auschwitz: The Nazi Assault on Humanity,* trans. Stuart Woolf (New York: Collier, 1961), 256.

3. Charlotte Delbo, *Auschwitz and After,* trans. Rosette C. Lamont (New Haven: Yale University Press, 1995), 286–87.

4. Anna Langfus, *The Lost Shore,* trans. Peter Wiles (New York: Pantheon, 1964), esp. 86. I should note that while these are experiences discussed by women (Levi's fears about erasure manifest themselves in a dream), male memoirists have also reported similar incidents, about which I have written from another angle in Carolyn J. Dean, *The Fragility of Empathy after the Holocaust* (Ithaca: Cornell University Press, 2004), 96–105. The major difference, as far as I can tell, is that in women's memoirs intimate partners are as likely to be agents of erasure as are friends, distant relatives, or acquaintances.

Not knowing, not understanding even when you do know, because you have a closed door inside you, and you only can *realize* what you merely know if you open it. That is the enormous drama of our age. Everyone is blind to those being tortured.[5]

An interesting set of essays by Christopher Browning about how historians might use both survivors' and perpetrators' testimony confirms these observations: Browning does not address how victims' experiences are always embedded in broader cultural discourses nor does he provide a way of recognizing these kinds of erasures, though he seeks to capture victims' experiences. He argues that there are essentially two ways of approaching testimony: from the critical perspective of the compassionate historian, or from the uncritical perspective of those who refuse to "sit in judgment" on survivors and transform history into a form of commemoration. He establishes the risks involved in the latter by reference to the fraud perpetrated by Wilkomirski and an Israeli court's conviction and then admission of error in the case of John Demjanjuk, a Ukrainian living in the United States who had been identified at the trial by survivors as the sadistic camp guard Ivan the Terrible. Later evidence proved survivors' memories wrong, though Demjanjuk was deported from the United States to Germany in 2009, this time to face charges of war crimes in Sobibor, a Nazi extermination camp.[6]

Browning insists that he wishes to examine not the content of testimony but the form, by which he does not mean its rhetorical style. He is less interested in "retelling and narrative construction," in "how survivors live their experience," or in trauma, than in how to construct a history from testimonies often contradictory and even erroneous.[7] He wishes to establish patterns of evidence whose preponderance points primarily to one conclusion rather than another. Browning does not dismiss testimony—to the contrary, he uses it in a gentle and compassionate manner and seeks to demonstrate its value—but reiterates at every point the necessity of

5. Hélène Berr, *The Journal of Hélène Berr,* trans. David Bellos (New York: Weinstein Books, 2008), 204.

6. Christopher R. Browning, *Collected Memories: Holocaust History and Postwar Testimony* (Madison: University of Wisconsin Press, 2003), 42.

7. Browning, *Collected Memories,* 37–38.

returning to a critical history that would do away with the idealizations and projections typical of commemoration.

Browning is too sophisticated a historian to draw a bold line between history and memory, as his effort to constitute patterns of evidence suggests. But if memory is always part of the reconstitution of the past, such patterns necessarily privilege some forms of memory over others because they are verifiable, and neglect other, messier, memory traces that might be extremely revealing.[8] In the end Browning insists finally on a neo-positivist use of as-empirically-verifiable-as-possible memories and reintroduces the divide between history and memory through the back door.[9] In so doing, he risks creating a presupposition of who is credible and who is not that potentially generates a story as phantasmatic (as characterized by denial, rejection, and repression) as those narratives obsessed by commemoration and the sanctity of survivors.

In contrast, literary theorists understand that traumatic memory in particular compromises history conceived as a straightforward narrative account of the unfolding of events, which the force of trauma by definition defers, represses, renders opaque or all-too-vivid but difficult to recount. Sidra DeKoven Ezrahi and Sem Dresden have both discussed how testimonies and memoirs complicate the divide between history and memory because of the very nature not only of trauma but also of language and the representation of atrocity itself.[10] More recently, Zoë Waxman has argued

8. Browning does, however, warn that Jan T. Gross's demand that we listen to victims first and corroborate their testimony later dangerously privileges testimony over facts. *Collected Memories,* 43.

9. For an assessment of historians' use of testimony that is critical of Browning, see Leonard V. Smith, *The Embattled Self: French Soldiers' Testimony of the Great War* (Ithaca: Cornell University Press, 2007), 193–202.

10. Sidra DeKoven Ezrahi, *By Words Alone: The Holocaust in Literature* (Chicago: University of Chicago Press, 1980); and Sem Dresden, *Persecution, Extermination, Literature,* trans. Henry G. Schogt (Toronto: University of Toronto Press, 1995). Historians have only recently begun to use this material, which they initially felt was too subjective to be useful. Regarding the literature on testimony and memoirs by literary scholars, a first generation of commentary beginning in the 1980s (though naturally similar concerns undergird all work about the Holocaust as it has transformed and changed foci) sought to construe memoirs and novels about the Holocaust as a category of literature, including a reassessment of realism and the construction of "a new order of consciousness." Alvin H. Rosenfeld, *A Double Dying: Reflections on Holocaust Literature* (Bloomington: Indiana University Press, 1980), 13. It also sought to define divergences between texts inscribed in a Yiddish collective and community-based literature and those belonging to a secular humanist European tradition. A second generation in the 1990s has been even more

that testimony that counts as documentary evidence must be conceived not in relation to its empirical utility, but as a mode of understanding how the constraints placed on victims may have altered the ways in which they speak. "The nature of the camps rendered obsolete" the "model of witnessing prescribed by Emmanuel Ringelblum and the staff of Oneg Shabat [in the Warsaw Ghetto]." She notes that "concentration camp life militated against" the kind of documentation of Jewish life still possible in the ghettos, and that physical and psychological suffering may well mean that testimonies from the camps were not necessarily written, as she puts it, with "objectivity" and "comprehensibility."[11]

When the literary critic Thomas Trezise questions the psychoanalyst Dori Laub's manner of interviewing survivors, he argues carefully that no understanding of victims can be divided neatly into what victims have told us and what historians have established happened (the former emphasizing a performative self-making before an audience and the latter aimed at

---

concerned with the nature of representation and aesthetics in this literature, in particular with the failure of representation and the vagaries of memory, including not just texts but also visual media. And a third now seeks to expand ever more widely genres of representation that fall under the rubric of 'Holocaust literature': third-generation work includes comic books and other cultural forms; explores the relationship between events and memories and the politics of memory; and approaches once controversial topics such as gender differences in the representation of survivors' experiences. Exemplary of second-generation approaches are Shoshana Felman and Dori Laub, *Testimony: Crises of Witnessing in Literature, Psychoanalysis, and History* (New York: Routledge, 1992); and Marianne Hirsch, *Family Frames: Photography, Narrative, and Postmemory* (Cambridge: Harvard University Press, 1997). For recent literature, see Michael Rothberg, *Traumatic Realism: The Demands of Holocaust Representation* (Minneapolis: University of Minnesota Press, 2000); and his *Multidirectional Memory: Remembering the Holocaust in the Age of Decolonization* (Stanford: Stanford University Press, 2009); Zoë Waxman, *Writing the Holocaust: Identity, Testimony, Representation* (Oxford: Oxford University Press, 2006); and Aukje Kluge and Benn E. Williams, eds., *Re-examining the Holocaust through Literature* (Newcastle upon Tyne: Cambridge Scholars Publishing, 2009).

11. Waxman, *Writing the Holocaust*, 86. On poetry writing in the camps, see Andrés Nader, *Traumatic Verses: On Poetry in German from the Concentration Camps, 1933–1945* (Rochester, NY: Camden House, 2007). Michael Rothberg and Jared Stark argue that the Yale Fortunoff Video Archive for Holocaust Testimonies constitutes rather than merely documents the past, and thus always has the potential to create new meanings. They call it a "living" archive. See Rothberg and Stark, "After the Witness: A Report from the Twentieth Anniversary Conference of the Fortunoff Video Archive for Holocaust Testimonies at Yale," *History and Memory* 15 (2003): 85–96. See also James E. Young, *Writing and Rewriting the Holocaust: Narrative and the Consequences of Interpretation* (Bloomington: Indiana University Press, 1988), 25–39.

developing a constative narrative of events).[12] Rather, these different levels of meaning-conferring language require consistent attention to how different aims of inquiry limit our full grasp of testimony's hybrid nature and in particular its multidimensional relation to various registers of language and thus world-making and unmaking. If our aim is to witness an individual experience *or* to understand testimony as evidence of a collective experience of persecution, we will fail to grasp, he argues, that "not all our memory-institutions, not even all the genres in which testimony might be housed, have proven or are likely to prove adequate to 'transmit the dreadful experience,' since the experience itself pertained to the very destruction of community and hence could only leave testimony to seek a temporary home in its cultural ruins, to haunt the remnants of genre just as more generally the Holocaust continues to haunt its own historical aftermath."[13]

History is not a set of empirical referents but the "ruins" within which orphaned memory dwells: history is thus made up of fragments of a world that cannot be recovered and is thus always in an uneasy and impossibly fraught relationship to the memory that will continue to haunt us and all genres within which the Holocaust might be represented. If this is true, we cannot explain how memory is figured by and embedded within a particular historical and social organization or location, and thus more specifically how the meaning of victimization is constituted at the nexus of victims' testimonies and a generalized set of cultural assumptions about what it means to be or have been a victim. That is, the incommensurable relationship between testimony and documentary evidence so elegantly asserted by Trezise fails to address how memory that does not correlate with a stable set of empirical references is embedded within and never fully separable from the rhetorical parameters within which victims' suffering may be defined at any given moment. When Trezise, for example, argues that the testimony of the victims and historians' efforts to document their stories are in and of themselves inadequate to "transmit the dreadful experience," he seeks to make a larger point about the necessity of interdisciplinary

---

12. Thomas Trezise, "Between History and Psychoanalysis: A Case Study in the Reception of Holocaust Survivor Testimony," *History and Memory* 20 (2008): 7–47; and Dori Laub's bitter response, "On Holocaust Testimony and Its Reception within Its Own Frame, as a Process in Its Own Right: A Response to 'Between History and Psychoanalysis' by Thomas Trezise," *History and Memory* 21 (2009): 127–50.

13. Trezise, "Between History and Psychoanalysis," 35–36.

inquiry in ensuring how the legacy of the Holocaust will be taught in the future. Selective listening to one kind of inquiry or another at the risk of missing the larger experience of victimization derives from an "anxiety of transmission," the power of which intensifies as those who lived through the events pass away.[14] Trezise is concerned primarily to address the consequences of selective listening rather than to dwell on this anxiety, and the reference to "anxiety" remains purely descriptive and suggestive. But however casual, his invocation of this anxiety is a reference to some organization of affective response channeled through disciplinary inquiry, in which questions and assertions about victims are already embedded. Thus, Laub, himself a survivor, seeks to support the victim at all cost, while historians, whose living witnesses are disappearing, are more than ever eager to get it right and often disdain the victim's testimony when it may not accord with the facts. And yet we might ask, is not the "anxiety of transmission" partially about who future audiences will be and what they will be capable of learning? In what rhetorical contexts will this "anxiety of transmission" be embedded? Such audiences remain abstract external referents in Trezise's account except insofar as Laub is a stand-in for those interlocutors who allow the victim to remake his or her world performatively through the act of testifying. But in this case the audiences are a stand-in for a larger context that remains unarticulated and through which anxiety is mediated.

Indeed, with no conceptualization of any cultural referents organizing affective response, it is not only impossible to grasp fully the meaning and impact of an alleged "anxiety of transmission." It would also be extremely difficult to account for how so many mainstream discourses about victimization across a wide array of disciplines turn memory into the figure of an abject, fetishized victim who feeds parasitically on the good will of those around him, or into a larger-than-life fantasy of having been victimized. Mainstream discourses that stress the centrality of suffering to identity presume that history constitutes a stable set of referents which memory somehow exceeds. But if there is no analysis of how memories may be mediated by and embedded in some conceptual and affective location, then there is no way of knowing why it is so difficult for many critics to envision injury except as a refusal to recover, a form of self-indulgence, or at worst, false

14. Trezise, "Between History and Psychoanalysis," 28.

or phantasmatic claims. Neither a conception of history as stable nor ever-unstable referent can begin to address why it is so difficult to fully recognize injury except when it conforms to a familiar moral economy that valorizes heroes and decency, courage and modesty, moderation and the virtues of the ordinary. To repeat, neither a concept of history "in ruins" nor a concept of history as metaphorical brick-building that always requires revision can account for extant constructions of victimization and their consequences. That is, without a concept of history conceived in terms of the social and rhetorical organization of affect, it is impossible to understand not only why we remember victims the way we do, but also why so many victims were and continue to be erased by contempt, overidentification, condescension, and other forms of projection or aversion attested to by Kluger, Hoffman, and others.

The extent to which historical and other forms of understanding not only reiterate but also depend on various erasures of victims' injuries remains underacknowledged, in spite of all the nuanced commentary on Holocaust memory, on testimony, and the many moving efforts in such work to grasp victims' experiences. Though we may possess extraordinary readings of victims' testimony, questions about what happens culturally when we know who is speaking, how they speak, and various investments in how we listen, all shape the reception of what is said. The more 'innocent' the speaker, for example, the more dramatic the injury inflicted will seem to be, and yet presumptions of victims' innocence and powerlessness may also be defenses against or anxieties about their rage.

The French historian and essayist Georges Bensoussan notes that victims are told not to hate in the name of being reintegrated into the community: "May your suffering be discreet," the victim is counseled; "May your memory be calm and your desire for revenge muted, for it is a matter of assuring the goodwill of humanity." Society, Bensoussan continues, "has little interest in taking charge of victims, and is only interested in the peace between its component parts."[15] Andrés Nader describes how the final stanzas of some of Ruth Kluger's poetry were removed from some German-language anthologies of poems from the camps because they suggested the desire for vengeance rather than depicted an "innocent victim

15. Georges Bensoussan, *L'Auschwitz en héritage: D'un bon usage de la mémoire* (Paris: Mille et une nuits, 2003), 206.

worthy of pity."[16] The preference among many critics for the gentle Primo
Levi over the angry memoirist and survivor Jean Améry also implies
greater comfort with familiar noble constructions of enduring suffering
discreetly rather than giving vent to rage. Améry argues that Nazi crimes
will be rendered indistinct by those who will want to move on, and writes,
"Everything will be submerged in a general 'Century of Barbarism.' *We,*
the victims, will appear as the truly incorrigible, irreconcilable ones, as the
antihistorical reactionaries in the exact sense of the word, and in the end it
will seem like a technical mishap that some of us still survived."[17]

As has been implicit thus far, testimony cannot be assigned either to history or to memory except as it has already been interpreted by the criteria
that define and legitimate these two categories of meaning. The cultural
imperative that opposes one to the other and the literary theoretical insistence, among some critics, on their infinite incommensurability reduce
the complexity of testimony either to contextualization or to incongruence,
rendering efforts to explain how their relationship might be affectively and
rhetorically constituted difficult to grasp. Without attending to these sorts
of questions about the cultural and psychic constraints that shape interpretation, we cannot understand how so much compassion for and knowledge
of victims can coexist alongside a profound suspicion of claims to injury
and thus cannot acknowledge powerful defenses against recognizing how
and why the reality of victimization itself is inextricable from the rhetorical fashioning of the exemplary victim.

The cultural preference among some critics for reductive minimalism constitutes one form of nonrecognition or erasure because it may artificially fold traumatic narrative back into everyday life as if it were an
experience already mastered and thus usable as documentary evidence.
The assertion that there is now a surfeit of memory about the Holocaust
also constructs a concept of unmastered memory that never defines what
'mastered' memory might be (two commemorative events a year? three?).
Nonetheless, reductive minimalism does rely on an undefined concept of

16. Nader, *Traumatic Verses,* 59. See also the interesting discussion in Pascale R. Bos, *German-Jewish Literature in the Wake of the Holocaust* (New York: Palgrave Macmillan, 2005), 71–88.
17. Jean Améry, *At the Mind's Limits: Contemplations by a Survivor on Auschwitz and Its Re-alities,* trans. Sidney Rosenfeld and Stella P. Rosenfeld (Bloomington: Indiana University Press, 1980), 80. The contrast between Levi and Améry is well known in the literature and discussed el-egantly by Nader, *Traumatic Verses,* 40–43.

mastery that renders some Jewish memory implicitly overwrought and histrionic, even if it never specifies what normative measure it exceeds. There are many other, equally powerful ways in which victims' experiences are explained by or assimilated into normative categories of everyday life even when those experiences exceed them. Indeed, the conceptually limited opposition between the Holocaust conceived as a figure of postmodern trauma and aporia and the folding of traumatic experience finally back into the everyday is itself a symptom of the failure to address trauma except as other-worldly or, most often, in culturally contained and thus normative forms. Primo Levi's exemplarity here, after all, begs the question of why self-control should be not only admirable in those who have suffered grievously, but also characteristic of the ideal victim.[18]

Among an increasing number of critics, the power of particular self-protective, normative rhetorical constructions of victims as modest, reticent (they proclaim their suffering quietly), and life-affirming stifles other possible representations, including those prominent in a great deal of victims' testimony.[19] In particular, this construction renders all but opaque the depth of cultural ambivalence toward victims underlying so many debates about Jewish victimization that have endured to the present: suspicion of victims, numbness or impatience with them, compassion tinged with revulsion, and revulsion yoked to attachment, some of which emerged in various forms in heated discussions about Jewish passivity during the Holocaust, to which we will turn shortly.

In a 1980 preface to a memoir by a Dutch survivor reminiscent of many critics' preference for minimalism in testimony, the psychiatrist Albert J. Solnit writes, "Dr. Micheels is low-key in personality, in writing, and in remembering. Yet his unhistrionic, matter-of-fact style of telling is itself a reassuring demonstration of the patience and indomitability of those who

18. On the question of Levi's complicated relationship to humanist thought, see Jonathan Druker, *Primo Levi and Humanism after Auschwitz: Posthumanist Reflections* (New York: Palgrave Macmillan, 2009).

19. Reticence is a useful way to describe some survivors' feelings about recounting their past, for fear, as Michael Pollak puts it, that they might render the extraordinary banal in the process of trying to represent their experiences. But it is hardly the only means of describing former victims' attitudes. See Pollak, *L'expérience concentrationaire: Essai sur le maintien de l'identité sociale* (Paris: Suites Sciences Humaines, 2000), 20. For a somewhat different view (which relates talking about the past and the shame it provokes), see Aharon Appelfeld's memoir, *The Story of a Life,* trans. Aloma Halter (New York: Schocken Books, 2004), 181.

survived and found a way to bring order out of chaos, coherence out of horror, and an affirmation of life out of mass murder."[20] Twenty-six years later, writing of his concerns about the exploitation of atrocity by false victims who claim to be real ones, the literary critic Charles Bigsby asserts:

> Nor is it so unusual for people to present themselves as victims, itself a familiar tactic of those who wish to deny responsibility for their own lives or seek compensation for their supposed sufferings. In the twenty-first century, this is a commonplace of an increasingly litigious culture. But something else is in play. Money does not seem to have been primary. They share something with the assassin whose marginal existence is transformed by attaching himself to history. They live vicariously. They live publicly. They lay claims to that twenty-first century grail—fame. They emerge out of the shadows into the bright light of attention...And so they synthesise memories, often extracting what seems to them to be the active ingredient of the concentration camp experience. Not for them the extraordinary reticence shown by so many survivors. They steal memories and when those memories are insufficiently dramatic they tend to show a preference for gothic horrors.[21]

Thus the preference for minimalist style is but one component of a much broader discourse about the exemplary victim. Over and over, the presumptive cultural demands of false victims (here recognized by the dramatic contrast between them and the putatively "extraordinary reticence" shown by many survivors) trump any inquiry into how some victims are deemed more credible than others since we are presumed to know that 'real' survivors would by definition be reluctant to seek attention. Reticence thus distinguishes real and false victims. Bigsby made this pronouncement before the headlines screamed a few years later about the very real Holocaust survivor who wrote a rather fantastic love story about a girl who threw him apples across the prison barrier. He meets her by pure chance after the war and they marry. The survivor's undoing was not that he had

---

20. Louis J. Micheels, M.D., *Doctor #117641: A Holocaust Memoir* (New Haven: Yale University Press, 1980), viii.

21. Charles Bigsby, *Remembering and Imagining the Holocaust: The Chain of Memory* (Cambridge: Cambridge University Press, 2006), 374. Bigsby's book explores the usefulness of varying literary constructions of memory, which proves in no way contrary to a notion of the exemplary victim.

made up having survived the camps, but that he had allowed this love story to be passed off as nonfiction, bringing him interviews, television appearances, and thus a great deal of attention.[22]

Jewish Passivity

If we ask how victims are rhetorically constituted as such, it becomes clearer how certain cultural truisms are shaped to conform to redemptive or at least to familiar moral narratives. The truism, for example, that all victims of genocide are fundamentally innocent obviously does not exclude passing judgment on them and distinguishes between some victims and others, and not only men in contrast to women and children. We should thus analyze under what conditions assertions of innocence appear to be more or less credible, of what innocence really consists, and what purposes it fulfills.

Presumably the judgments imposed on so-called innocent victims explain why there was and continues to be so much ambivalence about the behavior of Jewish victims. Some of its most familiar expressions are by now a relic of earlier, self-conscious efforts to address a presumptively anti-Semitic audience by survivors or heirs of victims worried about the narrative representation of Jewish death. One important example: the ongoing though now more muted discussions about the Jewish Councils in European cities and ghettos. The Councils were constituted normally by Jewish community elders and responsible for negotiating with the Nazis, including making decisions about who would be deported and who would not. Though Hannah Arendt's famous denunciation of the Councils as fundamentally complicit with the Nazis in *Eichmann in Jerusalem* may have been derided, the harsh judgment of or ambivalence about those Jews deemed to have been complicit cannot be denied.[23] Was the leader of the Jewish Council of the Warsaw Ghetto who committed suicide, Adam Czerniaków, guilty for having done so instead of having told his community

---

22. The survivor is Herman Rosenblat. See "False Memoir of Holocaust Survivor Cancelled," *New York Times,* December 29, 2008.

23. Hannah Arendt, *Eichmann in Jerusalem: A Report on the Banality of Evil* (New York: Penguin, 1994 [1963]).

what he knew to be true, or was he a martyr because he refused to sign the 'resettlement' edict knowing that children would be sent to Treblinka? His innocence hardly spares him judgment.

One might easily respond that knowing that all who participated were themselves victims does not and should not relieve them of all agency, and that those victims who decided, for example, to became Jewish kapos should indeed be judged for having chosen (for the most part illusorily) to save themselves by hurting others. Such judgments avoid asking difficult questions about the parameters of action in a radically redefined moral economy: the point is not to dismiss the idea that victims had agency (some victims had more than others), but to ask how agency might be evaluated in different contexts.[24] The debate about Jewish passivity in the face of annihilation provides more fodder for discussion, because it exposes to what extent assertions of 'innocence' appear to be more credible when victims

24. Calel Perechodnik's memoirs of having been a Jewish kapo include a letter from another survivor refusing to forgive him and condemning all those who made such choices; another survivor, Margareta Glas, refuses on the contrary to blame even some of the non-Jewish kapos in Auschwitz given the context. See Perechodnik, *Am I a Murderer? Testament of a Jewish Ghetto Policeman,* ed. and trans. Frank Fox (Boulder, CO: Westview Press, 1996); and Glas's testimony in Pollak, *L'expérience concentrationaire,* 75. One might also refer to Ruth Leys's effort to attribute agency to survivors by emphasizing their guilt. Leys, *From Guilt to Shame: Auschwitz and After* (Princeton: Princeton University Press, 2007), 1–16. Leys argues that recent discourses on trauma have diminished all the messy emotions associated with the "survivor guilt" generated by internalized identification—conscious and not—with the perpetrators that was often necessary to survival. Instead, she claims, psychiatrists have more recently argued that survivors' trauma is best represented not by unconscious, unbearable guilt, which emphasizes the opacity of consciousness to itself, but by "shame," in which a conscious subject is assaulted externally and thus retains spectatorial distance from his or her own humiliation. In this scenario, the camp survivor was diminished and stripped of his or her dignity, and carries the shame of that memory. At the same time, survivors also retain their ability to observe the inhumanity of their tormentors, to resist, and to carry on full lives afterward affected but not necessarily damaged by what they have undergone.

Leys's account of a shift from guilt to shame in the psychiatric construction of trauma victims seeks to demonstrate how victims' memories are transformed into passive screens in which time is compressed into the harrowing "space" of an assault, replayed again and again, much like the media objects Annette Wieviorka warns us survivors have come to be. In short, Leys's excoriation of the overly literalist construction of the traumatic flashback in the psychiatry of trauma is commensurate with new concerns not only about the transformation of the Holocaust into a media event and its victims into spectacles, but also with the inevitably passive humanity accorded to those survivors whose stories are objectified and become a focus of media fascination. For shame renders victims survivors, in her view, by depleting their ability to shape the outcome of events and experience. In the drive to sustain some form of agency for survivors other than having moved on, Leys prefers guilty and tormented survivors to passive ones.

have resisted their tormentors against the odds, especially when those victims behaved heroically and nobly rather than vengefully or in anger. Arendt was much denounced for having raised the biblical cry about Jews going like sheep to the slaughter in her 1961 reports from the Eichmann trial, though she had actually noted that Jews were no different from any other victimized group in this respect. Nonetheless, the controversy over her apparent insensitivity raged because the question about Jewish passivity clearly touched a very raw nerve.[25] Samuel Moyn has demonstrated to what extent the issue also resonated in the context of the French controversy over Jean-François Steiner's book on Treblinka some five years later. One of the central concerns of the controversy was whether Jews had been passive in the camps or had organized resistance, and how. Denunciations and defenses of Steiner were rampant.[26] Similarly, when André Schwarz-Bart won the Prix Goncourt for *The Last of the Just* in 1959, several prominent Jewish intellectuals believed not only that he had distorted Jewish religious tradition but also that he had presented the Holocaust in terms of Christian martyrdom, charges he bitterly rejected.[27]

Lucy S. Dawidowicz was still troubled in the early 1980s by the struggle among Jewish survivors and historians to prove that Jews had resisted the Nazi onslaught. She speculated, however controversially, that the 'blame the victim' mentality derived from a "modern sensibility which values activism and misunderstands the heroism of martyrdom" (meaning, as I interpret it, that heroism applies to the mass murder of innocents who could not fight back but went knowingly, and therefore heroically, to their deaths).[28] Her cryptic reference was to the ongoing ambivalence toward

25. Arendt, *Eichmann in Jerusalem*, 11–12.

26. Samuel Moyn, *A Holocaust Controversy: The Treblinka Affair in Postwar France* (Waltham, MA: Brandeis University Press, 2005), 117–18. Moyn also notes that Arendt's invocation of Jewish passivity was unjustly distorted (147–48).

27. André Schwartz-Bart, *The Last of the Just*, trans. Stephen Becker (New York: Atheneum, 1960). For a discussion of the debate, see Francine Kaufmann, "Les enjeux de la polémique autour du premier best-seller français de la littérature de la Shoah," *Revue de l'histoire de la Shoah / Le Monde juif* 176 (2002): 68–99. Also see the commentary in Ezrahi, *By Words Alone*, 132–37. For a defense of Schwartz-Bart, see Rosenfeld, *A Double Dying*, 70.

28. Lucy S. Dawidowicz, *The Holocaust and the Historians* (Cambridge: Harvard University Press, 1981), 134. The 2008 Hollywood movie *Defiance*, after the novel by Nechema Tec, also seeks to tell the story of Jewish resistance. The only purpose of the movie is to demonstrate that Jews fought back and were not solely a bunch of weak-kneed intellectuals (though such Jews make an appearance and need to be saved by a fearless leader).

Jews who did not evidently resist when rounded up to be shot or deported, but confirms the necessity of turning disempowerment itself into a form of heroism in order to cope with the shame associated with victimization, even when shame is related to industrialized murder.

The distinguished historian François Bédarida's 1992 preface to a book on the history of persecution under the Vichy regime manifests just how vibrant such questions remain, especially in Europe, even as they have been discredited. Bédarida notes that all the questions about Jewish passivity make no sense: "Without any doubt," he writes, "the heroes of the resistance saved Jewish honor, even if one may still ask what dishonor might reside in being the victims of a massive and systematic operation of extermination. Can one think of reproaching the hostages killed in reprisal for armed resistance to the Germans for having been shot? Or the victims of Oradour-sur-Glane, or of the Ardeatine Caves, for letting themselves be massacred?"[29] And Berel Lang has recently sought to dismantle questions about why Jews did not resist by proving them to be logical fallacies, emphasizing their continuing relevance.[30] One might also point to the historian Yehuda Bauer's preface to the first English version of Filip Müller's *Eyewitness Auschwitz*, in which Bauer leads the reader casually through a series of possible responses to the testimony that stand in stark contrast to established truisms. Some readers, he notes, "will notice the lack of successful resistance," a phrase which suggests that efforts to resist are prevalent in the memoir. He goes on gratuitously: "some will notice the fact that the author does not mention any case of Jews begging for their lives; some will emphasize the fact that most of the Jews going to the gas chambers had no inkling of what was happening to them; others will analyze the behavior of the SS murderers."[31] In short, Bauer anticipates and then 'corrects' any misapprehensions about Jewish passivity. Evidently Israel's military victory in 1967 did not put ideas about passive Jewry to rest. The military victory underscored a new fantasy that Jews, now embodied by the State

29. François Bédarida's preface to Adam Rayski, *The Choice of the Jews under Vichy: Between Submission and Resistance*, trans. Will Sayers (Notre Dame: University of Notre Dame Press, 2005), xiv.

30. Berel Lang, *Post-Holocaust: Interpretation, Misinterpretation, and the Claims of History* (Bloomington: Indiana University Press, 2005), 86–99.

31. Yehuda Bauer's preface to Filip Müller, *Eyewitness Auschwitz: Three Years in the Gas Chambers*, ed. and trans. Susanne Flatauer (New York: Ivan R. Dee, 1979), x.

of Israel, were all-powerful and generated the "tough Jew" phenomenon dissected by Paul Breines, but did not decrease the contempt for Holocaust survivors in Israel itself because of their alleged passivity.[32]

In intra-Jewish debate, post-Holocaust discussions no longer engaged with these questions nonetheless reiterate skepticism about victims, as if victim-blaming were no longer a cultural problem in reference to Jews. There appears to be confidence that skepticism about victims provides a welcome counterweight to victim-sanctifiers. The contemporary emphasis both on the phantom victim and on the so-called pervasiveness of the fantasy of wanting to have been a victim, in short, neglects how victims become objects of others' identifications, projections, and displaced anxieties, or objects of study to be treated with compassion but also skepticism. The questions we have mostly left behind (were Jews too passive? why didn't they resist? didn't some of them collude with the Nazis?) focused primarily on degrees of agency—projecting too much or too little of it onto victims rather than asking what kind of agency they had and how it might have been exercised. Some historians' sober assessments have had little impact on these questions, which are symptoms of a more profound cultural problem with and skepticism of constrained agency, constrained intention, and constrained will, even or perhaps especially in the context of the terrorized disempowerment that confronts so many victims.

Surely these questions were given their particular force by efforts both to fashion and to counter images of Jews as a group deserving of collective punishment, weak and parasitical: a group thought not unlikely to have sought to survive by parasitism or by selling out their own.[33] Thus many questions about Jewish passivity seem quaint or irrelevant now (though some critics still take time to respond to them) because, from the perspective of many contemporary critics, we are for the most part no longer in thrall to the stereotypes that motivated them: indeed, they say, we have sanctified the survivors and transformed the Holocaust into an icon of human-made catastrophe about which we want to speak endlessly. Most of these critics have not been too interested in exploring dimensions of

---

32. Paul Breines, *Tough Jews: Political Fantasies and the Moral Dilemma of American Jewry* (New York: Basic Books, 1990); Tom Segev, *The Seventh Million: The Israelis and the Holocaust,* trans. Haim Watzman (New York: Henry Holt, 1991).

33. Perechodnik, *Am I a Murderer,* xiii.

indifference, repulsion, and ambivalence toward Jewish victims except in terms of irrational fantasies that can be demonstrated empirically to be irrational, and thus determine Jewish attitudes toward gentiles to be either overblown and paranoid or reasonable, pausing before the extreme views of neo-Nazis and Holocaust deniers. That is why the historian Peter Novick dismisses Jewish claims about anti-Semitism in the United States as fueled by Jewish paranoia and the allegedly high status Western culture accords to victims.[34]

I do not wish to insist that victims should embrace their victimization. I wish simply to note that questions about Jewish passivity reveal as much about profound discomfort with or contempt for constrained agency and abjection as they do about anti-Semitic beliefs that Jews occupied a different moral universe than others. Attitudes toward victims are hard to grasp not simply because of various prejudices against them that could be clearly identified and challenged. They are also hard to grasp because scholars' and other critics' affective relationships with victims, especially with those already marginalized psychically and structurally, complicate the ability to do so. The rejection and sacralization of victims of catastrophe are rarely examined as modes of coping with the disruption of a secure moral universe in which people are presumed to struggle against their humiliation or in some fashion retain their honor (including their equanimity once liberated). Critics rarely address unconscious contempt, fear, and envy of victims that cannot be designated as a self-consciously irrational attitude and controlled for as bias.[35]

---

34. Peter Novick, *The Holocaust in American Life* (New York: Houghton Mifflin, 2000), 189. Those historians who have argued against this approach are rare. See note 46.

35. I might note here the unacknowledged attachment to abjection arguably manifest in the work of Giorgio Agamben, though I have discussed his work very little (or the tendency of some poststructuralists to transform trauma into a discourse of the sublime, which has been amply and persuasively criticized by LaCapra in his recent work). Agamben's influential work is informed by the presumption that victims are by definition abject, and perhaps irrecoverably so, and he focuses less on who or what consigned them to victimhood than on the corrosion of the human being in modernity: Auschwitz and the living-dead "Muslims" in the camp (those inmates who were barely alive but still moved, resembling, in camp idiom, Muslims at prayer) represent the summa of human degradation and become figures specifying less a particular moment in human history than a sign of how Agamben's attachment to abjection obscures his ability to conceptualize the plight of victims. Agamben, *Remnants of Auschwitz: The Witness and the Archive,* trans. Daniel Heller-Roazen (New York: Zone Books, 2000). For an interesting critical commentary, see Marc Nichanian, *La perversion historiographique: Une réflexion arménienne* (Paris: Éditions

All Too Human

The sadly condescending responses to survivors by those who deemed themselves superior to victims before much was known, or fears (like Primo Levi's) that one's own family will be indifferent, merely confirm the pervasiveness of these and other, equally insidious forms of nonrecognition, especially those most dramatic because they took place when knowledge about the Holocaust was already widespread. Ruth Kluger recounts an evening with her friend the famous German writer Martin Walser, who 'forgets' in spite of their friendship that she had survived Auschwitz and, in reference to the tragedy that befell German Jews, suggests that, after all, the fear of foreigners is deep-rooted and universal. "Martin," she writes, with a combination of weariness and pain, "says hatred of Jews was one of those variants of xenophobia which comes naturally to all men. No one wants to deal with differences if you haven't been brought up to tolerate them. I wonder, however: do I really act and look so different from him and his family, who have invited me into their house and at whose table I am sitting?" And she asks now more contemptuously, "Didn't our friendship come easily? Or did it really take virtue, courage, and deep insights on your part?"[36]

Walser's oscillation between knowing and not seeming really to know, between forgetting Kluger's past and remembering the general tragedy that befell German Jews is not driven (or does not seem to be) by awkwardness or guilt (it is Walser, we recall, who declared that the Holocaust had become a moral cudgel in postwar Germany that had outlived its purpose). If anything, Walser's own friendship with Kluger becomes, as she notes, evidence of his own particular virtue. Indeed, Walser explains prejudice as natural unless "men" are educated otherwise. His assertion not only naturalizes and thus reduces the impact of prejudice and difference and their effects but also diminishes the violence that was done and is now being replayed again, albeit in the form of a less lethal nonrecognition, to his friend Ruth. As questions about Jewish resistance and passivity

Lignes et manifestes, 2006), 211. See also Dominick LaCapra's trenchant critique of Agamben in *History in Transit: Experience, Identity, Critical Theory* (Ithaca: Cornell University Press, 2004), 144–94; and *History and Its Limits: Human, Animal, Violence* (Ithaca: Cornell University Press, 2009), esp. 163–78.

36. Ruth Kluger, *Still Alive: A Holocaust Girlhood Remembered* (New York: Feminist Press, 2001), 167–69.

denied the impact of terror under certain conditions in favor of motifs of courage and martyrdom, assertions that hatred of difference is tied to a universal human fear of foreigners also diminish the impact of this "fear" on victims, leaving them out of consideration. From the victim's point of view, this logic renders it impossible to understand the impact of having been a victim, of having been rendered abject, on recovery.

It is the absence of discussions of the abjection to which victims were reduced as well as its effects (in psychological rather than descriptive terms) that is most striking in discourses about victims: victims speak of contempt, of silence, of arrogance, and, of course, of their own fear (born of having survived something they knew would be difficult to believe). But those who surround and might even be sympathetic to them speak primarily in Walser's vocabulary. Thus, Walser's ideas about the naturalness of attitudes toward foreigners, however painful their effects on his friend, are extremely familiar: certain social attitudes, including that which involves inflicting pain on others, are naturalized so that from an ideological point of view they can be rationalized and explained. Prejudices can coexist with human decency and a commitment to universal rights because they have been transformed into a human attribute without cause: in this case Walser refers to a hollowed-out tribalism possessed by everyone and thus by no one (though more prominent, he claims, in the uneducated. He thus renders this particular trait even more profoundly human and universal because more primitive). Moreover, since so many murdered Jews were assimilated, Kluger's implicit question about why "foreign" is even applicable in this context reveals that Walser's logic is even more insidious because it renders anti-Semitic hatred and its effects benign.[37]

The naturalization of discrimination and its effects, including the abjection of the victim, occurs in a wide variety of contexts, and its flattening of the social world most dramatically obscures injury. The transposition

37. One consistent theme among many memoirists is that they were either surprised or had their worst fears confirmed when they realized that they had suddenly become "foreign." In the case of German, Austrian, and Dutch Jews, the realization that their friends would not help or suddenly saw them differently (or that they had to be inordinately grateful to those who did help) is constant. In memoirs by Polish Jews, the authors survive for the most part in spite of Polish hatred and exploitation. Many Poles who saved Jews were generous and courageous, but the literature teems with examples of Poles who helped Jews in order to exploit them further. Anna Langfus's memoir-fiction, *The Lost Shore,* confirms that the Polish resistance itself did not, as historians know, seek for the most part to save Jews and was often anti-Semitic.

from the historical to the trans-historical, the slippage from a conception of history as a brick-building-like narrative that attends only to the facts to a narrative about human history that is utterly dehistoricized in its assertions about how human beings are 'like that,' makes even traumatic injury part of the natural course of things. In Tzvetan Todorov's long essay about how Bulgarians saved Jews, there is little about the absence or presence of anti-Semitism, and a lot about human frailty, decency, and historical accident.[38] According to Todorov, Bulgarians are not particularly anti-Semitic and tend to be tolerant of minorities: the Orthodox Church opposed deportation (though particularly of converted Jews), and other Bulgarians did so because the Germans had not occupied the country and the regime still permitted opposition. When things heated up, some men emerged as heroes because they were decent, courageous, and unselfish, in spite of having once supported anti-Semitic laws. Todorov distinguishes Boris Peshev, a member of the Bulgarian National Assembly who publicly opposed the government's effort to deport Jews, "from other courageous and unselfish men" not by virtue of his conscience, "but [by] his strategy. He did what had to be done under these particular circumstances in order to achieve his goal." Peshev voted for anti-Semitic laws and thus presumably believed some of their premises and goals. But when he realized that the Nazis wanted to murder the Jews, he rose to the occasion, behaving virtuously, courageously, and exceptionally. Todorov's essay is finally about the virtues of decent men rather than about what happened to Jews, how, and why. Anti-Semitism has little to do with it: decent people, not necessarily destined for greatness, triumph or fail. Indeed, Jews appear in the narrative only as people who plead for help or who are already dead: "The sacrifice [*sic*] borne by the Thracian Jews would thus serve to save their brothers, because it would rouse the conscience of Bulgaria's legislators and high clergy."[39] "Under

38. Tzvetan Todorov, *The Fragility of Goodness: Why Bulgaria's Jews Survived the Holocaust,* trans. Arthur Denner (Princeton: Princeton University Press, 1999).
39. Todorov, *The Fragility of Goodness,* 30. Omer Bartov's review of Todorov's book argues that the view that we are all capable of goodness, sometimes in spite of ourselves, tends to flatten out important distinctions between real heroes and accidental ones. Bartov, "The Anti-Hero as Hero," *New Republic,* August 13, 2001, 33–38. Bartov is right. At the same time, while I don't wish to deny the significance of such categories, it is also important to note that simply contextualizing them does not do away with the normalizing tendencies they represent, in particular the negligence of what it means to be responsible for putting an exterminatory process in motion by voting for anti-Semitic laws. It grafts contexts instead onto a familiar moral universe.

other circumstances," Todorov adds, open dissent might have been "futile, even suicidal."[40]

In such accounts, ordinary people do extraordinary things when 'natural' and profoundly human attributes emerge under extraordinary circumstances. In other, more sophisticated historical and sociological accounts, this naturalization tends to be the result not of regression to some deep recess of what constitutes the human, for better or worse, but, paradoxically, of complex social processes that favor the development of distance between victims and perpetrators which turn presumably feeling people into numb ones. This post-Weberian argument in its mostly functionalist forms about the relationship between Nazism and modernity, and extermination and bureaucracy, is so well known (or perhaps by now so seemingly self-evident) that I will summarize it but briefly. The historian Christopher Browning argues in his work on Nazi perpetrators, "This approach emphasizes the degree to which modern bureaucratic life fosters a functional and physical distancing in the same way that war and negative racial stereotyping promote a psychological distancing between perpetrator and victim."[41] The sociologist Zygmut Bauman also argues that this enabling distance is socially produced by the institutions of modernity, in particular bureaucracy and its corollary, instrumental rationality.[42] Others

40. Todorov, *The Fragility of Goodness*, 39.

41. Christopher Browning, *Ordinary Men: Reserve Battalion 101 and the Final Solution in Poland* (New York: HarperCollins, 1992), 162. Browning's work, while generally functionalist, leaves room for ideological mobilization regarding how the eventual extermination of European Jewry developed in the Nazi bureaucracy. But he does not integrate these insights into his work on how the killing was rendered possible.

42. Zygmut Bauman, *Modernity and the Holocaust* (Ithaca: Cornell University Press, 1989). See also Elaine Scarry's description of torture in modern regimes: "The act of disclaiming is as essential to the power [of the state] as is the act of claiming. It of course assists the torturer in practical ways. He first inflicts pain, then objectifies pain, then denies the pain—and only this final act of self-blinding permits the shift back to the first step, the inflicting of still more pain, for to allow the reality of the other's suffering to enter his own consciousness would immediately compel him to stop the torture." That is, normal people do extremely cruel things because they don't realize what they're actually doing, or people do not perpetrate violence unless ideological fictions have so dehumanized the victim and so thoroughly shaped the mind of the perpetrator that he believes he is acting in the name of the law. Scarry even goes so far as to insist that if the experience of pain is pleasurable for either victim or perpetrator it cannot be conceived of as pain. Scarry, *The Body in Pain: The Making and Unmaking of the World* (Oxford: Oxford University Press, 1981), 57. The not entirely outdated functionalist concept of Nazism, in which killing Jews was a by-product of other military and state demands and had little to do with anti-Semitic ideology, simply mirrors

have criticized the lack of any attention to anti-Semitic ideology in such arguments.[43]

Here I want less to emphasize ideology than to note that for the purposes of explaining bystander or perpetrator behavior these functionalist arguments have more in common with the radically different but ideologically commonsensical approaches of Walser and Todorov than meets the eye. Of course, the reference to negative racial stereotyping and the modern bureaucracies and technologies which enabled its diffusion and implementation cannot explain why these institutions and tools were effective, as those who wish to focus on anti-Semitic ideology have long claimed. But it is also true that in spite of their efforts not to revert to ahistorical categories like 'human nature' and to put Nazi action into a specific historical context, these accounts finally explain how modernity turned Jews into things by reference to what human beings (in these cases, non-Jews) do under extraordinary circumstances. Thus, as Browning and others have noted, when circumstances generate an insuperable divide between communities, people do not wish to be excluded from the group to which they are designated as belonging.[44] It is perhaps not surprising that responses by social scientists to the question of how the vast majority in Nazi Germany or societies occupied by the Nazis allowed the Jews to be exterminated also use references to how humans behave universally under extraordinary circumstances: not wanting to know, indifference, tacit consent under pressure, and a focus on one's own deprivation and fear.[45]

It is not simply that none of these accounts provides explanations about how anti-Semitism took the extreme forms that it did, a particularly difficult question and one that has not been answered by those who focus on ideology, but that all of these accounts naturalize the responses of bystanders (and sometimes perpetrators) as quintessentially human behavior under

---

this approach in which the distantiation generated by modernity and its demands (or war and its imperatives) renders victims less than human.

43. The most famous example of an ideological approach is Lucy S. Dawidowicz, *The War against the Jews: 1933–45* (New York: Holt, Rinehart, and Winston, 1975). For a summary of the differences between those who emphasize ideology and those who emphasize functionalism, a now outdated divide, see Dawidowicz, *The Holocaust and the Historians.*

44. Browning, *Ordinary Men,* 188.

45. For a detailed discussion about how what historians referred to as "indifference" to German Jewry was really a form of violence rendered invisible or oddly agent-less, see Dean, *The Fragility of Empathy,* 76–105.

pressure.[46] They do so by universalizing human response, so that anti-Semitism disappears into the vast and self-evident history of how human beings behave, shorn of any historical specificity, aim, or object. Thus many social scientists as well as humanist writers do not address the sometimes hallucinatory quality of victims' experiences, especially those that cannot be assimilated into normative understandings of everyday life.

The recasting of anti-Semitism into human experience under pressure also fails to acknowledge the affective relations between Germans and Jews, for example, or between the writers we have discussed and the victims themselves. It is difficult to understand how these writers think about victims or if they do at all. Walser re-creates his and Kluger's past in his surely unconscious effort to exculpate Germans; and one has to presume that Todorov's desire to redeem Bulgarians comes at the expense, again unconsciously, of any attention to Jewish victims (other than those who were already dead). Other historians infamously don't address Jewish victims at all except as already other, already abject.

The scholarly reiteration of Martin Walser's erasure of Ruth Kluger's own experience of victimization (at least as I have characterized it here) has been decried in different terms by some historians of Jewish experience. They have noted not only that such accounts neglect anti-Semitic ideology (and thus the force of prejudice understood primarily in terms of stereotyping and the projection of fears about one's self onto alien others), but also transform Jews into figures in the background that are hard to make out, and focus solely on Nazi perpetrators (and bystanders to a lesser extent). Friedländer has suggested that such historians may even deflect their anxiety about the abjection of the victims by rendering them

---

46. Dan Stone and Alon Confino both seek to take fantasies about Jews seriously by returning to ideology (and thus away from social history) not simply as the history of anti-Semitism, but rather as the construction of shared mental space. Though both suggest in different ways that culture cannot be reduced to context (implying that fantasies about Jews not only exceed empirical referents but also cannot simply be reduced to stereotypes), their work falls short in addressing the opacity intrinsic in the Nazi extermination of the Jews, however crucial their interventions. See Stone, *Constructing the Holocaust: A Study in Historiography* (London: Vallentine Mitchell, 2003); and Confino, "Fantasies about the Jews: Cultural Reflections on the Holocaust," *History and Memory* 2 (2005): 296–322. See also Dominick LaCapra, "A Response to 'Holocaust Historiography and Cultural History' by Dan Stone," and Carolyn J. Dean, "Response to Dan Stone, 'Holocaust Historiography and Cultural History'," both in *Dapim: Studies on the Shoah* 23 (2009): 89–93 and 76–80, respectively. Even Phillipe Burrin refers to "regression" and to an "habituation to violence" when he seeks to explain Nazi Anti-Semitism. Burrin, *Nazi Anti-Semitism: From Prejudice to the Holocaust,* trans. Janet Lloyd (New York: The New Press, 2005), 67–69.

invisible or mass-like.[47] Most historians of anti-Semitism counter these tendencies primarily if not exclusively by documenting the victim's point of
view. But they often still engage testimony as exemplary of the verifiable
consequences of discrimination. Though literary theorists tend to focus on
texts and the representation of atrocity,[48] with only moderate interest in
its relationship to historical context, historians often bracket the quality of
testimony that exceeds contextualization (its often hallucinatory quality, its
gaps, its performative potential to heal), because it is insufficiently related
to the context that generated it.

To the extent that prejudice is defined as natural if regrettable, discrimination and its impact are evacuated of power to injure. To the extent injury
is acknowledged to disturb the putatively natural order of things (meaning
that injury can really be recognized as catastrophic), it is reduced for the
most part to a condition that must be documented rather than an ongoing
struggle to live and recover (I have argued that Friedländer and Gross try
to undermine this tendency with varying degrees of success, but that those
aspects of their work remain marginal or polemical in the eyes of historians). This tendency to bracket those aspects of testimony that exceed such
documentation and to identify them with memory goes far in explaining
how scholars as well as other critical commentators interpret this ongoing struggle to live or to recover in the form of a return to the ordinary,
that is to say, to a recognizable human condition characterized by all that
memory is not and history is: reticence, caution, modesty, and the absence
then of histrionics. Recall that Michael A. Bernstein argues that these experiences (or the event 'the Holocaust') should be rendered ordinary and
thus remain within the realm of the recognizably human and historical not
because they are ordinary, but because the Holocaust proves that human
beings react in extreme fashion to extreme circumstances.

This logic still begs the question not only of how ordinary or extreme
human response is constituted ideologically rather than as a natural re-
action to events as they occur, but also of what counts as ordinary and
extraordinary and thus how victims' experiences are evaluated and constituted as real injuries. It also begs the question of what these experiences tell us about the making and unmaking of social identity (a question

47. Saul Friedlander, *Memory, History, and the Extermination of the Jews of Europe* (Bloomington: Indiana University Press, 1993), 130–31.
48. Kluge and Williams, eds., *Re-examining the Holocaust through Literature,* 9.

which mostly literary theorists have pondered primarily in psychological or psychoanalytic terms, as Trezise has), as well as of how people might be made to disappear psychically and even literally. Most important, perhaps, we can see now that 'human,' 'history,' and 'ordinary' are tautologies whose impact is to cause the presumption that even extraordinary responses are ultimately ordinary because human and historical, leaving those experiences that cannot be so assimilated no conceptual space other than that of the thoroughly suspect realm of memory, now cast as a traumatic injury that has not been mastered. The failure to address these experiences, except for the most part from the bystanders' point of view, as human responses to crises embedded or not in modes of distantiation leaves theoretical room for a tendency to treat these experiences as things which are sacred and defy any sort of human understanding other than religious, or in terms of secularized forms of abjection that evoke fascination and pleasure. In short, under pressure of the so-called surfeit of Holocaust memory, the imperative to return to the ordinary and to history against memory has intensified at the expense of understanding how victims must be constituted to be credible and at what cost, and tends, as do all forms of neo-positivism, to deepen the abyss in which mysticism and things sacred reside.

The Social Organization of Affect

The human "body in pain" does not only symbolize violated dignity or provoke the desire to redeem suffering and render the body whole, but also often evokes anxiety, contempt, and pleasure that cannot be reduced merely to sadism. Nor can it be treated only as a violated, but sacred or profane thing (as does Giorgio Agamben, for example, by defining abjection as the only possible form of victim identity).[49] Hannah Arendt most dramatically addressed this complex set of problems from a perspective closer to understanding how the so-called redemptive power of violence as it was understood in the interwar period by figures such as Walter Benjamin and Georges Sorel may have perilous dimensions, especially when

49. Agamben, *Remnants of Auschwitz.*

embedded in institutions.[50] How, Arendt asks, does the affect associated with anti-Semitism—envy, revulsion, and so on—become an organized social form that replaces what we might call tolerance or assimilation (since liberal pluralism did not exist in continental Europe in its current Anglo-American form, and the status of Jews differed from nation to nation)? Arendt focuses squarely on promises of assimilation in late nineteenth-century France as a means of addressing aversion toward Jews, and in particular, the peculiar form that violence against them took and its consistency with the extermination to come.[51]

In the late 1930s, before fleeing Germany for France, where she escaped an internment camp, Arendt was concerned about the difficulty assimilated Jews and Zionists alike had in accepting that difference and sameness might coexist. She argued that Zionism was merely the other side of assimilation: it asserted a radical difference rather than the more complex interplay of difference and similarity that characterized the marginal Jew's relation to the land in which he or she was born.[52] Here she sought to provide a framework within which to examine the nature of discrimination and its consequences, in particular how it facilitates victims' desire to embrace either their own difference or their own disappearance (in the case of assimilated Jews).

In *The Origins of Totalitarianism,* Arendt provides a detailed account of how victims or, more broadly speaking, marginalized people permit their own erasure by believing in the promise of assimilation or, again more generally, by refusing to stand up for what they believe. She suggests that anxiety and contempt for Jews in interwar bourgeois Paris (a stand-in for modern European bourgeois life) took the social form of an "open secret"

50. Walter Benjamin and Georges Sorel in different ways attributed to violence world-creating or self-making powers rather than purely instrumental force. Though Sorel was called a fascist, he was a Marxist in a new guise who sought to blend Marx with Bergsonian thought. This redemptive violence was aestheticized and has a long and contested history.

51. Wendy Brown has defined tolerance as the social regulation of difference by focusing on culture, because the presumption that we are all equal before the law means, in liberal democracies today, that respectable political discourse cannot openly proclaim its aggression toward difference except by denouncing the cultural practices of others as barbaric (hence the hostility toward the Islamic "veil" in France). See Brown, *Regulating Aversion: Tolerance in the Age of Identity and Empire* (Princeton: Princeton University Press, 2006).

52. Hannah Arendt, *The Jewish Writings,* ed. Jerome Kohn and Ron H. Feldman (New York: Schocken Books, 2007), 48–59.

in which Jewish identity was known, privately permissible, and yet unspeakable. For the open secret combined the abhorrence of loudly proclaimed Jewishness (and fears of its contagiousness) with its quiet display.
Indeed, though her choice of Proust's fictional salons as a location to il-
lustrate the pitfalls of assimilation during the Dreyfus Affair may appear a
simple reference to the great half-Jewish gay ironist of social custom, Arendt uses Proust to draw an analogy between Jews and "inverts" that renders the concept of the open secret, used recently in contemporary criticism
to discuss homosexuality, useful. That is, the open secret was not only a
form of social regulation that turned the lives of those Jews who preferred
to pass as gentiles into private hells, breeding loneliness and isolation in the
form of the tolerance implicit in a policy of 'don't tell' (except among one's
brethren). Nor was it only a regime of "knowing," and "unknowing," as
the late Eve Sedgwick argues, that kept a threat paradoxically invisible and
yet always exposed: for Sedgwick, passing is the pained performance of
being like others (in her work, pretending to being heterosexual) that most
people understand to be a performance. Arendt also envisions the open
secret as a form of sadistic, institutionalized, entrapment.[53]

Indeed, Arendt addressed the idea that phantasmatic violence was an
important feature of open secrecy in her work on anti-Semitism and assimilation. Most interesting about Arendt's discussion is her emphasis on
the content of the threat posed by Jews and those she terms "inverts" and
on their impossible relation to the regulatory violence that puts them in
their place. In her discussion of anti-Semitism and the Dreyfus Affair in
turn-of-the-century Paris, she uses Proust to exemplify the promise of assimilation as a quintessentially bourgeois form of contempt. Proust's gay
character Charlus "rose to new social heights," "'notwithstanding his vice,'"
as Proust puts it. "Topics of conversation which he formerly would have
avoided—love, beauty, jealousy—lest somebody suspect his anomaly, were
now welcomed avidly 'in view of the experience, strange, secret, refined

53. Hannah Arendt, *The Origins of Totalitarianism* (New York: Harcourt Brace Jovanovich, 1976 [1951]). On the 'open secret'—or the 'closet' as a structural relation rather than a metaphor for loneliness and isolation, see Eve Kosofsky Sedgwick, *Epistemology of the Closet* (Berkeley: University of California Press, 1990). Sedgwick addresses the open secret as a pernicious and oppressive regime of "knowing." She draws on D. A. Miller's concept of "the open secret" in *The Novel and the Police* (Berkeley: University of California Press, 1988), 207.

and monstrous upon which he founded' his views."[54] But Arendt's enmity is directed not only at the French bourgeoisie, but also at Jews and gay men who mistook tolerance for acceptance. "The difference," she argues,

> between the Faubourg Saint-Germain, which had suddenly discovered the attractiveness of Jews and inverts, and the mob that cried "Death to the Jews" was that the salons had not yet associated themselves openly with crime. This meant that on the one hand they did not yet want to participate actively in the killing, and on the other, still professed openly an antipathy toward Jews and a horror of inverts. This in turn resulted in that typically equivocal situation in which the new members could not confess their identity openly, and yet could not hide it either. Such were the conditions from which arose the complicated game of exposure and concealment, of half-confessions and lying distortions, of exaggerated humility and exaggerated arrogance, all of which were consequences of the fact that only one's Jewishness (or homosexuality) had opened the doors of the exclusive salons, while at the same time they made one's position extremely insecure.[55]

In Arendt's view, the bourgeoisie harbored unconscious desires to murder those exotic creatures whom it had admitted into its salons at the fin de siècle. The compulsion of these "philosemites" to murder, she goes on, is a compulsion to "purge themselves of secret viciousness, to cleanse themselves of a stigma which they had mysteriously and wickedly loved."[56] This "viciousness" is embedded in a psychological quality she calls "Jewishness." Arendt's interpretation clearly focuses on an otherwise ungraspable dimension of violence embedded in the construction of an open secret that speaks to the complex way in which the revulsion toward Jewishness is inseparable from an attachment to it. Of course, she too demonstrates that open secrets, permissible concealment, privatization of a difference of

---

54. Arendt, *The Origins of Totalitarianism,* 81, citing from Marcel Proust's *Cities of the Plain.*

55. Arendt, *The Origins of Totalitarianism,* 82.

56. Arendt, *The Origins of Totalitarianism,* 86. I should note that Arendt interprets the Dreyfus Affair as having opened "society's doors to Jews," and the end of the Affair as the end of their "glory," which depended, in her view, on anti-Semitism, on a perverse attachment to and hatred of Jewish difference (86). From a historical point of view this argument is extremely idiosyncratic. It is difficult to argue that this complex affective relationship to Jews alone determined the degree of their assimilation or rejection, though it certainly helps explain the power of anti-Semitism and its institutionalization in affective terms.

which 'everyone is aware' are forms of institutionalized marginality. But she interprets the open secret not only as moral, sexual, and 'racial' regulation mirrored in the social practices of selective inclusion (the salons). Nor does she think it is merely a form of social control that reduces the threat of otherness and contains revulsion. Instead, in her view, open secrecy also manifests organized sadistic, even homicidal desires that cannot recognize themselves as such (a blindness that distinguishes these desires from the all-too-conscious violence of the proto-fascist mob on the streets).

Jewish identity marks the impossible humanity of those whose survival depended on how well they performed their disappearance—that they publicly shed their skins, their desires, their ethnicity, their selfhood. In Arendt, assimilation as open secrecy is a form of sadistic entrapment: the majority population asserts that difference is bearable, all the while becoming excited, gratified, and repulsed by its discreet display. Arendt's view underlines the continuity between fin de siècle constructions of the Jewish threat and those that emerged in more acute form after the Great War. As Arendt argued, what looked like the increasing acceptance of religious and sexual difference—invitations to the most exclusive salons—in fact signaled an intense desire to rid the world of Jews and homosexuals, even though she appears to describe that desire in the pretty conventional terms of projection.

If we speculate about Arendt's logic, the open secret is always a reminder and rendering of otherness, but it is never sufficient to deflect anxiety. Yes, as Arendt notes, the marked stylized exaggerations among the Jewish elite who entered the salons reflect a superior or overly deferential air that they cultivated as modes of self-assertion, self-protection, and self-identification. But this otherness was not a soothing reminder of difference contained but an enraging one: while Arendt conceives them as symptoms of Jews' real marginality, anti-Semitic critics turned these symptoms, including Jews' putative arrogance or unctuousness, into negative traits of a people who either had no right to make claims on its own behalf or masked its real lust for power behind a desire to please.

By addressing prejudice as a force not evacuated of affective power, Arendt suggests in the end that it is neither a 'natural' human response under pressure nor a simple projection of displaced fears or desires onto undesirable others, but a complex mobilization of affective relations that serves institutional purposes: shaping Jewish identity are modes of coping with aggression, whether it takes the form of defensive superiority or extreme, sometimes artificial, deference. In so doing, she implies that the ordinary or banal encounter between Jews and gentiles is in fact an extraordinary form of institutionalized violence, mirroring in other terms the less contained violence against Jews in the streets (though Arendt notes that the salons are peopled by those who profess their anti-Semitism openly as well, but clearly don't act on it). She also argues implicitly that assimilation in the form of what looks like tolerance illusorily resolves the modern tension between the idea that we are all equal before the law in spite of aversions some may have for others, and prejudice, or the aversion that impedes the practice of treating people equally. Arendt exposes a link between prejudice and an allegedly mature, democratically inclined citizenry that critics are loath to recognize, not by refusing to acknowledge that prejudice exists, but by revealing to what extent prejudice and civility coexist even when the latter appears to have, however problematically, overcome the primitive manifestations of the former embodied by the pogroms in the street.

Prejudice is thus ordinary in the sense that it may be institutionalized in various contexts but extraordinary in its capacity to wound, and the human response that putatively constitutes discrimination against others is not naturalized but constituted as a complex interplay of psychic and institutional forces whose violence is inseparable from the institutions that are supposed to contain it. The gratification afforded by higher social status merely signals the socialization of an explosive violence that is already present on the streets and in the transparently biased judgment of Dreyfus. Though Arendt is most interested in how violence is institutionalized, she demonstrates how it is so embedded in a way that sustains a conceptual space for injury which exceeds institutional forms (including the scholarly imperative of documentation). She thus rejects the critical effort to locate conceptual and emotional solace in history as a space free of projection, idealization, and other affective response. In her view, history is not just the documentation of the condition of injury but also the fashioning of injury in various and even opaque guises. In short, in Arendt's brief commentary, history, the ordinary, and the human are not a tautology because there is nothing self-evident or natural about how human beings respond under pressure and nothing at all ordinary about the power of prejudice.

Though Arendt is hardly the only major thinker to theorize about how violence is institutionalized, and how affect for better and worse is embedded in legal and social norms (one thinks of the many works of Theodor Adorno and, later, of Michel Foucault or Robert Coover in particular), her focus on Jews and on the tangible ways in which affect is mobilized makes her singularly compelling if we are to try and imagine other kinds of discourses about Jewish victims or even victims in general. Though the passages I have cited are short excerpts from a far larger book, she speaks eloquently about how *bystanders* are overly attached to the gratification afforded by the spectacle of those they wound.[57] If we follow her logic, perhaps critics' willingness to view victims as overly attached to their injuries might be a projection of bystanders' own powerlessness, guilt, or even complicity. Thus the Nazi occupation and the Holocaust, which in the West led to radically new conceptions of social death as well as efforts to grapple with irreparable individual and collective social and psychic wounds, fashioned Jewish victims as a projection of many of their compatriots' own experiences, that is, the majority who had not actively resisted or protested: they were innocent and yet guilty, terrorized into passivity and disempowerment, but nonetheless ashamed not to have struggled more than they did.[58] It is as if victims' own powerlessness and silence in the face of terror were projected onto bystanders, whose "fear" of foreigners, indifference, desire not to know, and fear of the state caused so much hand-wringing and rendered opaque any account of their own complicity. Surely the argument that by defining themselves as Hitler's victims Germans were unable to mourn or account for their actual complicity in the murder of European Jewry is but one more well-known version of this particular logic of projection.

57. In *On Violence* (New York: Harcourt Brace, 1969), Arendt is most concerned to distinguish between power and violence (the latter conceived in instrumental terms) and equates terror with the collapse of power and atomization, as she does in *Origins*. But in her discussion of rage, for example (63–64), she reiterates a theme we see throughout her work: admiration for a certain kind of self-making rage (since she associates dehumanization with terror and the subsequent numbing of emotions) whose real and psychological limits she nonetheless recognizes.

58. This is not to say that there was no shame at having been victimized. See Waxman, *Writing the Holocaust,* 102–3, 116.

Toward an Ethics of Writing about Victims

Now that trauma has become central to self-identity, and with it, of course, the dubious status of being or having been a victim, it is of great urgency that we not simply argue, as have Didier Fassin and Richard Rechtman, that trauma has replaced an older "moral economy" of sympathy and heroism.[59] In this inversion from one moral universe to a moral economy in which empathy itself requires an attachment to pain, all of us are now or wish to be potential victims. But the idea that we have moved from suspicion of victims to embrace them evades to what extent this new moral economy is a part of the ongoing historical refashioning of cultural attitudes to victims. These attitudes can be understood only in relational and affective terms in which suspicion, envy, attachment, and aversion are all in the process of being reformulated in reference to a new historical context in which the Holocaust of European Jewry has become the paradigmatic catastrophe. The new centrality and diffusion of injury have reinvigorated an older moral economy in which victims who demonstrated no agency under pressure of circumstances were least respected, least dignified, and perhaps even suspect. It is this narrative of human willfulness against the odds, of human willfulness and its power to make or unmake the world, that is always implicated in any discussion about victims and victimization, including a profound cultural investment in the moral soundness of those who suffer. Even the increased centrality of the victim since the nineteenth century presumes a victim-agent who seeks remuneration and protection for wrongs rather than a passive or abject subject who witnesses and lives through catastrophe. It is the introduction of the traumatized victim of catastrophe who, in his or her extreme disempowerment and traumatic, deferred, and thus often empirically indecipherable grief, appears to have generated as much aversion and suspicion as sympathy.

The diffusion of trauma to define all sorts of suffering is indeed problematic and is partially a consequence of the iconic status granted the Holocaust and the complicated affective relations of non-victims to those who have been victimized. The answer to the dehistoricization of memory and the leveling of injury thus generated is not to condemn a new moral

---

59. Didier Fassin and Richard Rechtman, *L'empire du traumatisme: Enquête sur la condition de victime* (Paris: Flammarion, 2007).

universe in which victims have taken center stage. Rather, it is to understand how this truism that suffering is now central to identity may be a more or less unconscious way of expressing a melancholic sense of loss or nostalgia—perhaps at times a process of mourning a redemptive construction of certain kinds of victims that was really no more or less sympathetic to victims of catastrophe than 'we' are supposed to be now. The most salient contribution of those critics in mourning has been to cast suspicion on all victims in the process of defining who really is a victim. To address fully these debates and their impact we must not only reveal to what extent they are embedded in and attached to a particular rhetorical constitution of exemplary victims: we must also draw attention to the deep cultural ambivalence about the state of being victimized that informs that exemplarity. In this context, we might recall that Dr. Louis Micheel's memoir, to which I alluded earlier, was extolled because it was not "histrionic," and was thus "reassuring" and "life-affirming." His words not only suggest that we cannot identify with victims who do not reassure and affirm life, but also beg the question of why we need victims to do so. This praise of Micheels, like the more pervasive praise of a far more famous memoirist like Primo Levi, avoids focusing on the aversion to their plight that victims themselves so often discuss.[60]

One might also note that those theorists who are not skeptical of victims, like Wendy Brown, still fail to diagnose why recovery is so difficult except in terms that reiterate the importance of insight, will, and agency in seeing through and resisting oppression. According to her, minorities believe that pluralistic political systems will better hear their grievances if they work within the system by defining themselves as having injuries they believe it might respond to. If neo-liberalism is the source not simply of wounds created by inequity, but also of an attachment to the wounds it creates, than only a willful struggle for what you want against a state that seeks to regulate your demands can make a difference. This argument, whether we

60. "I saw one of the soldiers bend over and vomit, and then another one. And then I understood. It disgusted them to look at us. They found us repulsive." Clara Greenbaum, liberated from Bergen-Belsen, quoted in François Bédarida and Laurent Gervereau, eds., *La déportation, le système concentrationnaire nazi* (Paris: Collections des publications de la BDIC dirigée par Joseph Hue, 1995), 201. This response to liberated victims is rarely discussed, and the impact of having been so degraded tends to be felt most often in the request that victims' dereliction not be put on display.

agree with its substance or not, does not address the existence of the deep cultural aversion to having been wounded, to the victim's debilitation (as opposed to the perpetrator's self-lacerations) and its impact on self-making and the constitution of exemplary and less desirable forms of personhood. The history of injury may be constituted by the patterns of survivors' testimony that correlate so that memories are verifiable and trustworthy and thus immune to the vagaries of victims' efforts to remember. But it is only criticism that embeds injury in the social relations that shape responses to it (and thus criticism which refuses to avert its eyes from injury) that will allow us to conceptualize impediments to recovery. In so doing, it might enable us to address from victims' points of view how a cultural aversion to or discomfort with their pain might generate the need for narratives that in one way or another reiterate that pain by denying, repressing, or erasing it, thereby compromising recovery.[61]

Cultural discomfort both with constrained agency and with fantasies about others' abjection is present even when victims are unmistakably survivors. Indeed, there is perhaps no better current statement of the discomfort generated by the state of having been victimized than the historian Annette Wieviorka's claim that it was as if, merely because she was a *historian* of Auschwitz, the subject matter would contaminate her, transform her "into a mournful being, living in between evil and death, forbidden the pleasures of life."[62] Surely Wieviorka's own denunciation of our "era of the witness" is informed by anxiety that media representations of survivors invoke and encourage such a response. If this is true, the idea that many people want to have been victims may very well be a symptom of critics' affective relations to victimization that requires further critical attention.

---

61. We should recall how both Saul Friedländer and Jan T. Gross have forcefully made attempts to address these problems from the victim's point of view. See chapter 3.

62. Annette Wieviorka, *Auschwitz: La mémoire d'un lieu* (Paris: Plurielle, 2005), 11.

Epilogue

How do dominant Western cultural presumptions that suffering is central to shaping identity, that injury confers social recognition, and that we all have a narcissistic investment in trauma obscure victims' sufferings? How might we acknowledge victims' pain in this context? The quest for the 'real' victim stresses ambivalence toward self-proclaimed victims and suspicions of their motives at a moment in history when images of pain no longer carry the force of self-evidence, when technologies of reproduction and media sensationalism contribute to fears of distortion and false claims, and when the intensified demands for redress by a wide variety of populations contribute to the powerful and pervasive rhetoric that victimization now confers status rather than shame. Of course, victims have always provoked disorientation, manifest in the numbness, denial, and discomfort of those who have not shared their experience, and we have discussed the dynamics of these relations in various ways. Indeed, we might note that the victims whose pain is most proximate and discussed in the United States—African Americans—are also those whose pain is often most contested by outright denial, if not of the legacy of slavery, then of its long-term impact and of the effects of discrimination. Even the sacralization of Holocaust survivors, more powerful in the United States than in most of Europe, need not necessarily reflect an embrace of victimization (though it may very well manifest narcissistic overidentification). It also arguably serves as evidence that victims provoke such deep discomfort that we insist on their distance by rendering them luminous—in this case sacred, in a transformed secular meaning of the term.

It is crucial to understand the overlap between American and French discussions of so-called victim culture in order to assess their pervasive power in the West. But it is also important to keep in mind how much the formation of minority rights in varying political cultures and different relations between state and society explain the nuanced differences between American and French critical perspectives. In the United States, liberal pluralism assumes that individuals and groups with diverse interests debate and define the meaning of the state. Structural inequities of all sorts may thus be acknowledged. At the same time, depending on their perspective, those engaged in such debates may also deny the existence of such inequities or their power to injure: some critics have argued that structural inequities or a history of suffering such as slavery are past, and have no impact on racism in the present; that words may or may not wound; that hate crimes need not necessarily require additional recognition when there exist laws to condemn the mistreatment of other human beings.

In France, critics' transformation of Jewish memory into the locus of excessive self-indulgence similarly contests even as it acknowledges Jewish pain by ascribing to Jews the power to make their suffering so central to Western culture that it obscures the pain of others. The specificity of French political culture and the French model of republicanism may explain why French debates target Jews differently than do American critics, though debates in both locations almost always involve phantasmatic projections about victims that only rarely engage with victims themselves. In France, the abstract individual represents the citizen and the nation, and his or her ability to be representative relies on the extent to which his or her particularities can be abstracted. Thus assimilation is not premised on the recognition of difference under certain conditions, but on the presumption that differences exist only as private concerns.[1]

---

1. The recognition of class difference and thus socioeconomic inequity is the exception in France, for historical reasons.

The strategy of claiming to have been victimized in order to secure rights is not particularly compelling in a context in which particularity and difference are already liabilities. As I have noted, Joan Scott argues that French opponents of Muslim girls' right to wear head-scarves to public schools constructed French citizens as victims of outsiders threatening the abstract equality and universality of French educational institutions.[2] Similarly, the historical legacy of anti-Semitism and the resurgence of memory about the Holocaust appear to have led French critics to project onto Jews claims related to the peculiar privilege of having suffered grievously. Here too critics become victims of minority groups who make what are perceived to be excessive claims on French citizens.

Surely, as I have insisted throughout, there are victims who exaggerate their claims, and others who seek to capitalize on having suffered or even who pretend to have done so. It is hard to argue against Wendy Brown's assertion that some minority groups in the United States develop attachments to their own suffering because it is an effective means by which second-class citizens receive state recognition. In keeping with the logic of Brown's argument, we might add that the tendency of some people to stage hate crimes against themselves is not only a pathological demand for attention, but also a misguided and disturbed acknowledgment that one's pain as an 'outsider' can be noted only when violence is perpetrated and a basic moral and social principle transgressed: the boundaries of the human body are in theory sacred, and it is prohibited to literalize by violent acts the discrimination that may be otherwise acceptable, even codified (thus the same people who condemn immigrants or gays in the United States and France only rarely condone extralegal violence against these groups, even when their otherwise inflammatory rhetoric encourages it). The revival of the legitimacy of torture in the context of fighting terrorism may call the body's sacredness into question, but the body's right not to suffer violence remains an important component of Western legal and moral self-representation. Here we might return to Marie L., the woman whose false claims to have been marked with swastikas by young French men of Arab and African descent I invoked at the beginning of this effort to understand the cultural fashioning of victims. If she had really been injured and had been Jewish, the fact of her ethnicity and the discomfort

---

2. Joan Scott, *The Politics of the Veil* (Princeton: Princeton University Press, 2007).

it provokes might have been taken seriously. But the response to her case may also highlight how easily discussion slipped from anti-Semitism and racism to a society in love with victims no matter who they are, as if the drama she enacted did not demand a broader discussion about attitudes toward the Holocaust, to Jews, and to those of Arab and African descent, immigrants or naturalized citizens.

Even if we acknowledge that some victims are not what they appear to be, the pervasive assumption that the experience and memory of Jewish genocide have dramatically undermined the rational contestation of grievances in democratic societies should be examined critically. In this book I have sought above all to focus on the peculiarity of critics' effort to return to an empirical history of injury deemed overwhelmed by memory, itself related to the iconic and thus ahistorical status granted Auschwitz and, by proxy, Jewish memory. The status of Auschwitz as an icon of evil in our time has directly and indirectly generated the evacuation of historical in favor of the moral content of suffering that leads to the peculiar concept of 'too much' memory. This pervasive reference to "excessive" or "surfeit" memory is surely the most problematic figuration of victims' demands for recognition: as I have sought to demonstrate over and over, the idea that there is a universal memory of suffering assumes that all memories are equal and equally recognized, and that demands for recognition of particular suffering might be excessive, disproportionate, and thus themselves aggressive and overwrought claims. The concept of surfeit memory should be recast and envisioned properly as a transformation of victims into aggressors who threaten the tranquility of those whose memories are acknowledged. Robert Meister argues that Abraham Lincoln resolved rhetorically the American Civil War by claiming that whites and blacks were equally victims, whites of their own inhumanity.[3] If correct, his is an excellent example of how universal memory cannot in fact take into account the historical differences in the treatment of victims and may in some cases even reduce all forms of victimization to the same moral content, as I have argued with regard to equations between Stalinism and Nazism, Jewish dead and German

3. Robert Meister, "Forgiving and Forgetting: Lincoln and the Politics of National Recovery," in *Human Rights in Political Transition: Gettysburg to Bosnia,* ed. Carla Hesse and Robert Post (New York: Zone Books, 1999), 135–76.

dead, Italian fascists and Italian partisans, and so on. Moreover, I hope to have shown that the fashioning of the exemplary victim, typically someone who has a quiet and controlled response to having been victimized and whose testimonial style is thus valorized, is a false measure by which to judge all victims. The exemplary victim is inextricable from an ideology of stoicism in the face of pain, and of suffering with honor. It may figure some ways of suffering. But this stubborn construct finally conceals cultural discomfort with pain and suffering in which societies often feel complicit. It tells us more about the projections onto victims of those who did not suffer than it does about the actual experience of victimization.

In the end victims cease to have identities and experiences and become projections of others' own anxieties—about injury, about vulnerability, about democracy. The historical experience of victims is erased in favor of figuring victimization as a form of too much memory. The surfeit of memory stands in for the erasure of real identity in favor of illusions about the singularity of one's own suffering. What, we might ask, is the investment in conceiving all Jews—and indeed increasingly other victims of catastrophe and hatred—as trying to take up limited space, as clinging to false identities, as narcissistic and responsible for the destruction of rational contestation in favor of histrionic and thus emotionally overwhelming claims? By examining these assertions critically we raise questions about the ethics of historical writing, for we might ask how we can shape responses to victims more effectively by dismantling cultural projections that erase the experience of the very victims in whose name we are supposed to speak. To do this much might help us to tackle the ongoing problems confronting victims whose suffering remains unacknowledged. It should also help us to question our own skepticism while remaining vigilant about would-be victims. Most of all, it opens up a critical field that allows us to investigate the limitations of historical and literary theoretical methods in confronting the overwhelmingly affective dimensions of institutionalized violence and its impact not only on victims' experience, but also on how victims choose to convey what happened to them.

I conclude with the memoir of Hélène Berr, who wrote about being a hunted Jewish woman in occupied Paris. She exemplifies how the cultural imperatives that define victims' credibility are often the same demands that sustain victims' aloneness and sense of abandonment. Berr, who throughout acted the part of the dignified and honorable victim and indeed behaved stoically to save children at great risk to herself, protests:

> Often I feel that I am playacting, and that my duty ought to be to appear not normal, to reveal it, to display the real gulf separating us [Jews] from other people instead of trying to ignore it or even avert my gaze, which I often do, out of respect, so others are not aware of my reproach. If only people knew what ruins are in my heart![4]

4. Hélène Berr, *The Journal of Hélène Berr,* trans. David Bellos (New York: Weinstein Books, 2008), 205.

INDEX

abjection, 32n4, 133, 160–61n35, 162, 166, 168, 177
abolitionism, 13
The Abuses of Memory (Todorov), 85, 88
Act and Idea in the Nazi Genocide (Lang), 134–42
Adorno, Theodor, 173
affective relationship with victims, 8, 19, 28, 102, 113, 143–44, 150, 160, 166, 171n56, 175, 177
African American slavery, 3, 6n17, 13, 17n50, 39, 41, 99, 178–79, 181
Agamben, Giorgio, 32n4, 160–61n35, 168
aggression, repressed, victims as objects of, 27–28
AIDS, as Holocaust, 3
Algerian War, 10, 59
Allied bombing raids in Second World War, 18, 62n13
Améry, Jean, 109n21, 152
animal rights activists, Holocaust comparisons by, 3
Antelme, Robert, 109n24
anti-identarianism, 93

anti-Semitism
    France, renewal in, 1, 48, 60, 61
    and Jewish perception of victimhood, 19, 31, 32, 42n31, 50, 160
    Lang, Berel, on, 140
    passivity of Jews during Holocaust, claims of, 160
    in Poland, 124
    redemptive, Friedländer's concept of, 74, 116–17, 140
    social organization and institutionalization of, 168–74
    surfeit of Jewish memory as projection of, 64n18
    of Vichy regime, 34
anti-victimism, 7
anti-Zionism and Zionism, 59n4, 91n107, 94, 169
"anxiety of transmission," 150
Appelfeld, Aharon, 32, 56, 102, 153n19
appropriation of/desire for victimhood, 2–4, 36, 37–46, 97, 154, 178–83

appropriation of Jewish identity, 2, 45–46, 53–54, 57, 132, 138, 146

Arab-Israeli War of 1948, 92n109

Arab-Israeli War of 1967, 15, 60n5, 158–59

Arad, Yitzahk, 115

Arendt, Hannah
   events shaping reception of work of, 11n28
   on Jewish burden of innocence, 41
   Jewish Councils, denunciation of, 155
   on Jewish passivity, 157
   on limits of human rights, 13
   on minimalism in victim testimony, 101
   on social organization and institutionaliza-
      tion of prejudice and violence, 168–74
   on totalitarianism, 65, 66, 92
   as universalist, 96

Aron, Raymond, 66, 67n28, 73n48, 75

ascetic minimalism. *See* minimalism

assimilation, 89, 98, 169–72

Aubrac, Raymond, 110–11

Auschwitz
   erasure of victims of, 143, 145, 156n24,
      160n35, 161, 177
   as icon of evil, 181
   identification with victims of, 3–4
   minimalism and, 102, 103, 107, 109n21, 129,
      132, 137
   "Muslims" at, 160n35
   Ravensbrück compared, 10
   surfeit of Jewish memory and, 59, 60, 82, 83,
      93, 94, 95n120

Austrian and German populations, rhetoric of
   victimhood applied to, 12, 18, 24, 40, 47,
   62n13, 112–13, 174

aversion, 8, 28, 30, 151, 160, 169, 173, 175–77

Badiou, Alain, 22–24, 63n15, 93

Ball, Karyn, 5, 63n15

Barbarism with a Human Face (Lévy), 66

Barbie, Klaus, 10n27, 18, 59, 67

Bardot, Brigitte, 3

Barkan, Elazar, 96–97

Barnouw, Dagmar, 35–36, 46

Bartov, Omer, 163n30

Baudrillard, Jean, 3–4, 20–21

Bauer, Yehuda, 158

Bauman, Zygmunt, 32, 40, 48, 164

Bédarida, François, 91, 158

Bellamy, Elizabeth J., 5–6n12

Beloved (Morrison), 39

Benbassa, Esther, 32, 42, 44, 55

Benjamin, Walter, 4, 101–2, 168, 169n50

Benoist, Alain de, 96

Bensoussan, Georges, 91, 151

Bergen-Belsen, 6, 145, 176n60

Berlant, Lauren, 22–24

Berlin Memorial, 6

Berlusconi, Silvio, 69n93

Bernstein, Michael André, 32, 47, 52–53,
   103–4n11, 167

Berr, Hélène, 145–46, 182–83

Besançon, Alain, 75–79, 82–83, 88, 89, 91

Betts, Hannah, 16, 17

Bigsby, Charles, 154

The Black Book of Communism, 68–72, 73, 76

Black slavery in U.S., 3, 6n17, 13, 17n50, 39,
   41, 99, 178–79, 181

blaming the victim, 33–34, 60, 157

blood libel, 42, 124

bombing raids in Second World War, 18, 62n13

Brauman, Romy, 61n10, 91n107

Breines, Paul, 159

Brossat, Alain, 92–98

Brown, Wendy, 22–24, 28, 169n51, 176, 180

Browning, Christopher, 114–15, 123, 146–47,
   164, 165

Bruckner, Pascal, 44

Bulgaria, 84, 86, 163, 166

Buruma, Ian, 2, 3, 43, 97

bystander/perpetrator behavior, naturalization
   of, 161–68

"camp universe" or *univers concentrationnaire,*
   10

Caron, Vicki, 64n18

carpet-bombing, 18, 62n13

Carroll, David, 48n44, 50n51

Chaumont, Jean-Michel, 89–91, 93, 96, 97

Chaunu, Pierre, 58–59, 62, 71, 73, 76

Ciampi, Carlo Azeglio, 25n75

Civil War, U.S., 181

Cole, Alyson M., 7, 33–34

Communism
   Nazism and. *See* Stalinism and Nazism,
      comparisons of
   supposed Jewish attraction to, 124

"competition of victims," 3, 6n17, 26, 29, 44, 50,
   67, 89, 91n107

Conan, Éric, 48–49, 51

Confino, Alon, 117–18, 120, 166n46

Coover, Robert, 173

Courtois, Stéphane, 69, 70–72, 73, 76

crimes against humanity, concept of, 13–14
culture of victimhood. *See* victims and victimhood after the Holocaust
Czerniaków, Adam, 155–56

Daniel, Jean, 76, 77
Dante, Levi's enjoyment of, 109n21
Dawidowicz, Lucy S., 157–58, 165n43
de Gaulle, Charles, 14
de Haan, Ido, 14n36, 37, 38
deconstructive performative, 39
Defiance (Tec), 157n28
Delbo, Charlotte, 53, 102, 145
Demjanjuk, John, 146
democracy, modern, totalitarianism of, 92–93
desire for/appropriation of victimhood, 2–4, 36, 37–46, 97, 154, 178–83
The Destruction of the European Jews (Hilberg), 103
Dieudonné, 42n31, 99
"dividends of Auschwitz," 60
Dössekker, Bruno (Binjamin Wilkomirski), 45–46, 53–54, 57, 132, 138, 146
Dresden, Sem, 106n15, 147
Dreyfus Affair, 170–71, 173
The Drowned and the Saved (Levi), 107

Edith P., 133
Ehrenbourg, Ilya, 69–70
Eichmann, Adolf, 15
Eichmann in Jerusalem (Arendt), 101, 155
emancipation in France, assimilation as Jewish price for, 89, 98
emotion and feeling. *See* minimalism
Engel, David, 125
entertainment, victimhood as, 5–6, 16, 20
erasure, 8, 143–77, 182
    assimilation as, 89, 98, 169–72
    critics' participation in, 7, 143–44
    defined, 144
    ethics of writing about victims and, 175–77
    Jewish victimization as stand-in for, 64
    literary theory and, 147–49, 152–55
    naturalization of prejudice and victimization, 161–68
    passivity of Jews during Holocaust, claims of, 153, 155–60
    reasons for, 28
    by sacralization of victims, 143, 160, 179
    social organization and institutionalization of prejudice and violence, 168–74

surfeit of Jewish memory and, 152–53
    transmission of victim memory, problem of, 147–52
    universalism, through concept of. *See* universalism
    victim memoirs on experience of, 144–45
ethics of writing about victims, 175–77
Evans, Richard, 118
exemplary versus literal memory, 84–88, 100
exemplary victims, 8, 30, 144, 152, 176, 182
Eyewitness Auschwitz, (Müller), 158
Ezrahi, Sidra DeKoven, 106n15, 147

Fackenheim, Emil, 90n102
Farber, Daniel, 8–9n23
Fassin, Didier, 21–22, 24n71, 175
Fear (Gross), 116, 123–28
feeling and emotion. *See* minimalism
Feher, Michel, 2, 43–44
Felman, Shoshana, 32n4, 160–61n35, 168
Ferry, Jean-Luc, 80n71
Findor, Andrej, 12n30
Finkelstein, Norman, 18, 60–61n9
Finkielkraut, Alain, 32, 43–44, 61n10, 91n107
First World War (Great War), victimhood discourse associated with, 9, 14, 47
Foucault, Michel, 30n84, 55n57, 92, 174
Fragments (Wilkomirski), 45–46, 53–54, 138
France
    assimilation as Jewish price for emancipation in, 89, 98
    Communist Party in, 65–66, 67
    concentration on French and U.S. discourse, 24–26
    differences between French and U.S. discourse, 179–80
    French Revolution, 58–59, 72, 82
    Marie L. case, 1–3, 180–81
    Muslims in, 21n62, 26, 34, 61, 62, 99n131, 180
    neo-liberalism in, 66, 67, 166
    renewed anti-Semitism in, 1, 48, 60, 61
    republicanism in, 26, 34, 44, 62, 179
    resistance in Second World War, 9–11, 18, 25, 158
    universalism in. *See* universalism
    Vichy regime, 2n4, 34–35, 49, 59–60, 67–68
    victimhood after the Holocaust in. *See* victims and victimhood after the Holocaust
Franklin, Ruth, 38, 56, 103

Friedländer, Saul, 74, 90n102, 103, 113–23, 126, 127, 140, 141, 166, 167
Furet, François, 64, 66, 67–68n28, 72–75, 77, 79, 82

Garapon, Antoine, 27n79
gays and lesbians, 3, 170–71
generalization of phenomenon of suffering. *See* universalism
German and Austrian populations, rhetoric of victimhood applied to, 12, 18, 24, 40, 47, 62n13, 112–13, 174
Gilbert, Martin, 129
Glas, Margareta, 156n24
Głowiński, Michał, 106–8, 110, 111n29
Glucksmann, André, 66
Goldberg, Amos, 5–6, 121–22
Great War, victimhood discourse associated with, 9, 14, 47
Greenbaum, Clara, 176n60
Grémion, Pierre, 64
Gross, Jan T., 113, 114, 116, 123–28, 141, 147n8, 167, 177n61
Grosser, Alfred, 58–59, 77
Grossman, Vassili, 69–70
Grynszpan, Zindel, 101
Gulag Archipelago (Solzhenitsyn), 66, 75

Hansen, G. Eric, 8–9n23
heroes/martyrs to victims, historiographic shift of focus from, 4, 15
heroism/martyrdom versus passivity of Jews during Holocaust, 155–60
Hilberg, Raoul, 103, 114, 119
historiography of victimhood, 9–19
    appropriation of Holocaust by other victimized groups, 17–18
    generalized "victims of fascism," 11–12
    in Great War, 9, 14, 47
    heroes/martyrs to victims, shift of focus from, 4, 15
    iconic status of Holocaust, development of, 15–17
    ideological meaning attached to suffering, 12–14
    patriotic suffering, narrative of, 14–15
    resistance fighters and Holocaust victims, tensions between, 9–11, 18
    surfeit of Jewish memory, emergence of concept of, 16–17, 18–19, 32
    victimology, as field, 33–34

Hoffman, Eva, 38, 39, 56, 144, 151
Holc, Jamie, 127
Holocaust
    appropriation by other victimized groups, 3–4, 17–18
    iconic status, development of, 15–18
    initial silence of victims of, 15–16, 32, 43
    passivity of Jews during, claims of, 153, 155–60
    sacralization of survivors. *See* sacralization of Holocaust survivors
    slavery and, 3, 6n17, 17n50, 41
    surfeit of Jewish memory regarding. *See* surfeit of Jewish memory
    uniqueness or singularity of, 63, 88–97
    victimhood after. *See* victims and victimhood after the Holocaust
"Holocaust envy," 3–4
Holocaust fatigue, 60
Holocaust literature, 147–48n10
Holocaust Testimonies (Langer), 128–34
homosexuality, 3, 170–71
Hughes, Robert, 8n23
Huizinga, Johan, 120
human rights
    as ideological concept, 13
    victim culture viewed as product of, 23, 43
Hume, David, 143
"hurbyn" and "Nakba," 92n109
Huyssen, Andreas, 4, 16

identity
    affective relationship to victims through, 8
    anti-identarianism, 93
    appropriation of Jewish identity, 2, 45–46, 53–54, 57, 132, 138, 146
    appropriation of victimhood by non-Holocaust survivors, 37–46
    erasure of. *See* erasure
    Holocaust envy and identity politics, 3–4
    memory and suffering, relationship to, 6–7, 21–24, 30
    passive rather than active construction of, 8
    proper relationship to past suffering, 46–51
    surfeit of Jewish memory as critique of identity politics, 33–36
    surrogate identity, victimhood as, 2
Ignatieff, Michael, 8, 13
innocence, Jewish burden of, 41–42, 90–91, 97, 151–52, 155–56

institutionalization and social organization of
  prejudice and violence, 168–74
intergenerational transmission of trauma,
  37–46
Israel
  Arab-Israeli War of 1948, 92n109
  Arab-Israeli War of 1967, 15, 60n5, 158–59
  compared to Nazi Germany, 56
  Palestinian-Israeli conflict, 15, 26, 29, 44, 50,
    56, 60n5, 61, 63n15, 91n107, 92n109, 94
  Zionism and anti-Zionism, 44, 59n4, 91n107,
    94, 169
Italy, 12n31, 18, 21n62, 25, 42, 62n13, 69n34,
  75, 182
Ivan the Terrible (camp guard), 146

Jaspers, Karl, 41
Jedwabne murders (1941), 123–24
Jewish Councils, 155–56
Jews and Judaism. *See also* anti-Semitism;
  Holocaust; surfeit of Jewish memory; victims and victimhood after the Holocaust
  assimilation of, 89, 98, 169–72
  emancipation in France, assimilation as
    Jewish price for, 89, 98
  innocence, burden of, 41–42, 90–91, 97,
    151–52, 155–56
  literal versus exemplary memory of, 84–88,
    100
  passivity of Jews during Holocaust, claims of,
    153, 155–60
  self-referencing of, 86, 87, 96, 97–98, 100
Joffe, Josef, 55
"Judeocentrism," 49

Kansteiner, Wulf, 5n13, 17n47, 103, 118,
  121n51, 135
kapos, 156
Kellner, Hans, 103, 135
Kielce massacre (1946), 124
kitsch, 97, 101
Kligerman, Eric, 104n13
Kluge, Aukje, 104n13
Kluger, Ruth, 53, 79n68, 128n68, 144, 151,
  161, 162, 166
Korean "comfort women," 43
Kuby, Emma, 10–11n28
Kula, Witold, 1

LaCapra, Dominick, 9n24, 105n14, 114, 160n35
Landsberg, Alison, 6n17

Lang, Berel, 31, 113, 114n33, 128, 134–42
Langer, Lawrence L., 113, 114, 128–34, 135, 138,
  139, 140, 141
Langfus, Anna, 145, 162n37
The Last of the Just (Schwarz-Bart), 157
Lášticová, Barbara, 12n30
Laub, Dori, 148–50
Le Pen, Jean-Marie, 76
Lefort, Claude, 66, 79–80
Levi, Primo
  on duty to remember, 64n17
  erasure experienced by, 144–45, 146, 152, 153,
    161, 176
  minimalism in testimony of, 106–10, 135–37
  ordinary, homage to, 52–53
  universalism attributed to, 85, 88, 89, 96,
    109n24, 135–36
Lévy, Bernard-Henri, 66, 99
Leys, Ruth, 156n24
Lincoln, Abraham, 181
Lindenberg, Daniel, 69
literal versus exemplary memory, 84–88, 100
Luckhurst, Roger, 5n15, 6

Maechler, Stefan, 53–54
Maier, Charles F., 31n1, 55
Malia, Martin, 73
Margolin, Jean-Louis, 70
Marie L., 1–3, 180–81
Martinet, Gilles, 66
martyrdom/heroism versus passivity of Jews
  during Holocaust, 155–60
martyrs/heroes to victims, historiographic shift
  of focus from, 4, 15
Meister, Robert, 181
memory
  historiographic shift and, 11
  Holocaust's dominance of memory studies,
    4, 16
  identity and suffering, relationship to, 6–7,
    21–24, 30
  Jewish memory as threat to other types of
    memory, 58–64, 69–70, 98–100
  literal versus exemplary, 84–88, 100
  reliable memory, determining, 46–47
  "too much." *See* surfeit of Jewish memory
  transmission issues, 147–52
Mendelsohn, Benjamin, 33
Michaels, Walter Benn, 2, 39–41
Micheels, Louis J., 153–54, 176
Milton, Sybil, 53

mimesis, 94–95, 105n14, 119, 138
minimalism, 8, 101–42
   as antidote, 102–5
   appropriateness of expressions of grief, 56–57
   defined, 101–2
   erasure of victims and, 147–49, 152–55
   Friedländer, Saul, 103, 113–23, 126, 127, 140, 141
   Gross, Jan T., 113, 114, 116, 123–28, 141
   Hilberg, Raoul, 103, 114, 119
   Lang, Berel, 113, 114n33, 128, 134–42
   Langer, Lawrence L., 113, 114, 128–34, 135, 138, 139, 140, 141
   Levi, Primo, 106–10, 135–37
   literary style, appropriateness as, 105–11
   objectivity attributed to, 114–15
   overemotionalism, suspicion of, 28–29, 108, 111–15
   privileging of, 52–53
   suspension of disbelief, 105–6, 119, 120, 123
Mitterrand, François, 60n7, 66
modern democracy, totalitarianism of, 92–93
moral economy of trauma, 5, 19–24, 47
Morrison, Toni, 39
Moulin, Jean, 10n27, 59, 111
Moyn, Samuel, 11n28, 67n27, 157
Müller, Filip, 158
multiculturalism, 9n23, 34, 43–44, 46
"Muslims" at Auschwitz, 160n35
Muslims in France, 21n62, 26, 34, 61, 62, 99n131, 180

Nader, Andrés, 108–9, 151–52
"Nakba" and "hurbyn," 92n109
Nanking massacre, 43
Naqvi, Fatima, 9n24
narrative fetishism, 112–13, 142
naturalization of prejudice and victimization, 161–68
Nazi Germany and the Jews (Friedländer), 116–23
Nazism. *See* Holocaust; Stalinism and Nazism, comparisons of
Neighbors (Gross), 123–28
neo-liberalism, 66, 67, 166
neo-positivism, 113, 147, 168
Niederland, William G., 38n20
Nietzsche, Friedrich, 4
Nolte, Ernst, 86n93
Nora, Pierre, 21, 35

normalized nature of catastrophe in modern world, 92–94
Novick, Peter, 2, 3, 17n50, 32, 49, 50, 160
Nuremberg Tribunal, 27n79

objectivity attributed to minimalism in victim testimony, 114–15
Oneg Shabat, 148
"open secret," prejudice as, 169–72
ordinary, privileging of. *See* minimalism
The Origins of Totalitarianism (Arendt), 65n20, 169

Pagis, Dan, 52
Palestinian-Israeli conflict, 15, 26, 29, 44, 50, 56, 60n5, 61, 63n15, 91n107, 92n109, 94
Papon, Maurice, 60, 67
partisans in Second World War, 9–11, 18, 25, 158, 162n37
The Passing of an Illusion (Furet), 72
passivity of Jews during Holocaust, claims of, 153, 155–60
patriotic suffering, enfolding narrative of, 14–15, 52
Perechodnik, Calel, 156n24
perpetrator/bystander behavior, naturalization of, 161–68
Peshev, Boris, 163
Poland, 14, 119, 123–28, 144, 145, 162n27
Pollack, Michael, 153n19
Popkin, Richard H., 90n102
pornography, suffering as, 99, 102n5
postmodernism and victimhood, 4, 5
posttraumatic symptoms, 21, 38, 112
Power, Samantha, 13
privileged status, victimhood viewed as, 1, 2–4, 34, 36–37, 43, 49–50, 85, 88–89
Proust, Marcel, 170–71
psychiatric discourse, adoption of, 21–22, 33, 37–38

Raczymow, Henri, 39, 63, 70
rape victims, as complicit in own victimization, 33
Ravensbrück, 10
real and would-be victims, distinguishing, 20–22, 36, 51–57
Rechtman, Richard, 21–22, 24n71, 175
"redemptive anti-Semitism," 74, 116–17, 140
Reid, Donald, 9–10

reparations/restitution for victims, 27–28, 38
repressed aggression, victims as objects of, 27–28
republicanism, French, 26, 34, 44, 62, 179
resistance fighters in Second World War, 9–11, 18, 25, 158, 162n37
restitution/reparations for victims, 27–28, 38
Revel, Jean-François, 76–77
rhetorical constraint. *See* minimalism
Rigoulot, Pierre, 71
Ringelblum, Emmanuel, 148
Robin, Régine, 45, 58
Romano, Sergio, 31
Rosenblat, Herman, 155n22
Rosenfeld, Alvin H., 35, 102n5, 106n15, 147n10
Rosenfeld, Gavriel D., 4n9
Roth, Michael S., 22n66
Rothberg, Michael, 6n17, 13n35, 35n13, 148n11
Rousset, David, 10, 15, 85–86
Rousso, Henry, 48–49, 51, 60, 71–72, 91
Runia, Eelco, 57
Russian Revolution, 72–73

sacralization of Holocaust survivors
    erasure and, 143, 160, 179
    minimalism, privileging of, 104, 110, 113, 116, 140
    Stalinism and Nazism compared, 64, 74, 91, 93, 97, 100
    surfeit of Jewish memory and, 32, 46, 48, 52
sacrifice, 9
Sakowicz, Kazimierz, 115
Santner, Eric, 4, 40, 112, 142
Sarkozy, Nicolas, 99n131
Scarry, Elaine, 164n42
Schindler's List (film), 132–33
Schoenfeld, Gabriel, 32, 34–35, 50
Schwarz-Bart, André, 157
Scott, Joan Wallach, 21n62, 180
Sebald, W. G., 101–2
Second World War
    carpet-bombing by Allies in, 18, 62n13
    Holocaust. *See* Holocaust
    resistance fighters in, 9–11, 18, 25, 158, 162n37
self-reference, Jewish, 86, 87, 96, 97–98, 100
Semprun, Jorge, 110, 111
sexual abuse victims, as complicit in own victimization, 33
Sherry, Suzanna, 8–9n23
Shoah. *See* Holocaust

Sicher, Efraim, 36
Simon, Jonathan, 55n57
slavery, 3, 6n17, 13, 17n50, 39, 41, 99, 178–79, 181
Sobibor, 146
social organization and institutionalization of prejudice and violence, 168–74
Solnit, Albert J., 153
Solzhenitsyn, Alexander, 66, 75
Sophie's Choice (Styron), 102n5
Sorel, Georges, 168, 169n50
Speer, Albert, 107
Spiegel, Gabrielle, 4n9
Stalinism and Nazism, comparisons of, 18, 58–100
    The Black Book of Communism and, 68–72, 73, 76
    contamination of victims by, 79–81
    Jewish claim to uniqueness of Holocaust and, 63, 88–97
    Jewish memory as threat to other types of memory, 58–64, 69–70, 98–100
    literal versus exemplary memory and, 84–88, 100
    normalized nature of catastrophe in modern world, 92–94
    opacity of Communism/Stalinism versus clarity of Nazism, 72–79
    totalitarianism, concept of, 64–68, 75
    universalism as phenomenon and, 58–64
    universalist approach to, 82–84
Stark, Jared, 148n11
Steiner, George, 90n102, 129n73, 133
Steiner, Jean-François, 157
Stella, Frank, 101n2, 134
Stone, Dan, 166n46
Styron, William, 102n5
Suleiman, Susan, 110–11
surfeit of Jewish memory, 8, 31–57, 181
    boundaries between real and would-be victims, establishing, 20–22
    as concept, 28–29
    critical discourse on, 3–4, 31–37
    defined, 31–32
    erasure of victims in claims of, 152–53
    historiographical emergence of concept of, 16–17, 18–19, 32
    identity politics, as critique of, 33–36
    non-Holocaust survivors' appropriation of victimhood, 36, 37–46, 97

surfeit of Jewish memory *(continued)*
  proper relationship to past suffering and,
    46–51
  real and would-be victims, distinguishing,
    51–57
  as threat to other types of memory, 58–64,
    69–70, 98–100
  universalization/generalization of phe-
    nomenon of suffering in response to. *See*
    universalism
"survivor syndrome," 38, 156n24
suspension of disbelief, 105–6, 119, 120, 123

Tec, Nechema, 157n28
Tillon, Germaine, 10
Toaff, Ariel, 42
Tocqueville, Alexis de, 67n28
Todorov, Tzevtan
  goodness, focus on, 84, 128–29, 163
  on minimalism in victim testimony, 106–8,
    109n21
  naturalization of prejudice and victimization
    by, 163–66
  on privileging of victim status, 2, 34, 43, 85,
    88–89
  on Stalinism and Nazism, 80, 84–89, 91,
    93–94, 96–97
  on surfeit of Jewish memory, 3
"too much" memory. *See* surfeit of Jewish
  memory
totalitarianism, 64–68, 75, 84, 92
Touvier, Paul, 60, 67
Treblinka, 11n28, 88, 156, 157
Trezise, Thomas, 148–50, 168

United States
  Civil War, 181
  concentration on French and U.S. discourse,
    24–26
  differences between French and U.S. dis-
    course, 179–80
  slavery in, 3, 6n17, 13, 17n50, 39, 41, 99,
    178–79, 181
  victimhood after the Holocaust in. *See* vic-
    tims and victimhood after the Holocaust
univers concentrationnaire or "camp universe," 10
universalism, 8, 58–100, 181–82
  as concept, 8, 58–64
  human potential for good and evil, narra-
    tives of, 25

Jewish memory as threat to other types of
  memory, 58–64, 69–70
literal versus exemplary memory, 84–88, 100
naturalization of prejudice and victimization,
  161–68
patriotic suffering, enfolding narrative of,
  14–15
resistance fighters and Holocaust victims,
  tensions between, 10
Stalinism, universalist approach to, 82–84
uniqueness of Holocaust, claims regarding,
  63, 88–97
Vendée rebellion compared to Holocaust,
  58–59
Using and Abusing the Holocaust (Langer), 132

Vendée rebellion, 58–59
Vergès, Jacques, 59
Vichy regime, 2n4, 34–35, 49, 59–60, 67–68
victim-blaming, 33–34, 60, 157
victimology, as field, 33–34
victims and victimhood after the Holocaust,
  1–30, 178–83
  affective relationship with, 8, 19, 28, 102, 113,
    143–44, 150, 160, 166, 171n56, 175, 177
  aversion to, 8, 28, 30, 151, 160, 169, 173,
    175–77
  "competition of victims," concept of, 3, 6n17,
    26, 29, 44, 50, 67, 89, 91n107
  concentration on French and U.S. discourse,
    24–26. *See also* France; United States
  contemporary cultural narratives and, 26–27
  critical approaches to, 2–9
  erasure of. *See* erasure
  ethics of writing about, 175–77
  historiography of. *See* historiography of
    victimhood
  moral economy of, 5, 19–24, 47
  relationship between memory, suffering,
    and identity, 6–7, 21–24, 30. *See also*
    identity; memory
  repressed aggression, victims as objects of,
    27–28
  surfeit of Jewish memory and. *See* surfeit of
    Jewish memory
  universalist approach to. *See* universalism
Villiers, Philippe de, 50

Wachnich, Sophie, 12n30
Walser, Martin, 18, 161–62, 165, 166

Warsaw Ghetto, 60, 70, 148, 155
Waxman, Zoë Vania, 15, 16, 147–48
Weill, Nicolas, 60, 64n18, 70
Weinreich, Harald, 108
Weissman, Gary, 53, 128n68, 129–30
Werth, Nicolas, 70
White, Hayden, 103n9, 105n14, 135n87
Wiesel, Elie, 61n9, 90n102, 129n73
Wieviorka, Annette, 3, 15, 16, 20, 70, 104,
    109n24, 156n24, 177
Wieviorka, Michel, 61
Wieviorka, Olivier, 14–15, 63n17
Wilkomirski, Binjamin (Bruno Dössekker),
    45–46, 53–54, 57, 132, 138, 146
Williams, Benn E., 104n13
Williamson, Joel, 25n77

Winter, Jay, 14n37
Wolf, Joan, 60, 68n32
World War I (Great War), victimhood dis-
    course associated with, 9, 14, 47
World War II
    carpet-bombing by Allies in, 18, 62n13
    Holocaust. *See* Holocaust
    resistance fighters in, 9–11, 18, 25, 158,
        162n37
Writing the Book of Esther (Raczymow), 39

Yad Vashem museum, 6
Yannakakis, Illios, 71
Young, James E., 109n22

Zionism and anti-Zionism, 59n4, 91n107, 94, 169

www.ingramcontent.com/pod-product-compliance
Lightning Source LLC
Chambersburg PA
CBHW020533270326
41927CB00006B/560

* 9 7 8 1 5 0 1 7 0 5 6 3 2 *